Teaching Mindfulness-Based Groups

The Inside Out Group Model

Trish Bartley and Gemma Griffith

Teaching Mindfulness-Based Groups
The Inside Out Group Model

Published by:

Pavilion Publishing and Media Ltd
Blue Sky Offices, 25 Cecil Pashley Way
Shoreham by Sea, West Sussex
BN43 5FF

Tel: 01273 434 943
Email: info@pavpub.com
Web: www.pavpub.com

Published 2022

A catalogue record for this book is available from the British Library.

ISBN: 978-1-803880-84-6

Pavilion Publishing and Media is a leading publisher of books, training materials and digital content in mental health, social care and allied fields. Pavilion and its imprints offer must-have knowledge and innovative learning solutions underpinned by sound research and professional values.

Authors: Trish Bartley and Gemma Griffith
Production editor: Mike Benge, Pavilion Publishing and Media Ltd
Cover design: Emma Dawe, Pavilion Publishing and Media Ltd
layout and typesetting: Emma Dawe, Pavilion Publishing and Media Ltd
Printing: CPI Antony Rowe

To Charles (TB).   To my family (GG).

This book is dedicated to all the groups we
have taught, trained, and learned from –
and all mindfulness-based groups
that cultivate interrelatedness
wherever they may be.

May they offer benefit that grows and endures.

Also by Trish Bartley:

Holding Up the Sky: Love, Power and Learning in the Development of a Community

Mindfulness-Based Cognitive Therapy for Cancer: Gently Turning Towards

Mindfulness: A Kindly Approach to Being with Cancer

Also co-edited by Gemma Griffith:

Essential Resources for Mindfulness Teachers

Praise for this book

"An elegantly and compellingly elaborated exploration of an essential feature of all mindfulness-based clinical and non-clinical programs, namely that they unfold within collections of people gathered for a limited time in common aspiration for relief and perhaps release from suffering. Even if this book doesn't help you become a better mindfulness teacher, which it undoubtedly will if you live inside it and take its direction to heart, you can't possibly read it without becoming wiser and more skilful in all your human interactions, including, and perhaps especially, with yourself."

Jon Kabat-Zinn, PhD, founder of MBSR, author of *Full Catastrophe Living* and *The Healing Power of Mindfulness*

"A rich and enduring resource for both beginning and experienced teachers of mindfulness, that is rooted in the deep and personal experience of the authors. Change, as they point out, is born not just of learning techniques but also of reteaching ourselves what is needed for us to flourish and thrive rather than survive or endure. Every mindfulness group is a gathering of stories of both the teacher and the participants. Stories of vulnerability and uncertainty, often fear and pain. The group also holds the human, universal story of the longing for kindness, respect and healing. A great responsibility rests upon the shoulders of every mindfulness teacher to hold those stories with skill and compassion. This book guides every teacher through that journey, and the lessons we are asked to learn and to embody. This work is a gift to the mindfulness community."

Christina Feldman, co-founder, Bodhi College, senior insight meditation teacher, co-author of *Mindfulness: Ancient Wisdom Meets Modern Psychology*

"The work of becoming a mindfulness teacher involves embodying what we are teaching, understanding groups, holding and facilitating group processes and unlocking the potential that groups can have in teaching and learning. Trish Bartley and Gemma Griffith draw on their wealth of experience to provide the field with a map, a compass and a set of skills for teaching Mindfulness-Based Programs."

Willem Kuyken, Riblat Professor of Mindfulness and Psychological Science, University of Oxford, co-author of *Mindfulness: Ancient Wisdom meets Modern Psychology*

"This is a wonderful book, bringing together the practical wisdom of two pioneers of mindfulness teacher training with the lived experience of both novice and experienced teachers. The authors offer a clear framework for teachers, so that – whatever our level of experience – we may come to discern the many ways in which participants in any class are relating to themselves and others, and how teachers can increase their sensitivity by 'reading' (rather than judging) their own reactions. This is not just about skilfully navigating a class 'group process', but cultivating the core attitudes of not-knowing, kindness, compassion, curiosity, balance and appreciation in order to teach and to live with transformational depth and insight."

Mark Williams, Emeritus Professor of Clinical Psychology, University of Oxford, co-author of *Mindfulness: A Practical Guide to Finding Peace in a Frantic World*

"Discovering how to harness the power of the group to cocreate new learning is essential for mindfulness teachers. Trish and Gemma have gifted us a treasure trove of wisdom on this theme. Their writing offers key insights into ways of facilitating groups that are gateways to transformation, and that embody more of what the world deeply needs."

Rebecca Crane, PhD, Professor in Psychology and Director, Centre for Mindfulness Research and Practice, Bangor University

"The beauty of *Teaching Mindfulness-Based Groups* stems from the communion of depth and simplicity. Trish Bartley and Gemma Griffith are the first to foreground the group dimension that is so foundational, so crucial, so essential in mindfulness-based group dynamics. Its importance has been evident to anyone working in this field since the very beginning, yet no one has previously devoted such in-depth inquiry into the several layers of the group process. Perhaps because what is in full light is often not seen. However, the most innovative and generative aspect of this necessary book is the opening of a new horizon: to consider the MBIs also as a vehicle that enables participants to experience glimpses of the reality of the dimension of awareness which is beyond the contraction of the 'self', the reality of non-separation."

Antonella Commellato and Fabio Giommi, Associazione Italiana per la Mindfulness

"Trish and Gemma have drawn on their extensive experience of teaching mindfulness-based groups to offer a wonderful 'hymn' to what can arise when humans come together with wise intention to explore the big issues of life – both individually and collectively. We are in essence social creatures, and learning and practicing mindfulness in groups can take our explorations to much greater heights and depths than when walking the path alone. Trish and Gemma are wonderful guides to this journey."

Vidyamala Burch, mindfulness teacher, author, and co-founder of Breathworks

"With *Teaching Mindfulness-Based Groups*, Trish Bartley and Gemma Griffith have brought the mindfulness teaching community a gift that is inexhaustible. As you learn, page by page, to keep each group's co-creation of mindfulness as a key focus, you will find that it brightens and deepens your teaching – continually refreshing the curriculum and your own practice and commitment."

Donald McCown, PhD, Director of the Center for Contemplative Studies, West Chester University of Pennsylvania, author of *Teaching Mindfulness: A Practical Guide for Clinicians and Educators*

"Teaching mindfulness in the complex Southern African context requires sensitivity to trauma, and deep understandings of safety and inclusivity. I am so grateful that Trish and Gemma have shared theory and practice that will support both upcoming and established teachers in our African context. They tackle the challenges of running MBP groups as well as highlighting the huge potential of this inner work, that can enhance the outer work of social justice and sustainability. This is a much-needed resource that we can keep dipping into again and again and fills a gap for teachers and trainers alike."

Linda Kantor, PhD, Founding Director of the Institute for Mindfulness South Africa (IMISA), Adjunct Senior Lecturer at the Graduate School of Business, University of Cape Town

"The group is a powerful influence in mindfulness teaching, but how does this work? This book brings much needed clarity to the group element of mindfulness teaching and will be a great help to teachers in working skilfully with group processes to maximize participants' learning."

Ruth Baer, Professor Emeritus of Psychology, University of Kentucky, Director of the Master of Studies in Mindfulness-Based Cognitive Therapy, University of Oxford

"*Teaching Mindfulness-Based Groups* is a nice resource for both novice and experienced mindfulness teachers. The book is organized into different parts describing the inside out group model frame for facilitating mindfulness groups in easy-to-understand language. These are finished with chapters describing personal experiences by mindfulness teachers in running mindfulness-based groups. The authors have embodied mindfulness in their writings and have demonstrated sensitivity and care to potential readers who are about to or have run mindfulness-based groups. Overall, this is a very useful resource guide for any mindfulness teacher."

Samuel Y.S. Wong. Professor and Director, JC School of Public Health and Primary Care, Hong Kong. Director, Chinese University of Hong Kong, Thomas Jing Centre for Mindfulness Research and Training

黃仰山教授

香港中文大學醫學院　　賽馬會公共衛生及基層醫療學院院長

香港中文大學敬霆靜觀研究與培訓中心總監

"This book is about a subject close to my heart. For some reason, the contribution of the group setting to the pedagogy has lacked thorough methodical description. This is unfortunate, since the group adds great value to the learning process in mindfulness training. With this book, Trish Bartley and Gemma Griffith now fill in this gap. The book is a gem, as it is well grounded and eloquently written. A must-read for every teacher of mindfulness-based groups!"

Rob Brandsma, author of *The Mindfulness Teaching Guide: Essential Skills and Competencies for Teaching Mindfulness-Based Interventions*

"There is increasing evidence that mindfulness and global sustainability are more connected than we think, but we need to know more about the link between them. It's high time to explore the practical relevance that contemplative practices such as mindfulness and compassion can have on sustainability across individual, collective and system levels, and how we can tap into this potential to drive sustainable transformation. Looking into the relevance of dyads, triads and larger-group dynamics to support transformative capacities such as perspective-taking, and interconnectedness more broadly, is an important step forward in this context – all aspects that are presented in this new and inspiring book."

Christine Wamsler, Professor of Sustainability Science at LUCSUS (Lund University Centre for Sustainable Studies), Director of the Contemplative Sustainable Futures Program

"This wonderful, insightful book is the first of its kind to delve deeply into the significance of the group in Mindfulness-Based Programs (MBPs). The MBP group is a powerful vehicle for participants to do their inner work and experience interconnection as they relate to and are supported by other group members. The authors offer a detailed description of the Inside-Out Group (IOG) model with its core components of the MBP teacher embodying mindfulness, reading the group, holding the group and befriending the group. There are many rich examples and practical applications presented for the use of each of these components in the group setting. There are also specific practices for the teacher to deepen their personal practice and capacity to befriend themselves and others. *Teaching Mindfulness-Based Groups* is an invaluable resource for anyone teaching or aspiring to teach Mindfulness-Based Programs. A deep bow of appreciation to Trish Bartley and Gemma Griffith for sharing the gems of their wisdom and compassion in writing this book."

Diane Reibel, PhD, Director of the Center for Mindfulness at Thomas Jefferson University Hospital, co-author of *Teaching Mindfulness: A Practical Guide for Clinicians and Educators*, co-editor of *Resources for Teaching Mindfulness: An International Handbook*

"This book is a delight. Using the Inside Out Group (IOG) model – embodying, reading, holding and befriending – the authors beautifully describe how the mindfulness-based teacher can approach facilitating a mindfulness-based group with intention and wholehearted engagement. This is a book I will enjoy recommending."

Susan Woods, Senior Faculty, The Centre for Mindfulness Studies, Toronto, Canada

"I remember one of our first pieces of research on the role of the teacher in mindfulness based cognitive therapy, and our surprise about the participants pointing out they learnt a lot more from the group than from their teacher! This made us awkwardly aware of a not unimportant blind spot of ours, or may I call it vanity? A problem that Trish Bartley and Gemma Griffith do not appear to suffer from: they are fully aware of the importance of the group context in mindfulness-based programmes. With this inspiring and stimulating book they invite us to develop both our sensitivity and skills in this area. It marries theoretical background and up to date research evidence with extensive practical experience and personal revelations. I warmly recommend it and hope that it will contribute to our interrelatedness and humanity, not only as mindfulness teachers but also as citizens of a world in social and environmental crisis."

Anne Speckens, Professor of Psychiatry and founder and director of the Radboud University Medical Centre for Mindfulness

Audio resources

A series of recorded practices to accompany this book are available for download at www.pavpub.com/teaching-mindfulness-based-groups-resources

Contents

A series of recorded practices are available for download at
www.pavpub.com/teaching-mindfulness-based-groups-resources

Acknowledgments

We are very grateful to our students, trainees, and all the mindfulness-based programme participants over the years who have taught us so much about the nature of groups and what they need from us, as their teachers or trainers – and also to all the other groups we have worked with over many years.

We are also indebted to our colleagues in the Centre for Mindfulness, Research and Practice at Bangor University, and within the Mindfulness Network core training team – for their support, guidance, valuable feedback and shared learning. In particular, we want to single out Rebecca Crane, who co-developed the inside out group model and read a draft of this entire book, and also followed up with further feedback. Her insights were invaluable, and we very much appreciate her time, encouragement and generosity. We also want to give special thanks to Eluned Gold, Bridgette O'Neill, Christina Shennan, David Shannon, and Sophie Sansom for their helpful feedback and kind support. We want to mention all current members of our training team, including Taravajra, Estrella Fernandez, Karunavira, Bethan Roberts, Pamela Duckerin, Sud Ubayasiri, Ciaran Saunders, and Alison Evans for supporting our ongoing learning.

Our grateful thanks go to Willem Kuyken for his foreword. We very much appreciate his kindness in finding the time to write this and are especially happy and proud to have his input at the very front of our book.

There are others who we are very grateful to, who have offered their support in terms of personal encouragement, incredibly helpful advice, and invaluable feedback. Significant amongst these are Ursula Bates, Rob Fellows, and Paula Sonrisa Sturmer, who looked at several iterations of various chapters and greatly supported their development. Franca Warmenhoven and Rob Vincken have been very generous with their time, feedback, and good counsel – and through See True Mindfulness in The Netherlands, they have contributed a great deal to several of the experiential group learning processes described in this book. Very grateful thanks and appreciation also go to Christina Feldman, Tina Usherwood, and John Teasdale for their wise guidance and mentoring recently and in the past. Christina Feldman has offered guidance and direction to many of the practice chapters and for that we are especially grateful to her. A few further people have been very generous with a range of support and encouragement. These especially include Ursula Bates, Rob Vincken, Linda Kantor, Diana Allanson, and Tina Usherwood.

Our grateful thanks go to our four interviewees, Thandi Glider, Dave McCormack, Paula Sonrisa Sturmer and Pauline Gibbs. Their perspectives offer a fresh and very valuable addition to this book. We are so appreciative to all four for their time, wisdom, and willingness to do this.

Our thanks also go to Pavilion Publishing and everyone who has been involved in bringing this book into print – especially to Darren Reed for his kindness and patience.

From a personal perspective, Trish wishes to make special mention of two co-trainers who she has been very lucky to have worked with. Jody Mardula, former colleague and friend, is highly skilled in groupwork. They shared much learning, fun and an unusual level of intuitive connection during their extensive work with training groups. Christina Shennan is another colleague and friend who in a similar way offers a level of direct insight, heart, and connection that is very enriching to the groups we work with, and to me personally.

Finally, many thanks and love to our families and friends for their support and encouragement. They have seen less of us during some busy writing periods.

Foreword

"We have advanced from canoes to galleys to steamships to space shuttles – but nobody knows where we're going. We are more powerful than ever before, but have little idea what to do with all that power.

Yuval Noah Harari (2011)

When I read Yuval Harari's 2011 book *Sapiens*, his thesis resonated with me. He starts by summarising seventy thousand years of human history. He ends the book with the question, "Is there anything more dangerous than dissatisfied and irresponsible gods who don't know what they want?"

There is no doubt that in seventy thousand years our species has made extraordinary progress. Across the seven billion people that inhabit our planet today, the average life expectancy is seventy-two, compared with the low thirties at the turn of the twentieth century. People can travel the world; a hundred years ago most people never travelled more than a few miles from their birthplace. The internet grants us all access to information that would have been unimaginable not long ago.

But this progress has come with real challenges and the COVID-19 pandemic has reminded those of us who needed reminding of our vulnerability. While many people are living longer, this means they often need to learn to live longer with one or more health conditions, typically with some degree of disability and pain. And although there has been remarkable progress in treatments for communicable diseases, heart disease and cancer, this progress has not been matched in mental health. As many as one in five people – that's one billion people alive in the world today – will experience a significant mental health problem such as depression, anxiety or addiction at some point in their life. Though we have some good treatments, most will never access these treatments. Moreover, progress is not distributed equally; stark health, social, gender and economic inequalities in many parts of the world are becoming larger, not smaller. Human migration is creating tensions and conflict across the world. Information and the internet are being misused to further nefarious agendas. Population growth is also unequally distributed, with striking correlations with poverty, women's rights and education. Human colonisation of the planet has raised the very real spectre that the current trajectory of growth is not sustainable in terms of the earth's resources, nor its effects on climate change. These are not remote, abstract ideas. They are real and play out for all of us in one form throughout our lives.

Trish Bartley and Gemma Griffith open their book with a quote from Victor Hugo, which suggests that the most powerful ideas come at time when they are most needed. Our minds and hearts literally and metaphorically create our world, moment by moment, through where we choose to place our attention, how we experience what we attend to and our choice of words and actions. So, the solutions to the problems we face will have to come from human minds and hearts. A trained mind is better able to see clearly, make good choices and speak and act discerningly. At this juncture in the arc of human history, a systematic training for the human mind and heart is exactly what is needed. A growing body of evidence suggests not only that mindfulness-based programs cultivate foundational skills and qualities of attention, wisdom, compassion, discernment and pro-sociality. They also have the potential to be part of the solution.

Perhaps the most significant development in programmatic mindfulness training was the work of Jon Kabat-Zinn in the 1980s. Kabat-Zinn had studied meditation in a range of Buddhist traditions and was working as a young molecular biologist in the laboratory of a Nobel Laureate, Salvador Luria. While attending a meditation retreat taught by Christina Feldman, he had a compelling vision to use all his training and experience to develop a mindfulness curriculum that could be taught in mainstream Western settings. Over several years he developed an eight-session MBP, Mindfulness-based Stress Reduction (MBSR), that provided a vehicle for people to learn mindfulness in the "Stress Reduction Clinic" at the University of Massachusetts General Hospital. Perhaps one of the most striking and innovative aspects of MBSR is the way it uses systematic mindfulness training, taught over eight sessions, that draws on and weaves together much of the richness of the meditative traditions Kabat-Zinn had studied, but in a way that is accessible, relevant, and useful to people in Western settings. Kabat-Zinn also had an extraordinary talent for inspiring and communicating the potential of mindfulness in the mainstream, not just for those with chronic health problems, but also as a different way of being and living (Kabat-Zinn, 2011). MBSR has now been extensively researched and disseminated around the world to people with longstanding health problems as a way to better manage their pain and disability (Kabat-Zinn, 1990). It has been taught to a range of other groups, and the evidence base for its effects on psychological and mind-body outcomes is continually evolving (Bohlmeijer, Prenger, Taal, & Cuijpers, 2010; Demarzo et al., 2015; Khoury, Sharma, Rush, & Fournier, 2015).

Mindfulness-Based Cognitive Therapy for depression (MBCT) built on the structure of MBSR and worked with its central premise that mindfulness practice can be a powerful vehicle for understanding and transforming the mind. It was originally developed with a particular focus on people with recurrent depression who were at significant risk of depressive relapse

(Segal, Williams, & Teasdale, 2013). It had a particular cognitive science formulation of depressive relapse and was carefully adapted to help people learn skills to prevent depression from recurring and stay well. It has been shown to be effective in numerous randomized controlled trials. Like MBSR, it has been adapted and extended to a range of new groups and contexts, and the evidence base for this broader family of mindfulness-based cognitive therapies is evolving.

MBPs are informed by theories and practices that draw from a confluence of contemplative traditions, science, and the major disciplines of medicine, psychology, and education. They are underpinned by a model of human experience that addresses the causes of human distress and the pathways to relieving it. They develop a new relationship with experience characterized by present moment focus, decentering, and an approach orientation. They engage participants in a sustained intensive training in mindfulness meditation practice, in an experiential inquiry-based learning process and in exercises to develop insight and understanding. And finally, which brings us to this book, they tend to be taught in a group format, with one or two teachers and between twelve and thirty participants.

Caricatures of mindfulness portray it as an individualistic, even "selfish" pursuit that misunderstands the problems we face and provides an inappropriate solution. But this is to profoundly misunderstand the ethical foundations, theory, and context for MBPs. We all live in relation to others – our family, our friends, our colleagues, and the wider community. These broader influences are shaped by and shape our experience, our behavior, and our lives. MBPs intention is to support a process of understanding, training and transformation that enables us to live well in relationship with others, the wider community, and the world.

This is not easy work. Consider the work of a heart surgeon, an airline pilot or a gardener. Each requires a lot of knowledge, extensive and experience to do their work well. Teaching MBPs is no different. Like a crucible used to meld ingredients at high temperature, the group aspect of MBPs supports learning and transformation. Trish Bartley and Gemma Griffith draw on their wealth of extensive and complementary experience to provide the field with a map, a compass and a set of skills for teaching MBPs. Becoming an MBP teacher involves embodying what we are teaching, as an individual, in dyads and in groups, understanding groups, holding and facilitating group processes and unlocking the potential that groups can have in teaching and learning. This wonderful book makes Trish Bartley and Gemma Griffith's wealth of knowledge and experience available to mindfulness teachers so they can teach MBPs with embodiment and skill, unlocking the power of a group to support participants' learning.

If the science of mindfulness and MBPs continues to progress as it is currently, the next fifty years will see important breakthroughs in our understanding of the relationships between our mind-body, our health and well-being and the ways in which we are shaped by and shape the world. This in turn will enable us to continue to develop MBPs so they can support the work of addressing the challenges of the contemporary world.

Willem Kuyken

Ritblat Professor of Mindfulness and Psychological Science

University of Oxford

About the authors

TRISH BARTLEY has been involved in MBCT since its early development in the UK. She is a founding member of the core training team at the Centre for Mindfulness, Research and Practice (CMRP), Bangor University, UK, teaches on the Mindfulness Network's teacher training pathway, and trained on the Bangor University master's programme for 15 years. She has been leading mindfulness training workshops in Europe since 2010. She supervises mindfulness teachers and has taught MBCT for Cancer to people with cancer since 2001. Trish is the author of *Mindfulness-Based Cognitive Therapy for Cancer and Mindfulness: A Kindly Approach to Being with Cancer*. She has long had a passion for working with groups and has a background in community work in the UK and rural development in South Africa.

GEMMA GRIFFITH, PhD, is a Senior Lecturer and mindfulness teacher in the Centre for Mindfulness Research and Practice (CMRP), Bangor University, UK. She is director of the Master's in Mindfulness-Based Approaches and Master's in Teaching Mindfulness-Based Courses at the CMRP. Research interests and publications include group process in mindfulness-based programmes, qualitative research, the role mindfulness plays in parenting, and the adaptation of mindfulness-based programmes for people with learning disabilities. She is co-editor of the book *Essential Resources for Mindfulness Teachers* (Crane, Karunavira & Griffith, 2021).

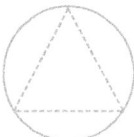

Introduction

Welcome to this book! We hope that it will be of benefit to you and your teaching of mindfulness-based groups in whatever form and context they take place.

In this introduction, we explain our thinking behind the book and offer some signposts for reading and using it. As the title makes clear, it has been written for mindfulness-based teachers who work with groups.

- You may be starting out as a mindfulness-based teacher – perhaps still in training.
- You may be more experienced but feel that you could make more of your mindfulness groups.
- You may already have a well-established group practice in another field and are curious as to how it might translate into a mindfulness-based teaching context.

Whatever your entry point, we have written out of our own mindfulness-based group teaching and training experience, whilst also including the latest research and pedagogical literature so that it is as relevant as possible for you. Most of the book is built around the inside out group model[1], which has four key capacities:

- inside out embodying
- reading the group
- holding the group
- befriending the group

We offer a brief précis of this model later in this introduction. Mindfulness-based groups offer us endless opportunities to learn about our interrelatedness and humanity – and teaching them can be both fascinating and challenging.

---

1   Griffith GM, Bartley T & Crane RS (2019) The Inside Out Group Model: Teaching Groups in Mindfulness-Based Programs. *Mindfulness*. https://link.springer.com/article/10.1007/s12671-019-1093-6 (accessed January 2022).

The Mindfulness-based programme (MBP)

You will find the text is littered with the initials MBP. This is an abbreviation of mindfulness-based programme. We use this term very broadly. We see it as referring to 'classical' eight-week programmes such as Mindfulness-Based Stress Reduction (MBSR) and Mindfulness-Based Cognitive Therapy (MBCT), and also encompassing other forms of teaching mindfulness – whatever the population, duration of the course, and context (online, blended or in person, clinical or community, workplace, school, and so on). There are also occasions when mindfulness is taught in a group setting in taster or introductory sessions, during drop-in sessions, or within an ongoing process such as regular mindfulness-based practice sitting groups. Many of us also bring mindfulness practice to inform our professional roles. We are not able to cater for all the different permutations and forms of groups (closed, open, one off, etc.), but we hope that what we have covered will support the mindfulness-based groups that you are involved with – understanding that you will need to translate what you read so that it applies to the particular context and groups that you are teaching or working with.

Setting the scene

Mindfulness practice offers individuals the resources and potential to enhance their well-being, by learning to change the way they relate to challenging experiences, enjoy more of what they value, and make wiser choices in how they act. As is well known, there is growing evidence for the efficacy of MBPs for a variety of clinical populations, as well as for the general public, in relation to stress, and in contexts such as workplaces and schools. However, this potential for personal well-being is not realized by everyone, since currently MBPs are only partially accessible to the wider community. Issues of inclusivity and relevance are significant challenges for the mindfulness field and there is an urgent need to find ways of widening access with integrity and respect.

Mindfulness practice is essentially relational on an intrapersonal level. That is, we learn to relate to our own internal experience in ways that are more kind, responsive and flexible. This learning within an MBP evolves out of formal and informal mindfulness practice, and from the connections that unfold in the group, through inquiry, discussion, small group processes, and through shared curriculum exercises.

Most MBPs are taught in groups, which are relational on an interpersonal level. We sit in a circle with other members of the group. When working online, we see each other on the screen. We learn about ourselves and our experience alongside others, as they learn about theirs. The potential for interconnectedness and interrelatedness is available through the mindfulness-based group.

The experience of being in a group appears to be a key feature for MBP participants in the feedback they give (formally and informally). However, the influence of the group on participants' experience of the session is not yet reflected in the research on MBPs, although this field of research is developing (see Chapter four). This is a curious paradox, although part of the reason for this lies in the difficulty in researching the impact of the group within the MBP due to the many variables involved. However, since the group is the usual context within which participants learn mindfulness, we can assume that the group has a significant influence.

The term 'gestalt'[2] describes the phenomenon that we find more meaning from appreciating the whole of something than we do when we break it down into its constituent parts. All the parts of the MBP group – participants, physical and social context, population vulnerabilities, MBP programme, teacher and much more – are the ingredients that come together to form the group and its potential to hold its members. Since there is so much complexity involved, every group is inevitably different – yet we tend to find that most MBP groups function well in the hands of a well-trained mindfulness teacher.

As we learn in Chapter 14 – befriending the group – the group amplifies opportunities to cultivate the warmer qualities of mindfulness, such as befriending, empathy, compassion, and appreciation of self and others. These are nurturing to the whole MBP group process and the individuals within. They also nudge us towards the potential of a wider collective benefit that ripples out beyond the MBP group.

However, we have to add that groupwork practice is a huge and complex topic. There are some notable giants such as Irvin Yalom, who have written at length, brilliantly and in a highly accessible way, about the theory and practice of the psychotherapeutic group. We see our efforts here in relation to mindfulness-based programme groups as very modest in comparison. Our intention is to focus attention on the group, in line with the Mindfulness-Based Interventions: Teaching Assessment Criteria (MBI:TAC)[3] (initially developed as a teaching assessment tool), which puts group learning as one of six domains of teaching competence. In this vein, we hope that this book will stimulate more interest in the mindfulness-based group and contribute to MBP teachers discovering more about how the group supports people to learn mindfulness.

We now offer a précis of the Inside Out Group Model.

---

2   https://gestaltcentre.org.uk/what-is-gestalt/

3   Crane *et al*, 2013

The Inside Out Group (IOG) model

In this section, we sketch an outline of the IOG model to give you a sense of the whole model, before going into more depth in the chapters that follow. The Inside Out Group (IOG) model was published in Springer's Mindfulness journal after about two years of development[4]. Our aim was to create the simplest and clearest model possible that would encapsulate the complexities of group process in MBPs, and at the same time offer pointers as to how the teacher might use this to cultivate mindfully enabling relationships within the MBP group.

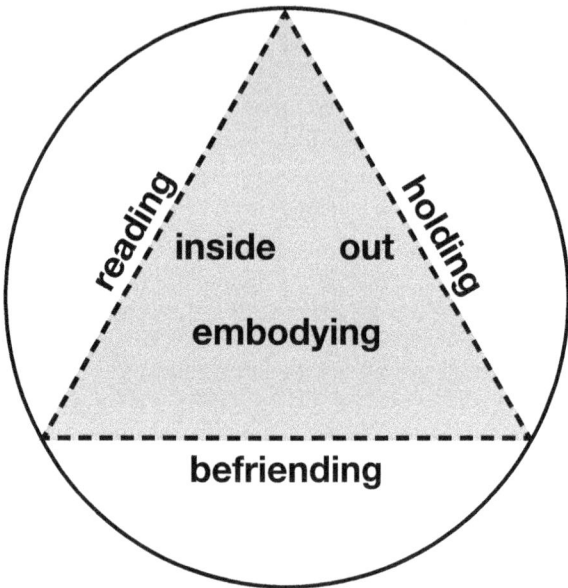

The centre of the model illustrates the inside out, mindful embodying of the MBP teacher, in touch with the three capacities of holding, reading, and befriending the group. This is within the entire 'learning context', which in our original IOG article was symbolised by an additional circle surrounding the group circle. The eagle-eyed amongst you may have noticed that in this book we no longer show an additional 'learning context' circle surrounding the IOG model. This is deliberate, because our thinking around this has developed over time. The learning context is huge, and encompasses everything outside of the space of the group circle (societal influences, the particular context of the MBP course, what participants bring with them into the class, the teacher's training, practice, ethics etc.) and thus the container of an additional circle was unnecessary, and seemed to imply that there was a fixed boundary to the learning context – when in reality, this is unlikely to be the case.

---

4   Griffith *et al*, 2019

There are four sections to the model:

1. **Inside out embodying:** Mindful embodying arises from the personhood and mindfulness practice of the teacher, and points to a key aspect that influences the group and the class. It can be a difficult concept to grasp, and indeed may be one that needs to be felt or seen in others before we can have insight into what embodying mindfulness means.

   In our original article about the IOG model, we defined inside out embodiment thus:

   "Inside out embodiment is the arising of non-judgmental present moment awareness within the teacher. The 'inside' encompasses phenomena arising within the boundary of the body of the teacher, such as thoughts, the felt sense of the body, and emotions, and 'out' refers to phenomena arising outside the body of the teacher, such as what is seen and heard in the group while teaching. In a sense, these boundaries are arbitrary and in constant flux, and the main point is that the teacher is able to be aware of and purposefully direct attention to the range of phenomena that arises while teaching."[5]

   Inside out embodying therefore points to the interface between the 'inside' of the body of the teacher (the internal felt sense), and the 'outside' of the body of the teacher (awareness of what is happening in the group). By noticing where our attention goes, and by bringing it into connection with our direct experience when teaching, we are able to notice our habitual patterns of mind (for example, we may have a running background commentary about a particular participant as we teach). This can take us into thoughts 'inside', and away from connecting with the immediacy of sensory experience and with the whole group we are teaching, which is 'outside'. Inside out embodiment is central to the IOG model as it underpins the teacher's ability to read, hold, and befriend the group whilst teaching.

2. **Reading the group:** The teacher can viscerally sense or 'read' what is happening in the group and in their own being as they teach. This connection is supported by an understanding of the theories of group process which allows the teacher to place what is happening in the group into a context of wider understanding – which includes signs and symbols from the body language of group members – and an understanding of the different potential influences that affect what participants bring with them into the group.

3. **Holding the group:** The teacher establishes a learning container by consciously holding awareness of the group as an entity in its own right as they teach. With this awareness, the teacher can support the conditions that are needed to facilitate the participants' learning as the

---

5   Griffith *et al*, 2019, p.1318.

group progresses. This includes cultivating an environment in which participants are encouraged to choose what is right for them (e.g., choosing an anchor point that is most helpful during meditating practice) and where participants can take risks if they choose to, in terms of what they share with the group and how they learn.

4. **Befriending the group:** The teacher holds an intention and cultivates their practice to befriend all experiences that occur in the session – both towards participants and, importantly, towards their own experience whilst teaching.

   Our intention is that the IOG model will support MBP teachers to facilitate a dynamic and creative group process, embedded in mindful awareness, with the aim of that this will facilitate the relational potential of the MBP group. It is too early to tell what influence the IOG model may have in the field. We hope that it will inspire MBP teachers and trainers to take the development of this groupwork skill to heart, and that this will enable them to make the best use of the promise of the group in MBPs. This book aims to expand the model and show how it can be used when teaching MBP classes, in the hope that it will dial up the visibility and potential of the interrelatedness of group process in MBPs.

There are a number of recorded practices for mindfulness teachers that align with this book available to download at www.pavpub.com/teaching-mindfulness-based-groups-resources

The article and the book

We first published the Inside Out Group (IOG) model in *Mindfulness* in 2019[6]. We always planned to follow the paper with this book in which we would have more space to draw out the theory and practice of MBP groupwork. It has taken longer than we intended, mainly due to the pandemic and all the new priorities that hove dramatically into view (such as shifting the entire Bangor mindfulness master's programme online in March 2020).

The Inside Out Group model frames most of this book. It is offered as a way of supporting and understanding the MBP group as mindfulness-based teachers. After this introduction we have four chapters that set the scene and underpin the rest of the book. In the first chapter, we write about the value of MBP groups to the personal and wider collective well-being of those who attend them – and the interrelatedness that a mindfulness-based group can potentially offer in the face of social and environmental crises. Indeed, mindfulness is attracting much interest as a key support for the vital

---

6   Griffith *et al*, 2019

'inner work' that is needed if the 'outer work' of policy implementation is to succeed in supporting the planet's long-term sustainability and bringing social justice into reality.

We then move to Chapter Two, which explores the wider context, including some stages in the MBP teacher's development; some aspects of the MBP itself, and those who are drawn to come onto programmes. Chapter Three looks at the history of how the MBP group became more important in the pedagogical literature over time. Chapter Four continues in this vein, drawing out the current research in this field such as it is, including the MBP group as a common factor in participant outcomes.

Part One starts to explore the IOG model in depth, beginning with the core practice of embodying mindfulness as an MBP teacher, from the inside out in Chapter Five. We then move on to draw out the ways that we can support a healthy launching of the MBP group in Chapter Six, with the key enablers of safety[7] and inclusivity as central ingredients.

Part Two explores the first of the three capacities of the IOG model – that of reading the group which offers a number of ways of understanding the MBP group and how to interpret what the group needs from the role of the teacher. Chapter Seven includes an overview of the underpinning group development theories that can be helpful to the MBP teacher. Chapter Eight considers group membership issues and Chapter Nine looks at the MBP teacher's understanding the role of body language.

Part Three considers the second capacity, that of Holding. Chapter Ten looks at many aspects of the MBP teacher's holding of the group, and chapters 11 and 12 reflect on the key teaching practices of inside out guiding, inquiry and facilitation. Online considerations in holding the group are highlighted in Chapter 13.

Finally, Part Four moves to explore the third capacity in the IOG model; that of Befriending. Chapter 14 draws out aspects of the MBP teacher's practice of befriending and outlines some qualities of befriending through the Four Friends for Life[8] in Chapter 15.

At the end of the book, in Chapter 16, we outline some aspects of supporting the ending of the mindfulness-based group.

Finally, in the brief conclusion, we invite a reflection of what you are taking away and what small steps you might put in place in your future teaching of mindfulness-based groups. The book finishes with a personal afterword from Trish, where she reflects on her experience of mindfulness-based groups – and what they might offer the world.

---

7   Safety as a key group enabler is explored at the end of Chapter one and in further depth in Chapter six, Launching the Group

8   van den Brink & Kostler, 2015

Teachers' interviews

Between these chapters, we have interviews with four MBP teachers. They share their ideas about their teaching and learning of MBP groups. Thandi Glider speaks of how the IOG model influences her teaching, and of her commitment to helping people in MBP groups learn how to be more fully human. Dave McCormack draws parallels between adult learning literature and mindfulness pedagogy, the value in forming a learning community, and his sense of the potential value of the MBP group. Paula Sonrisa Sturmer challenges us as MBP teachers to do our inner work if we genuinely want to widen inclusivity in our MBP groups. She speaks of her commitment to tend to the collective as well as the individual. Pauline Gibbs talks about diversity and her wish to reach deeper into diverse communities, in support of social justice and what she feels is needed to achieve this. These conversations offer grounded perspectives about how the IOG model can support MBP teaching, as well as wider considerations of the work of teaching groups.

Ways of writing

In the early days of starting to write, we, Gemma and Trish, spent pleasant afternoons with tea and cake in a Welsh garden centre forming ideas and shaping how we might bring them together. This was a rich process, and the cake was delicious! Later, when Trish moved to north Oxfordshire, around the time that Covid-19 and the first UK lockdown arrived, we resorted to Zoom for our discussions.

Gemma took on the major role of writing the IOG article, with Trish and Rebecca Crane as co-authors. The actual writing is the straightforward part – but as many of you may know, getting an academic article to publication involves a lengthy process of receiving peer feedback and reviewing and adjusting the text, responding to further reviews, and so on, until finally it is accepted for publication. The process of getting the IOG article published was around two years. We are happy that since publication, it has been read and downloaded over 10,000 times.

The process of writing a book is rather different from writing an article. This one has taken a similar amount of time to actually write (around two years), but most books seem to require a good deal of 'cooking' before a single word is written. This one is no different. It is a book that Trish has thought about writing for a long time. She has written two earlier books that relate to mindfulness and cancer (one for teachers[9] and one for people with cancer[10]) and a first earlier book that was written about her experience of

---

9   Bartley (2013)

10   Bartley (2017)

development research after a year with local people in rural South Africa[11]. Groups have held an abiding interest for Trish and her work has involved her in enabling groups in many different contexts over more than four decades. Most of these groups have shared common themes (such as poverty, stigma, exclusion, women's issues, and, significantly, health and well-being). Most also shared ways of working involving 'bottom up' participatory processes that sought to empower, connect, and promote a sense of personal dignity and collective collaboration. Much of the writing in this book is drawn from the learning from these groups.

While Gemma has explored the research and theory of MBP groups in her writing, Trish has written about teaching practice and group process. Gemma was first author for the IOG article – and Trish has taken the lead for this book. As co-authors, Gemma and Trish have offered feedback to each other's chapters as the writing has progressed. We have drawn on our individual skills and experience in order to bring the book to completion. If an academic perspective on the IOG model is needed, the IOG article is the primary place to go. If there is a focus on applied mindfulness-based teaching perspectives, come to the practice chapters in this book.

Some explanations

We have chosen to use non-binary pronouns throughout – so instead of referring to teachers or participants as 'he' or 'she', 'him' or 'her', we refer to the teacher or the participant as 'they', 'them' or 'their'. This in line with APA recommended formats, but more importantly it reflects our own principles.

In most of our writing, we step into being practitioners alongside you as you read this book – by using 'we' throughout. This is not just more invitational – it is also quite genuinely how we see ourselves as ongoing learners rather than experts. However, the 'we' of writing can often be problematic. Many of you may not necessarily identify, feel included, or perhaps find aspects of the text relevant. It is so tempting to assume a commonality amongst 'us mindfulness-based teachers' that may not exist. With this in mind, we want to write that, if there are places where we have been insensitive, lacked awareness, or made any unhelpful errors, we do genuinely apologise. We have sought feedback and taken care to write in ways that are inclusive and thoughtful as best we can, but with the best of intentions, things get missed or come across in ways that we did not intend, but were not sufficiently aware of. As white, middle-class, cis-gendered women, there may well be places where we lack insight, and we have tried to acknowledge this as best we can throughout the book. We both continue to seek to widen awareness around what we bring with us into our work. We truly hope that this book might make some contribution

---

11   Bartley (2003)

to dismantling some of the barriers to accessing MBP groups, but we are well aware that wishing it were so is not necessarily enough.

There are a number of sections in this book that describe reflective exercises which we invite you to explore. Many of these come from workshops[12] on teaching mindfulness-based groupwork that Trish and others offer through the Mindfulness Network (in the UK), See True (in the Netherlands) and other places in Europe and further afield. We encourage you to partner with another MBP teaching colleague on a similar teaching path, or take them to your mindfulness supervisor to explore together. This will offer you a much richer experience than exploring them on your own.

And finally...

We are strongly of the opinion that you, as readers of this book, already have a lot of knowledge, understanding and experience of groups, drawn from the scores of groups that you have been members of, and the many different roles that you have taken in those groups. However, it is also true that many of us feel nervous about leading MBP groups. In the early days of teaching, there may be some sense of alarm at the exposure of teaching in front of others. Our education tends to be based on an 'expert' model of imparting knowledge 'from the front' – rather than one of facilitator and enabler of learning, as with the MBP teacher. It feels important to appreciate that all the group learning we have absorbed over the years is a valuable and transferable resource in helping us gain more understanding of what MBP groups need.

The process of groups – their chemistry, connectivity and social potential – is fascinating. Almost every group offers a challenge at some point – a moment that brings halting uncertainty and doubt. Things happen within groups that can be hard to fathom, and at times as MBP teachers we can wonder where on earth to go next with what is emerging in front of us. Yet, in pausing, calling on intention and finding courage, we discover that on a good day we can work mindfully with what is emerging – and when the page turns, we may discover moments of deep connection and common humanity in the room. When this evolves, the MBP group can sometimes come together like a fine orchestra making music. This has potential to change lives and contribute to a little mending of the world, one moment at a time.

---

12   https://www.mindfulness-network.org/

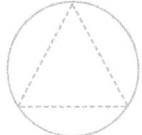

1. The value of the mindfulness-based group

Exploring the continuum of personal and collective well-being

Trish Bartley

> *"Nothing is more powerful than an idea whose time has come."*
>
> Victor Hugo (1802-1885)

This chapter looks at the potential for the mindfulness-based group to connect personal well-being with the collective, community, and global well-being which the world so urgently needs. Social scientists in the fields of sustainability, social justice, and community participation are looking at mindfulness as a means of supporting new ways of addressing ecological challenges and creating a more just, compassionate, reflective, and sustainable society[13]. It is early days, yet there is growing interest that mindfulness has (for example) 'the potential to foster climate adaptation at multiple levels, from individual to global.'[14] We offer the hypothesis that the mindfulness-based group has an important contribution to make in realising this focus from the personal to the personal *and* collective well-being.

In attempting to draw some of these threads together, we start with Jon Kabat-Zinn's vision of an orthogonal shift[15] of consciousness and lay this alongside the critical challenges we face concerning social inequality, discrimination, and the climate emergency. Mindfulness practice is viewed as supporting pro-social behaviour, and we share some early examples of social and climate action projects that are mindfulness-based. In looking more closely at the contribution that the mindfulness-

---

13 Frank *et al* (2019)

14 Wamsler (2018)

15 Kabat-Zinn (2019)

based group has to offer, we identify two key group enablers of *Safety* and *Inclusivity* that sustain the qualities needed to support relational spaces that empower participants to take their learning beyond the MBP and out into the world.

Setting the scene

When Mindfulness-Based Stress Reduction (MBSR) was first developed, Jon Kabat-Zinn framed his programme around the alleviation of stress, a universal human experience[16]. Later, when Mindfulness-Based Cognitive Therapy (MBCT) was developed (out of MBSR and Cognitive Therapy), it narrowed its focus to a clinical population[17]. Research by the founders of MBCT (Zindel Segal, Mark Williams, and John Teasdale) established an evidence base for the treatment of people with recurrent depression and put MBPs on the map in a new way. Many developments of MBCT and MBSR followed – and MBP research now has transformed what was sceptically seen by some as a passing 'fad', into respected mainstream approaches that are helping thousands of people across many continents and in many different clinical, community and workplace contexts.

However, Jon Kabat-Zinn has always had a vision that goes a lot wider. In his first book, *Full Catastrophe Living*[18], he wrote about his hope that, when enough people had learned to live mindfully, there would be a tipping point, which he called an orthogonal shift in consciousness that would impact society as a whole.

Mindfulness, he wrote:

> '*could be the most important evolutionary opportunity for humanity ... to know ourselves in our wholeness and our interconnectedness as a species, and to be able to act out of the wisdom of a larger wholeness rather than out of a more small minded ... sense of self- interest.*'

Jon Kabat-Zinn[19]

Participants on an MBP have the opportunity which Jon Kabat-Zinn refers to – that of knowing their own humanity through experiencing a connectedness both with their own vulnerability and with the vulnerability of others. I may discover that 'my' experience is similar to 'yours' or that it is different and distinct – yet I can learn that it is possible to be with that, without needing to contract into judgement or separate out into a personal world view that has 'me' and 'mine' as the central concern.

---

16 Kabat-Zinn (2013)
17 Segal *et al* (2013)
18 Kabat-Zinn, 2013
19 Kabat-Zinn, 2019

Ubuntu is a form of African humanist philosophy that reflects this 'knowing'. An approximate translation from Xhosa is "a person depends on other persons to be a person"[20]. Archbishop Desmond Tutu expanded on this: 'A person is not basically an independent solitary entity. A person is human precisely in being enveloped in the community of other human beings, in being caught up in the bundle of life. To be is to participate.'[21]

In an introductory mindfulness session for a small group of women affected by HIV and Aids in rural South Africa, two key questions are being explored. You might want to reflect on them for yourself:

What keeps you awake at night? – is the first question…

Worrying (was the universal answer) – *'Will there be enough food for the family this month? – how can I find money for my child's school uniform?* (attendance at school is conditional on having uniform) – *will my sister live?'* (she was very ill with HIV and Aids).

What makes your heart sing? – is the second question…

Being happy – *'When someone in the family is getting well – when the veggies in my garden are growing nicely – when the children are happy – when we sing together – when there is love amongst us.'*

We can make much of our differences, yet it is our worries that keep us awake at night – and our joys that make our hearts sing. The content of what worries us and what brings us joy may be very different in context and impact but at this fundamental level of love, family, and well-being, it is easy to connect in empathy for others.

However, there are many instances where understanding and awareness are lacking, and opportunities for well-being are markedly different. In most forms of discrimination, the domination of those in the majority automatically confers certain powers and privileges that are denied to the rest. Sometimes these come in very subtle ways (and sometimes they are all too evident), yet they are deeply embedded in personal and national histories, and in belief systems. This is systemically and systematically damaging to those being marginalised. Where the majority fails to recognise the impact that words and actions might have – including in an MBP context, whether deliberately or completely without awareness – the impact is very real to those being marginalised. This directly threatens feelings of safety and inclusivity in an MBP group, which we write about later in this chapter.

In many countries of the world, including the US and the UK, racism is a clear example of this – resulting from the momentum of history and endemic within the colonial institutions that pervade every facet of society. Everyone needs to be aware that they may not have adequate knowledge or sufficient awareness

---

20   Battle, 1996
21   Tutu, 1972

of these impacts; and whilst many people feel a great 'awkwardness' about this, we all need to commit to uncovering and dismantling our own personal and social biases, and unconscious prejudice. In the UK, this is especially true for those racialised as white. Recognition, understanding and change inside society are urgently required – in our organisations, and in our MBP teaching and training. These issues are explored in two interviews in this book:

Can we have conversations that widen understanding of what racism involves and how we perpetuate it? – as Pauline Gibbs proposes in her interview in this book (see page 199).

Can we hold an intention to learn, rather than close up and defend ourselves, when our implicit biases show themselves? – as they surely will, in the 'social smoke', that Paula Sonrisa Sturmer mentions in her interview (see page 149) in this book.

This has implications not just within our societies but also for us as global citizens. TS Eliot suggested that humans cannot bear very much reality. His words are relevant today. Poor food security in some areas of the world contributes to a probable climate apartheid, where 'the haves' are better resourced and protected, and 'the have-nots' struggle to survive the floods, the fires, the droughts, the crop failures, the wars and the pandemics. At the time of writing, the United Nations World Food Programme[22] (WFP) suggests that 768 million people were chronically hungry in 2020[23]. WFP was awarded the Nobel Peace Prize in 2020 for its work in feeding the hungry, malnourished and starving in many parts of the world. Over 80 million people were displaced in 2020[24] and many are refugees, living in camps or on the move, hoping there is a better life somewhere else.

As readers, you may wonder why these statistics are relevant to a book about teaching mindfulness-based groups? We would argue that, as teachers, it is vital, ethically and practically, for us to be aware of our context both locally and globally in the interrelatedness of the issues that affect us all as humans. Mindfulness has a part to play, and as Kofi Annan[25] said, 'co-operation and partnership are the only routes that offer any hope of a better future for all humanity'.

---

22 https://www.wfp.org/

23 See World Food Programme hunger map https://hungermap.wfp.org/?_ga = 2.250346691.455719 855.1640773062-370757625.1633014776

24 International Rescue Committee tweet on 19/6/21

25 Kofi Annan was Secretary General of the UN 1997-2006. He and the UN were co-recipients of the Nobel Peace Prize in 2001.

Pro-social mindfulness

Mindfulness practice helps us to widen beyond the individualism that besets us, to encourage more pro-social behaviour that connects us to nature and compassion for others[26]. Ruth Baer wrote about this potential back in 2015:

> *'Mindfulness itself is inherently ethical, and the practice of mindfulness cultivates kindness and compassion towards self and others… The experimental psychology literature provides a strong foundation for working with personally meaningful, prosocial values in MBIs.'*[27]

Global empathy has been used as a term to suggest that responsive pro-social behaviour enables a move from bystander to upstander[28] and to an inclusive sense of 'we'[29]. This might be an example of Jon Kabat-Zinn's 'acting out of the wisdom of a larger wholeness'.

Md Anisur Rahman, a Bangladeshi development visionary, wrote in a similar vein about the importance of the development of the person[30]. He believed that a 'consumerist' economic view trapped people in a culture of dependency and insufficiency. He championed a 'creativist' view that emphasised *'the value of organic life with nature, standing up and moving forward in communal solidarity, in search for life and self-determination… and the primacy of human dignity'*. His words echo the 1948 Universal Declaration of Human Rights[31].

The United Nations' 17 Sustainable Development Goals (2015)[32] stand on the shoulders of that 1948 declaration, to provide a map for the structural change needed to lead to a better world. There is an increasing understanding in UN circles of this need for 'inner work', such as mindfulness, to happen alongside the 'outer work' taking place in governments, organisations and civil society.

Mindfulness practice supports individuals to connect with a sense of their personal agency. The Mindfulness Initiative is a UK charity bridging contemplative practice and public policy. In a discussion document, *Mindfulness: Developing agency in urgent times*,[33] mindfulness is portrayed as a foundational capacity – 'a way of being in relationship with the world which supports agency, our individual and collective capacity for intentional action'.

---

26   Grossman, 2015

27   Baer, 2015

28   Bystander is someone who holds back to observe the event – upstander is therefore suggesting someone who steps up and responds to what is needed.

29   Matoba, 2021

30   Bartley, 2003

31   www.un.org/en/about-us/universal-declaration-of-human-rights

32   https://sdgs.un.org/goals

33   Bristow *et al*, 2020: www.themindfulnessinitiative.org/agency-in-urgent-times/

A growing recognition of the potential of mindfulness as a foundational, pro-social capacity may not be enough. We need to find ways of harnessing MBPs to be much more pro-active in contributing to global change by seeing our personal well-being as situated within and intimately connected with our wider collective well-being.

Mindfulness – personal and collective well-being

Prof Christine Wamsler at Lund University's Centre for Sustainable Studies (LUCSUS) is a leading academic in the area of sustainability research, teaching and impact. She challenges us not to leave it to science and governments to solve these global challenges alone, and is interested in looking at what a personal practice of mindfulness can offer this area:

> *"The vast majority of sustainability practice, scholarship, and education has, so far, focused on the external world of ecosystems, wider socioeconomic structures, technology, and governance dynamics... A critical second aspect has been neglected: the inner dimensions of individuals... and transformation (embodied in notions such as consciousness and compassion are emerging as a potential new area of exploration)."*[34]

Christine and her colleagues advocate the importance of linking individual, collective and system change[35]. They propose that the root causes of climate crises need addressing, i.e. the individual and collective mindsets and associated inner personal qualities – such as openness, self-awareness, empathy, relationality, agency, and values-based courage.

Bethan Roberts and Rebecca Crane, in their chapter in *Essential Resources for Mindfulness Teachers* (2021), write about "the potential limits of current MBP curriculum models in terms of their dominant emphasis on the inner personal causes of suffering and lesser emphasis on contextual and social causes."[36] They write that mindfulness has a role in supporting people to become individually and socially mindful – and highlight a number of important areas such as: reflecting on underpinning assumptions and social contexts; considering MBP teaching from a pro-social orientation (forming intentions to find ways of including examples of everyday behaviours in teaching sessions that involve sustainable living); and developing understanding of non-discriminatory practice.

---

34   Wamsler, 2018
35   Wamsler *et al*, 2020a; Wamsler *et al*, 2020b; Wamsler *et al*, 2021
36   Crane *et al*, 2021

Targeted programmes and initiatives looking at sustainability and social justice

Although it is early days, there are some promising examples of new MBPs and other initiatives that incorporate mindfulness practice for environmental and social benefit.

Bruce Barrett and his colleagues have developed Mindful Climate Action (MCA), an eight-week group-based programme that is designed to help people improve their health whilst simultaneously lowering their carbon footprint[37]. Early research in two pilot studies is encouraging and a randomised controlled trial is planned. Their MCA sessions last for two and a half hours with two hours spent on mindfulness-based training and roughly 30 minutes on learning about the science of climate change and other sustainability issues such as energy, transport, and food.

The Dutch Environmental Education and Learning for Sustainability Policy produced a framework to develop 'ecological mindfulness'. They saw 'vital coalition' as a key element in a process where educators and policy makers come together to understand how to engage young and old within the community to collaborate in sharing common concerns and transitioning towards sustainability and ecological mindfulness through specific projects such as the greening of local playgrounds[38].

Paula Sonrisa Sturmer and others have been working with the Ulex Project in Spain delivering Mindfulness and Social Change courses as part of a European wide activist education programme, by integrating socially engaged mindfulness with anti-oppressive pedagogy[39].

Joanna Macy, an eco-Buddhist pioneer in the field of social and environmental change, draws on many years of involvement with an empowerment network known as *The Work that Reconnects*[40]. In a book with Chris Johnstone, *Active Hope*, they write about three dimensions of what they call 'The Great Turning'. The first – *Holding Actions* – is designed to raise awareness, slow down the damage, protect what is left, and care for all that are impacted by war and injustice. *Life Sustaining Systems and Practices* invites rethinking and transforming the systems that cause harm and find ways to live that bring benefit. Finally, the third dimension brings about a *Shift in Consciousness*, drawing on what they call our *connected self* so that we have a deepened sense of belonging in the world[41].

---

37   Barrett *et al*, 2016
38   Sol & Wals, 2015
39   Wreford & Haddock, 2019
40   https://workthatreconnects.org/resources/about/
41   Macy & Johnstone, 2012

The Welsh Parliament (Senedd Cymru) brought in the 'Well-being for Future Generations' Act 2015. This sets out a blueprint to change behaviours, align culture, and promote values-based collaborative decision making from a 'power over' to 'power with'. This is far reaching, involving everyone in the supply chain, not just those directly involved in government. Mindfulness is included as a foundational skill to support the development of inner personal awareness and new perspectives, thus enabling the outer work of changing the system at every level.

These are just a few of the mindfulness initiatives that are looking at new ways to take action on ecological sustainability and social justice – with mindfulness increasingly being seen to offer a valuable ingredient in what Paul Hawken describes as *'the largest social movement in history that is restoring grace, justice and beauty to the World'.*[42]

The mindfulness-based programme group

"The moment we stop listening to diverse opinions is also when we stop learning. Because the truth is, we don't learn much from sameness and monotony… Echo chambers ration knowledge … limit wisdom: wisdom that connects the heart, activates emotional intelligence, expands empathy and understanding, allows us to reach beyond the lonely confines of our own minds and engage with the rest of humanity, to listen to them and learn from them."

Elif Shafak[43]

Increasingly, mindfulness is valued in new contexts of learning, research and action that connect the domains of the personal and the collective to the needs of environmental sustainability and social justice. These initiatives and MBPs themselves inevitably involve people coming together in groups. We believe that the mindful group dynamic is fundamental in enabling the learning of those involved and to supporting the 'orthogonal shift' described above. This next section explores what is needed within the mindfulness-based group for this potential to be realized.

We propose that there are two key group enablers – *Safety* and *Inclusivity* – which in our view offer the greatest chance of creating a culture within which learning and connection leads to interrelatedness – enabling personal and collective well-being to ripple out into the world.

---

42   Hawken P, 2008
43   Shafak E, 2020

Cultivating SAFETY: the involvement of the MBP group

We first look at *Safety* through the lens of what takes place at the start of an MBP.

Most people feel some level of anxiety, apprehension, and uncertainty at the beginning of an MBP. As teachers, we may also experience something similar – with sensations of nervousness and a busy mind. This is all quite normal. Whenever something unknown and challenging is experienced, all species take steps to protect themselves. Animals of every kind share primal reactions of 'fight, flight, freeze'. As humans, neurons in the brain fire up our threat system, which is triggered both by cues in our environment, *and* by our internally felt thoughts, emotions and body sensations. Our reactions often end up adding to the challenges we feel.

Paul Gilbert's formulation of three different emotion regulation systems is helpful to us here[44]. The *threat or self-protection* system helps us detect and respond to threats. When anxious, most of us tend to ruminate – often moving into self-criticism and comparing ourselves adversely with others. The *drive and resource seeking* system helps us discover, engage in, and enjoy the things that enable us to survive, such as finding food, partners, sex, friends, money, and work. This system is all about wanting, consuming, and achieving. Finally, the *soothing and affiliation* system is linked to feelings of contentment when we are not threatened or driven. Emotions such as safeness, feeling connected, and peaceful well-being are included. These three systems can help us make sense of what is happening for participants early on, and at times throughout MBP sessions, and what we can do as MBP teachers to support safety in the group.

We explore this more fully later (Chapter 6: Launching the MBP group) but for now, we can acknowledge that showing kindness, slowing things down, and holding the group in ways that are grounded and boundaried all help to influence ways of thinking and being that can soften anxiety and open into slower, more gentle mind states. This is vital in promoting safety in the group and represents important learning to take out into in the world when uncertainty and threat is present.

Experiencing safeness in a group is empowering – people are more confident about engaging and expressing their ideas. However, feeling safe in the group (and outside in the world) is not a given, even in benign circumstances. We may not know what has occurred for participants in the past that may trigger painful reactivity in the moment.

---

44 Gilbert & Chodon, 2013

Horizontal inquiry[45] (see Chapter 12) is a form of inquiry that can follow a mindfulness practice where experiences are shared around the group in single words or phrases linking up with others who may have experienced something similar. Horizontal Inquiry is a valuable way of normalising experiences and cultivating safety in the group. A colleague of ours recently suggested that we need a new word for normalising. "It is so important and yet the term itself doesn't sound all that significant." When we let go of taking things personally, as facilitated in horizontal inquiry, there is a chance of deepening into a sense of connection with others and this in itself can support safety. It is a bit like an echo, bouncing off a surface (others in the group) to be heard in a way that confirms and validates. Normalising enables group members to relax and open up, involving the whole group and helping participants feel that they can belong and be included. This opens the door to learning and connection – two vital ingredients for personal and collective well-being.

Facilitating INCLUSIVITY: Interconnection within the MBP group

We look at this second enabler, *Inclusivity*, in two ways: initially through a general understanding of inclusivity within the MBP group and then through the perspective of diversity and discrimination. We use the example of racism, whilst recognising that MBP teachers within the UK are most likely to be racialised as white and be in the majority.

We start by returning to Paul Gilbert and his third classification of the *soothing and affiliation* system. We linked soothing to safeness. 'Affiliation' is variously defined (outside legal contexts) as close connection or family related. In evolutionary terms, this is the system that helps us form bonds of attachment, which are essential for our survival. In everyday contexts, feeling connected supports us to feel calm, settled and safe, which enables us, as humans, to care and be cared for. "It helps us understand how and why feeling cared for can be innately calming for us and is associated with a sense of well-being."[46]

The second domain (relational skills) of the Mindfulness-Based Interventions: Teacher Assessment Criteria (MBI:TAC) underlines this[47]. (This is a tool to enable MBP teaching to be assessed for adherence and competence. It is increasingly used as a supervision and reflective tool.) Key features in this second domain are the MBP teacher's relational skills, which include qualities such as connection, acceptance, compassion, warmth, authenticity, respect, and mutuality. When trust and safety are nurtured in

---

45 Horizontal inquiry is a way of exploring the mindfulness practice experience of group members that includes and acknowledges other group members' experience, rather than staying with one group member (vertical inquiry).

46 Gilbert & Chodon, 2013

47 Crane *et al*, 2013

the MBP, connecting with others is easier and the group is more likely to be experienced as an interconnected whole. Safety and inclusivity are closely related. When they come together, MBP group members can learn as much or more from each other as they do from us, their teachers.

If feeling safe (through normalising) is a bit like an echo that bounces back from the group to validate the experience of the participant, then inclusivity and interconnecting might be more like a sound that resonates around the circle of the group, tuning the participants to a shared wavelength[48].

Inclusivity and diversity

Issues of diversity are vital to consider when looking at inclusivity. Just as the climate crisis is coming onto MBP agendas, so is an awareness of society's failure to embrace concepts of diversity and inclusion.

All forms of discrimination intersect and overlap, rather than being experienced as isolated and distinct[49]. Systemic discrimination favours the dominant group (which, in the example of racism in the UK, might be 'white British'[50] ethnicity). It may appear less overt and more subtle in nature than individualised discrimination, but the impact is pervasive and plays out in all aspects of society, including the mindfulness sector.

In the UK, recognising that the majority of MBP teachers come from the majority ethnic background, it is important to understand the forces of power and privilege at work that favour white people compared to people of colour/indigenous people and other marginalised groups. This understanding is vital if there is any hope of widening the accessibility, relevance, and inclusivity of MBPs. A first step is to engage in personal learning *and* unlearning – for example by fully appreciating the way that the struggles of black people are often 'airbrushed' out of history and tend to be taught in schools without rigor and with poor quality materials[51]. There is a need to commit to understanding what this actually means, and to notice the little and not so little moments when something is said and done from a place of implicit bias. This commitment to notice more, and act more often on what we notice, will be needed for as long as society is unequal.

As MBP teachers, it is important to appreciate that the cumulative effect of discrimination impacts on a sense of belongingness. This applies to all forms of discrimination whether they involve 'visible uniqueness'

---

48   This resonance metaphor is the same as that used by McCown *et al*, 2010. *Teaching mindfulness: A practical guide for clinicians and educators*. Springer.

49   Lean & McKinsey (2020)

50   This is a debatable term to use, and we include it here only as an example of a dominant group, whilst acknowledging that there may well be population groups within the British Isles who feel discriminated against, now and in the past.

51   https://hub.jhu.edu/2021/02/10/black-history-curricula-lacking-rigor-and-quality/ Johns Hopkins Magazine February 2021 (accessed April 2022)

(gender, race/ethnicity, language, ability, age, and other aspects of physical appearance) or less visible differences (medical conditions, religious adherence, class, education level, profession, sexual/relational orientation)[52]. Even the spaces that we teach in are not neutral (see our interview with Paula Sonrisa Sturmer on page 149). They tend to reflect the values, attitudes, background, class, sexuality, race, gender and so on, of the MBP teacher/s who teach in them. So, as well as engaging in the personal learning that each of us needs to do, we also need to look with new eyes at the messages we are giving our participants, implicitly and explicitly, about the MBP space, social context, the materials we use, and the programme we wish to welcome people into (see Chapter 6 in which we explore this further).

The aspiration to have a safe, inclusive process implies that all group members need to be able to participate in the MBP at whatever level feels comfortable and possible for them at the time. This is especially relevant if we are to be successful in widening the representation of people currently accessing MBPs. This intention goes in both directions. We wish to widen access and we also need to learn how to do this in ways that are relevant, respectful, and culturally aware – with an understanding of all that is needed. With the best of intentions, we will be bound to fall down at times, and when we do, our task is to see this as another opportunity to peel back a layer of unconscious bias that we had been previously unaware of, and to learn to respond differently next time.

In the UK, we are a long way from having balanced representation in the MBP teaching community, and the pathway to becoming a mindfulness teacher can take many years. It will take time to redress the current unbalanced demographic in the mainstream mindfulness community. However, MBP groups can play their part to encourage the rich diversity of their participants by becoming spaces that are as safe and inclusive as possible, where the norms usually framed by the dominant mainstream are transformed into ways of being together that are much more aware, open, collaborative and respectful. Vital collaborations are needed if we are to join together to contribute to the social justice issues that really matter, personally and collectively – in our hearts and minds – and in the wider planet as a whole.

Beyond the mindfulness-based group: ripples moving out

'This is a watershed moment in history where all of humanity has come together, whether we realise it or not. The heating planet

---

52   From The Work that Reconnects Webinar (August 2021): An exploration of De-escalating Patterns of Harm in White Dominant Spaces (workthatreconnects.org)

is our commons. It holds us all. To address and reverse warming requires connection and reciprocity… it means listening intently and respectfully, stitching together the broken strands that separate us from life and each other. It doesn't mean hope or despair; it calls for action that is courageous and fearless… the ultimate power to change the world does not reside in technologies. It relies on reverence, respect and compassion – for ourselves, all people, all life.'

(Paul Hawken, 2021[53])

We now consider what the mindfulness-based group itself offers to our urgent social agendas, if our two key enablers of safety and inclusivity are realized as far as possible.

Let us not forget in the work involved in delivering an MBP that we are supporting our participants to invest in their futures on a personal, collective, relational and societal level. A number of sustainability academics have written about their interest in mindfulness in connection with cultivating relatedness, inner personal qualities and different mindsets that engage empathy and values-based courage. We suggest that the ripples from the MBP group have the potential to extend far and wide, from the experience of belonging to a mindfulness-based group, to enriching the personal (family, close friends and neighbours), the collective (local community, schools, workplace, wider organisations), the systems (social networks relating to nature and the environment, social and political activities, etc.) and even the future (the state of the world being left to our grandchildren's children and future generations)[54].

We bring this together by highlighting:

- the *group skills and experience* gained through being in a mindfulness-based group
- the opportunities to *clarify personal values* whilst relating to others
- the *interrelatedness* that supports *inner personal work*
- the links between *the personal and the collective* out in the world.

Group skills and experience

Mindfulness-based programmes offer a rather different experience of being in a group. We learn new skills that start with cultivating more grounded-ness in response to our experience. We learn to listen in the MBP group with more of ourselves, which helps us to be more aware when the mind wanders off, or when we disagree with what is being expressed. The MBP group exposes us to new ideas, perhaps finding our voice alongside others who

---

53 Hawken, 2021
54 Wamsler, 2020a

may also be finding new voices, in a mindful setting that values respect, empathy and inclusivity. A group experience that embodies these mindful values can be strongly empowering to the individual and offer insights that can be taken out into other groups.

"When you feel alone, don't look within, look out and look beyond for others who feel the same way, for there are always others and if you can connect with them and with their story, you will be able to see everything in a new light.[55]*"*

Elif Shafak

Clarifying personal values while relating to others

In their seminal paper *Mechanisms of Mindfulness*, Shapiro *et al* (2005)[56] suggest that "personal vision or intention is dynamic and evolving". As we practice mindfulness and 'reperceive' habitual patterns of mind, we may also come to "recognise what is meaningful … and what (we) truly value". Participants may come to an MBP with the intention of learning how to better manage their stress, and later connect with a strong wish to get involved in making a difference in their community, locality or even country. Jon Kabat-Zinn writes, "your intention sets the stage for what is possible".[57]

Many MBP teachers guide a practice at the start of the group that helps participants draw out their intentions for learning mindfulness. Engaging with these inner reflections alongside others in the group can affirm, support and clarify personal values. This helps MBP group members to stay on track with their values and co-opt their ongoing practice to support actions and behaviours that are in tune with them.

Our personal values (what really matters to us) inevitably develop throughout our lives. What matters to a young adult may be rather different to what matters to someone in middle age. Our values are influenced by upbringing, events, people, culture, community, the groups we belong to and the ideas we come across. The widespread tendency (in much of Western society) to emphasise the individual may be quietened through the experience of practicing mindfulness and belonging to an MBP group, where values and intentions are clarifying, and there are opportunities to join with others in empathy and compassion.

As MBP teachers, our personal values and intentions will influence the form of the MBP that we teach and some of the emphases that we choose to include within the programme. We are likely to see many more examples of explicit and implicit elements of social agendas coming into MBPs – either via direct curricula, as teaching examples in context, and/or woven into the

---

55 Shafak, 2020
56 Shapiro, 2006
57 Kabat-Zinn, 2013

entire teaching language and process. This is very welcome and bound to deepen in response to the crises of the present world.

> *"Mindfulness has the potential to become both a core part of a collective vision for society, and a way to help make that vision a reality… From all quarters we are called urgently to a better understanding of ourselves, each other, and our role in shaping the world… to reclaim and reorient attention towards what matters, reflect more wisely, and act from a place of collective purpose."*

(Jamie Bristow and Rosie Bell[58])

Interrelatedness that supports inner personal work

We use reflective questions in the MBP group to become more aware of inner experience. Emergent discussions that flow in small groups are gathered up into the larger group. They serve to nurture reflective capacities that use the whole range of personal experience as a guide (body sensations, emotions and thoughts, and reactive urges). In MBP groups, we talk about the undercurrents that drive our lives in ways we may never do in everyday life. We learn to take a pause, individually and as a group, when emotions are stirred, or something is triggered for us or for another. We discover the value of getting the ground under our feet when we feel unsteady, uncertain, angry or fearful – and the value of this is affirmed when we see the benefit it offers others. We learn to use words to describe our experience, to heighten awareness, and choose to respond mindfully rather than react habitually. All these resources and more are strengthened by the interrelatedness of the MBP group.

This is confirmed by the current interest in 'relational thinking'. A number of researchers in the sustainability field consider that relational approaches offer a basis for integrating inner and outer, and personal and collective dimensions of sustainability. Walsh *et al* (2020) make a "call to action for sustainability scholars and practitioners to co-develop a research agenda for advancing a relational paradigm within sustainability research practice and education based on relational ways of being knowing and acting"[59]. In a study looking at environmental and climate policies and practices in Swedish municipalities, five complementary strategies were identified which "revealed an increasing need for relational approaches that require individuals to develop cognitive/emotional capacity to establish trust, communicate inclusively and promote social learning while at the same time dealing with increasing complexity and uncertainty"[60].

---

58 Bristow *et al*, 2021
59 Walsh *et al*, 2020
60 Walmsler *et al*, 2020

This description mirrors what is taking place in the MBP group: inner work and personal learning taking place through interrelatedness with others. These are essential partners to support the outer work needed to respond to the urgent social and environmental agendas that exist.

Making the links between the personal and the collective out in the world

Mindfulness practice helps us to join up what before has been separate. We learn to relate to the experience of the body, which helps us find ways of turning towards what is challenging and responding with kindness, as best we can. We learn to connect with moments of present awareness as we sit with our MBP group colleagues and learn that they too have their own struggles and habitual tendencies. This embeds a culture of allowing empathy and understanding, and the possibility of friendliness, which is much needed both personally and collectively.

The ripples that move out beyond the MBP group travel into the individual lives of MBP group members, and through the layers of their personal relationships and social networks – including partners, children, wider family members, neighbours, local community networks, work colleagues, and so on. These ripples of mindfulness learning and experience move out to join up with some of the strangers in the lives of group members – the new mother at the school gates, the cashier at the supermarket, the person next to them in the queue. There are many people out there to connect with if we choose, and these small moments of connecting can profoundly change the experience of that moment. The MBP group can also deepen appreciation and relatedness to non-humans – the bee collecting pollen from the centre of the flower, the spider weaving its web in the corner of the window, the clouds chasing across the sky, the trees losing their leaves one by one in autumn.

Relatedness is key to all this. The MBP group offers an experience of forming a learning community with others who – not many weeks before – were strangers. Sharing perspectives and our diverse longings to be free of suffering brings us together in ways that help us become aware of the relatedness between 'me', 'you', 'us', and the world beyond. These edges are not fixed. To move from this shared experience in an MBP group to a worldview of humanity need not be such a huge step. It helps so much to see and care that the issues that relate to us, also relate to others.

> "We have the potential to participate in... ...a flowering, not only of ourselves as individuals but of society as a seamless whole."[61]

Jon Kabat-Zinn

---

61 Kabat-Zinn, 2000

We can act in ways that are life enabling for future generations without knowing whether our actions will be successful or not. Doing this now gives our life meaning and is arguably the most life affirming way of spending the time we have.

> *"If we want to be good ancestors, we should show future generations how we coped with an age of great change and great crises."*[62]

Jonas Salik

It is easy to get disheartened when we become aware of all that is missing; of all that is wrong and much needed for individuals, societies and the planet as a whole. It is naïve and idealistic to suggest that mindfulness and MBP groups can heal the ills of the world – but as Robert Chambers famously wrote:

> *"Big, simple solutions are tempting but full of risks. For most [of us] … most of the time, the soundest and best way forward is through innumerable small steps and tiny pushes, putting the last first not once, but again and again."*[63]

Robert Chambers

The wisest way forward seems to need us, as MBP teachers, to stay close to our intention to do our best with each group and each programme – supporting the conditions for good practice, knowing that this opens the door to many possibilities.

> *"The key question is not how can I make a difference? But how can we make the difference? A mere shift of pronoun has the power to change the world."*[64]

Roman Krznaric

Summary

Mindfulness practice helps us to widen beyond the individualism that besets us, and to support pro-social behaviour that connects us to nature and compassion for others[65,66]. Researchers, practitioners, and policy makers in the fields of sustainability and social justice are showing interest in mindfulness as a way of enabling personal inner work to partner the outer work urgently required in the world.

---

62 Jonas Salik's 1977 speech: 'Are we being good ancestors'.
63 Chambers, 1983
64 Krznaric, 2020
65 Grossman, 2015
66 Baer, 2015

We have recorded a practice for teachers that links to this chapter and your teaching intention. It can be downloaded at www.pavpub.com/teaching-mindfulness-based-groups-resources

The MBP group is a significant vehicle for participants' learning and interconnection. *Safety* and *inclusivity* are presented as the two key enablers of the mindfulness-based group. As a result, the relational skills gained from the MBP group can underpin a sense of interrelatedness between the personal, social, and environmental spheres of life – and links can be made between personal and collective well-being.

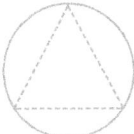

2. Dimensions of mindfulness-based programme teaching

Understanding the context

Trish Bartley

In this chapter, we introduce the different dimensions of MBP teaching and some central themes that relate to this. This will help to clarify the frameworks that mindfulness-based group teaching sits within.

The separate dimensions of MBP teaching can sometimes seem to be in creative tension with each other. They are the voices, if you like, that champion a particular corner and pull at us, as MBP teachers, with their different demands. As we get more familiar with them we find that, on reflection, they can help us to contemplate the different aspects of MBP teaching that include the complexity of working with mindfulness-based groups.

Of course, each voice, as it appears here, may risk seeming a bit fixed and two dimensional. In reality they are much more multi-layered. However, by offering these outlines, we hope to set the scene and help to kindle an appetite for exploring further into the MBP group and what follows in the later sections of this book.

The dimensions of mindfulness-based teaching that we consider in this chapter include:

- The new and more experienced mindfulness-based teacher.
- The mindfulness-based programme.
- The mindfulness-based programme participants.
- A mention at the end of the chapter of the mindfulness-based group, as a segue into what follows.

The new mindfulness-based teacher

As a new teacher, you are probably still engaged in training – whether on a recognised teacher training pathway or via your own individually tailored pathway. You may have started to offer some mindfulness taster sessions, perhaps in your workplace or local community. This seems to be an obvious place to begin – short, limited introductions with a mix of presentations and short practices. However, later, when we have more teaching experience, we come to realize that running a taster session can be one of the hardest things to do for people who often know very little about mindfulness (except what they have read, which is often a misrepresentation of the approach). However, we have to start somewhere, and those of us who are new to teaching MBPs need to find ways of 'warming up' before teaching a full programme.

Later, as a new teacher, you offer your first eight-week group-based programme. You are probably amazed to discover just how much work is involved in recruiting participants, booking a venue (or sorting an online platform), arranging orientation session/s, gathering course materials (practice recordings, handouts or workbooks), finding a supervisor and arranging sessions, and sorting out any number of practical details like payments, insurance, arrangements to cover things at home, responding to participants' queries and so on. Sometimes, when programmes are arranged through your work context, some of these tasks seem easier (venue, networking, promoting the course etc.), but then other complexities appear, such as referral expectations, accurate orientation information, organisational hierarchies, safe assessments and so on.

In amongst all of this, as a novice teacher you may well be beset with doubt and fear (most of us are). *Is this what I am meant to be doing? Am I getting it right? How on earth do I manage that?* A lot of these concerns are focused on the tasks – things that have to be accomplished. However, mindfulness-based teaching, as we discover, is only partly about 'doing'. Much more challenging is the business of working through all the tasks and then dropping into the present moment, and teaching in an aware 'being mode of mind'.

The business of trying to find out what we need to know reminds me of one of my son's school assemblies, many years ago.

In his second year of infant school, his rather gifted teacher, Mrs. Wilde, was helping his class learn about different forms of knowledge and how they are acquired. The class was divided into three groups. The first group shouted out examples of things that were known and could be looked up and proven (the world is round; Alexander Fleming discovered penicillin in 1928; and so on). A child in the second group then held up a packet of cornflakes and a number was held up on a card by another child, which she explained was how many →

cornflakes they had found in the packet. They were demonstrating that we can find things out for ourselves by asking questions and discovering/researching the answers. (I wondered at the time how many corn flakes were eaten by the children as they counted!) The third group explained that there were things that we don't yet know – and my son got his turn to shout out 'Is there life on Mars?' I felt very proud!

Of course, impressive as it was, the children had missed out an important group of questions. They were too young to move into complex philosophical matters where vast areas of knowledge are not just unknown, but which we are not even aware that we do not know them. The planets not yet discovered. The new skill that we have never heard of. And this is where we are as we start out as new mindfulness teachers – unaware of all the layers involved in the craft that we imagine, in time, we can perfect.

It is inevitable, at some point, that doubt and its first cousin, the inner critic, dig in. The more we realize just how much there is to learn, the more the inner critic appears in view. And this is painfully uncomfortable – sabotaging the learning we are embarking on. The Learning Stages (Burch, 1974)[67] or the Conscious Competence learning theory helps us make sense of this. It is a developmental model in four stages: unconscious incompetence, conscious incompetence, conscious competence, and unconscious competence. The first two are probably the territories we inhabit as new mindfulness-based teachers.

1. *Unconscious incompetence – we don't know what we don't know.* This is the stage of the 'holy innocent', unaware of not knowing what we do not know. We are blissfully naïve, possibly even a little complacent. It is inevitably a young place, whether through age or inexperience.

2. *Conscious incompetence – we know what we don't know and start to realise how much we have missed and how much more there is to know.* This is the most uncomfortable of the four stages. Here, we have arrived at a place that holds more experience (enough to know more about what is needed) only to become aware of just how much more there is to learn. This might be termed 'beginners' mind', but there is a great challenge in staying open and immediate to all that is unfolding – and for many there is a marked tendency to move into debilitating periods of 'inner critic', rather than the freshness of 'beginners' mind'.

We will consider the other two layers of conscious competence and unconscious competence in the next section.

---

67 "The Learning Stages" were created by Mr. Noel Burch, co-author with Thomas Gordon of the *Teacher Effectiveness Training Book*, 1974. This is disputed and an earlier citation is also quoted Martin M Broadwell 1969 in the *Gospel Guardian*, an American Christian periodical published 50s-70s

The experienced mindfulness-based programme teacher

When we have gained some experience, we are able to bring a level of reflection into our teaching and learning. The MBI:TLC[68] (known as The TLC) helps us with this. Some of you reading this book may be bringing years of skills in reflective practice into this work – but however this has developed over time, as MBP teachers we are bound to be influenced and informed by all the training and learning we have assimilated from our participants, peers, teachers, and trainers. We may be more able to hold in present moment awareness the content of the programme; the process of facilitating the group learning; and the response of our participants as they land into their practice. We are cultivating the capacity to be more discerning about the session just taught, and probably less convinced now by global labels of 'good' or 'bad' teaching. Instead, we can see the nuances of how things could be different, and of the many dimensions and choices that are involved in almost every moment. We are more able to draw learning from the times when we fall short of what our participants need from us.

> I use a device to help me reflect, which I've often shared with trainee teachers. Fred (or Freda) sits on my shoulder as I teach or train – a part of me, but with a wider view than I might have moment by moment. Fred is not actively involved in the ongoing happenings in the room or on the screen. In this way, it is as if he is able to freeze frame salient moments in the session and, with practice, I can use them later when I have the time and space to reflect further. 'Fred' is my reflective observer assistant.
>
> There might be some questions that can help with this process such as:
>
> - what was going on at that point?
> - what was I doing as teacher, and what was happening in the group/with the individual participant?
> - how did the content of what was being taught impact on what was happening in the room?
> - How did it feel? In my body and in terms of a felt sense of unpleasant experience (very unpleasant, quite unpleasant, not at all unpleasant etc...)
>
> In this way, I can learn from the session and bring that learning into aspects of future sessions (remembering that new learning tends to take time to integrate).

As more experienced teachers, we are aware that there is always more to learn. We know that the craft of teaching MBPs is highly involved, full of layers of meaning and significance, asking for integrity in knowing that what we do within the space of the mindfulness-based group matters to each individual participant. This awareness is in no way depressing, although the sense of responsibility can be sobering. At times, it can even be inspiring and humbling

---

68   Griffith, 2021

to connect with. We can continue to teach MBPs, even for the rest of our lives, and at the end there would still be a huge amount to learn.

If we are lucky, we belong to a peer teaching practice community, such as a SiTT group[69]. These are colleagues with whom we can discuss books, talks and training, chew over thorny teaching issues, share ideas for next retreats, and importantly, we can also practice alongside. They are the ones with whom we build trust, who are available for support when a session has been tricky. They are there for us as we are for them. Now that many of us are more familiar with online gatherings, we are no longer limited by geography to make these connections.

As we develop as teachers, we seem to evolve a growing awareness that it is less about us and our competence as teachers (although this is clearly important), and more about facilitating the programme itself, in ways that are aligned as much as possible with the wisdom and intention of those who have shaped the approach, over many tens and even thousands of years. So, although we start from a position of not knowing, which borders on complacency, and move through some discouraging layers of trying hard to get things right, some years down the line we may come to a place that holds genuine humility, realizing that it is less about 'me as teacher' and more about my intention to teach the programme with integrity and in ways that benefit others.

The experienced teacher probably falls into one of the later two stages of the Conscious Competence model:

- *Conscious Competence – we are trying out the new skill – practicing, becoming more familiar, acquiring competence.* This is a more secure position, more confident of knowing what is needed, with the capacity to deliver much of what is required. However, there is a tangible sense of effort involved, of the need to remember what is important, and perhaps some hard work to bring it all together.

- *Unconscious Competence – after much practice, our teaching skills have a sense of flow. It is internalized. We don't have to think about it so much anymore.* This stage involves a teaching practice that has flow and grounded intuition. The MBP teacher has developed a confidence that is embodied, authentic and natural; that seems to arise with almost effortless effort. To the uninitiated, this stage can look a little like the first – disarmingly simple yet confident. However, unlike the first stage, the experienced practitioner knows what they are doing. Their ease is justified and comes with a measure of wise discernment and mindful embodying.

The only risk in seeing learning through this prism is that it presents the stages as incremental, a bit like climbing a ladder step by step to the top. Although this is partly true (we definitely improve with experience given the right conditions), it is not entirely helpful as a take home message. It is true that the world tends

---

69 https://www.sitt.community/

to see the acquisition of knowledge and learning in this way – but mindfulness-based teaching, more than anything, needs present moment awareness that is embodied and kindly. Once we slip into complacent, automatic habits of teaching, and stop investing in regular practice, ongoing learning, retreat and supervision, we risk losing intention, integrity, humility, and heart.

The Reflective Competence model[70] below develops the conscious competence model a little further. Will Taylor (2007) proposed that it might be more useful to consider this way of looking at learning to be more as a spiral than a hierarchy, with reflective competence underpinning all. This perspective works well in our MBP teaching context, which privileges the practice of reflection and continuous development as an important part of sustaining integrity as an MBP teacher.

The reflective competence model also parallels the developmental layers of competence in the MBI:TAC[71], where each stage (beginner, advanced beginner, competent teacher, proficient teacher, and advanced teacher) has its own characteristics with growing levels of embodied intuition and a reduced need to hold the structures and roles in such firm attention.

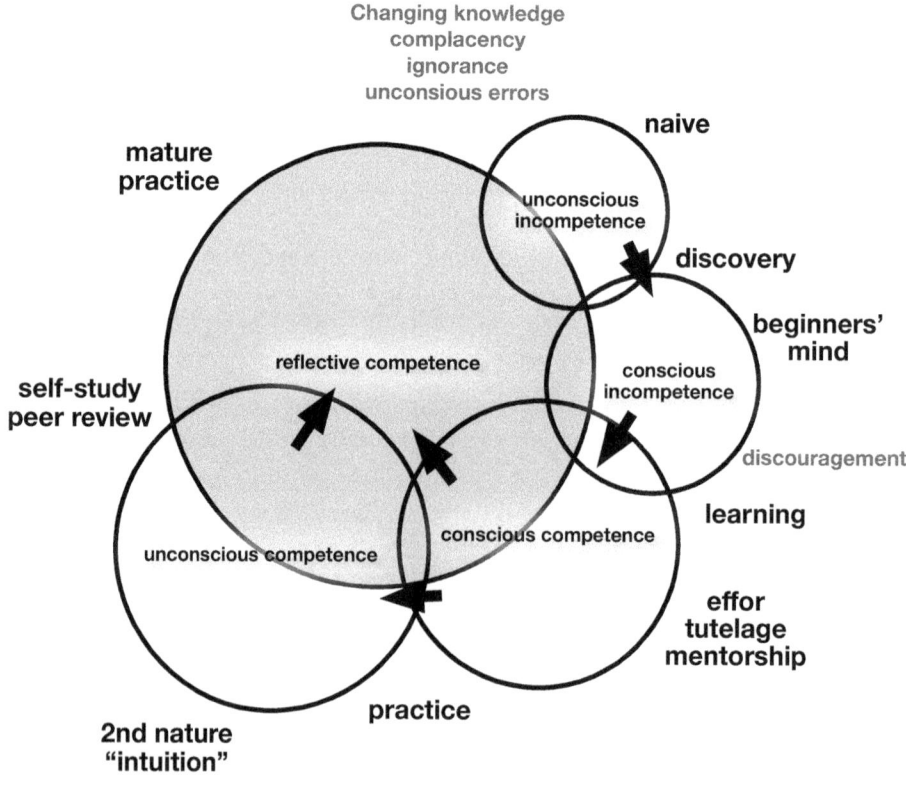

---

70 This model is courtesy of Will Taylor, Chair, Department of Homeopathic Medicine, National College of Natural Medicine, Portland, Oregon, USA, March 2007

71 Crane *et al*, 2013

The participant

We now look at some contexts and issues for MBP participants to draw out another dimension within MBP teaching. We do this through the lives of Ayesha, Glenroy, and Nia.

Ayesha has been feeling dissatisfied with life in general – especially in relation to how things are going in her job and her social life. She was told about mindfulness from a friend, who is concerned about her. She discovers that she might be able to access a programme through her work in a large legal firm. This has many advantages, until when she realizes that she will be doing it alongside a manager she is not keen on. She is motivated to learn mindfulness to help her manage periods of anxiety, which relate to her personal life and also to a growing sense of unease and uncertainty, especially in relation to the climate crisis.

Then there is Glenroy. He has had a number of episodes of depression. He has tried CBT (Cognitive Behavioural Therapy) and it was helpful. His key worker is now encouraging him to go on the next MBCT programme. Glenroy lives in the city, in rented social housing, with his partner and their two growing children. He works as a chef in a local restaurant and his wife is a waitress at the same place. Both their jobs are part time, so the family struggles to manage at times – especially when Glenroy is less well. The future of the restaurant looks uncertain due to the Covid pandemic. They have a large extended family, who originally came over to the UK from the West Indies in the early 60s.

Nia is also interested in mindfulness. She has been concerned about her health for some time. She is in her 60s, has debilitating COPD (chronic obstructive pulmonary disease) and is worried about the risks of Covid, even though she has been fully vaccinated. She tried an introduction to mindfulness that was being run by her health trust's Recovery College[72] and got on quite well, but is not sure that she can manage all the daily practice or the online platform. She lives on her own in a low-rise council flat and is quite lonely. She would love to be more involved in what is going on in her local community.

Although Ayesha, Glenroy, and Nia are imaginary participants, their different backgrounds, health needs, income, social and family networks demonstrate the range of those who might find their way to MBPs. Indeed, it is a widely held aspiration that, as clinical, community and workplace programmes become more widely available, participants from diverse communities and backgrounds will be able to access MBPs more easily. Ways of teaching MBP groups skilfully have an important role to play in this. We need to move steadily towards a place where there are fewer barriers to coming onto an

---

72 Recovery Colleges are offered in some UK Health Trusts within the NHS (National Health Service) and offer a range of educational courses and one-off workshops that are designed to improve health and wellbeing by increasing knowledge and skills and promoting self-management.

MBP, where mindfulness-based groups are genuinely inclusive, and teachers are drawn from all backgrounds, levels of income, and identities.

Ayesha, Glenroy, and Nia will each bring with them a bundle of habitual ways of reacting that cause them to suffer. These will include a diverse mix of universal vulnerabilities that are shared by everyone (such as the way we seek to avoid what make us feel anxious) and individual vulnerabilities specific to each one of them. These specific patterns are formed through upbringing, life events, illnesses, background, gender, identity, and the matrix of personal and socially constructed histories that impact on our lives. Some MBP groups are formed from people who share a specific vulnerability – for example, a history of recurrent depression. In this instance, the programme taught to the group would be MBCT, which was developed and tailored from MBSR specifically to intervene with the patterns of vulnerabilities experienced by people with recurrent depression. However, much of the MBCT programme includes work with the diverse universal vulnerabilities that lie at the root of all our suffering.

So, each MBP participant brings with them patterns that will be broadly shared by others – and their own mix that are particular to each one of them. Overall, we share more similarities than we have differences – and yet it is so important for us, as MBP teachers, to honour, respect and be sensitive to the uniqueness of each participant and to the difference that they bring.

The day arrives for the start of the programme. The participants enter the room, the MBP teacher has everything prepared and all is ready to begin this collective and individual encounter with the practice of mindfulness and how it intervenes with the habits and patterns of body and mind. None of them can be sure what this will offer. We hope that it will bring different degrees of personal benefit and well-being to them all – and that it will also link with wider collective benefit and well-being out in the world.

The mindfulness-based programme

The founding mindfulness-based programme was mindfulness-based Stress reduction (MBSR), an inspired intervention created by Jon Kabat-Zinn in the 1980s. Many programmes have since been developed, shaped and adapted out of that original legacy. So whatever MBP is being taught, providing it has the integrity of MBSR, MBCT, or one of the other carefully formulated, evidence-based MBPs, then we can usually be confident about the authenticity of the programme.

An important paper by Crane *et al* defined this beautifully[73]. It took many years to write and used the weaving metaphor of warp and weft to help make clear what was integral to MBPs. The warp elements

---

73   Crane *et al*, 2017

are regarded as essential, without which a programme cannot be said to be mindfulness-based. The weft elements are the contextual and developmental elements that are needed to carefully adapt the MBP to suit the needs of the context or population.

The essential (warp) and flexible (weft) ingredients of MBPs[74]

WARP

The essential ingredients of MBPs:

1. are informed by theories and practices from contemplative traditions, science, medicine, psychology and education
2. are underpinned by a model of human experience that is characterised by present moment focus, decentering and an approach orientation.
3. are supported by the development of greater attentional, emotional, and behavioural self-regulation, as well as qualities such as kindness, compassion, wisdom and equanimity.
4. engage the participant in sustained intensive training in mindfulness meditation practice, in an experiential inquiry-based learning process and in exercises to develop insight, learning and understanding.

WEFT

The flexible ingredients of MBPs:

1. The core essential ingredients are integrated with adapted curriculum elements and tailored to specific contexts and populations.
2. Include variations in programme structure, length and delivery, and are formatted to fit the population and context involved.

The eight-week MBP may appear clear in terms of curriculum themes, but as we understand it more deeply we come to appreciate the complexity and rich potential that lies within it. The sequencing of the learning is based on pedagogy that has been taught and tested over hundreds of years (i.e., The Four Foundations of Mindfulness[75]). This implicitly holds frameworks for understanding the human mind, its potential and its vulnerabilities.

A programme with this level of complexity inevitably takes time to learn to teach. We train to become aware of moments of reactivity, which move us into automatic unhelpful reactions – and learn to interrupt those moments by coming back to present moment awareness that offers the possibility of responding more skilfully and choosing more kindly.

---

74 Ibid
75 Analayo, 2003

In the intense busyness of our lives, with ever-increasing distractions and a tendency to lean towards instant solutions, it is inevitable that teachers and organisations will want to truncate the programme into fewer weeks, shorter sessions, and reduced practice times. Indeed, early-stage teachers report this[76]. On the one hand, in our current social context, it might be possible to justify a programme that is four or six weeks long instead of the 'classical' eight weeks. We do need to adapt to the changing needs of the people we wish to reach. However, on the other hand it is vital that we stay in touch with the 'warp' of the MBP and not compromise the programme. We always need a clear rationale of what it is we are seeking to achieve, why we are seeking to do it and what will be lost if elements are removed. There is a danger that MBPs can be adapted too quickly before a mature understanding is in place of the different steppingstones needed to build the full structure of the intervention. The history and complexity of MBPs means that any adaptations need to be made with care and with grounded, evidence-based knowledge.

Of course, the historical origins of the programme go back long before Jon Kabat-Zinn and the creation of MBSR. One way of looking at the mindfulness-based programme is through the metaphor of a bridge with twin footings on two vast 'continents' of knowledge and teaching[77]. The earliest of these land masses come from contemplative traditions, which we have loosely termed the Dharma (the ancient teachings). The key foundations of MBPs are drawn from early Buddhist teachings (namely the Four Foundations of Mindfulness, or the Satipatthana Sutta, which include the body, feeling tone, the mind, and the conditions/core teachings that help or hinder practice and matters relating to ethical integrity). The relational qualities of mindfulness (such as friendliness, empathy, compassion and kindness) come from all contemplative traditions. These cannot be viewed as the sole domain of Buddhist psychology, although the Brahma Viharas – kindness, compassion, appreciative joy and equanimity – lay out this ground very clearly.

The other footing of the 'mindfulness-based programme bridge' rests in the territory of science, another vast continent of knowledge and exploration. This includes contemporary psychological underpinnings (such as the universal tendency to ruminate, the experience of aversion etc.). Science in this context includes research, relevant theoretical models, neuroscience, and much else.

---

76   Bowden, 2020

77   The analogy of the Dharma and science flowing into each other was first conceived as an hourglass at a gathering of European MBP teachers arranged by Professor Mark Williams at Merton College, Oxford, UK in early 2000s. Initially the discussion ranged around which way the hourglass might stand – with Dharma on top flowing into and influencing science or the other way around. Later Melanie Fennell developed this further by suggesting that the relationship of MBPs to science and the Dharma was more like a bridge straddling two continents, as suggested in the figure above. This metaphor has been further developed since then.

At first glance, it looks as if the landmass of the Dharma, originating from ancient teachings, has a fixed size, while the territory of science is increasing all the time. However, we might challenge this view and suggest that both areas are expanding, but not necessarily at the same rate. To stay fresh and relevant,

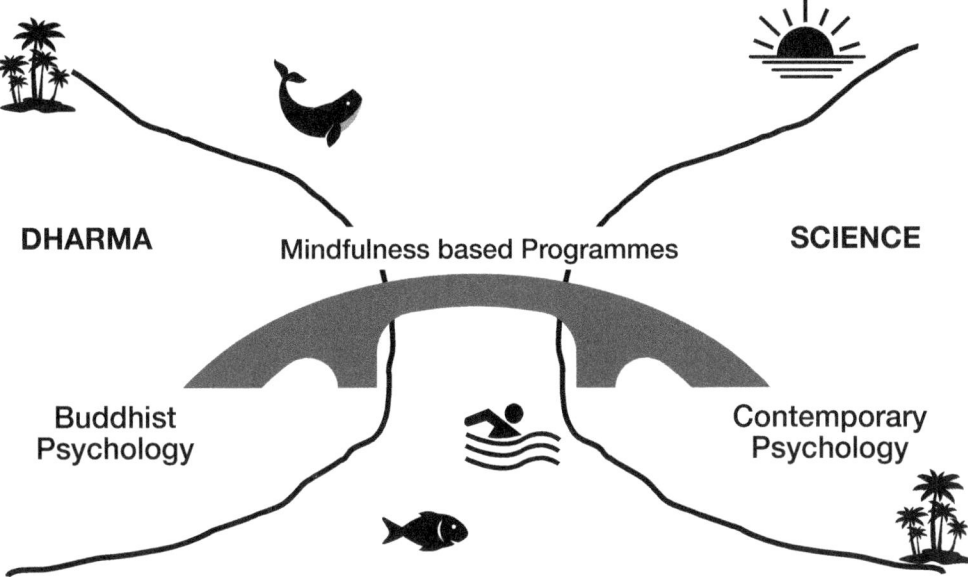

Buddhist and other contemplative teachings are continually being translated and adapted for modern times – and science, of course, is constantly going deeper and expanding into new territory.

When this way of seeing the twin influences of MBPs was first conceived not long after MBCT was first published, it was as if the mindfulness-based bridge was narrow, a bit like one of those rickety rope bridges that you might find spanning a Himalayan valley. You need courage and resolve to walk across, holding your nerve as it sways alarmingly!

Later, when the evidence base was being established, especially in mental health, MBPs might be characterised as having morphed into a new and sparkly footbridge, well designed and much more secure, but still less significant when compared to the substantial bridges alongside, such as CBT (Cognitive Behavioural Therapy) and conventional evidence-based treatment approaches. So where are we now? The MBP bridge certainly seems to have become more substantial – perhaps with two lanes going in each direction and carrying a high volume of traffic, which is increasing all the time. There have been a few repairs needed, when outside challenges have questioned the robustness of the safety barriers (e.g., do MBPs ignore the ethics implicit in the Buddhist practice of mindfulness? Are MBPs too Buddhist/not Buddhist enough?) However, the MBP bridge has shown its capacity to stand up to some stormy weather, with its feet planted firmly in both territories, which continue to support, inform and interact with each other.

> *"This interface is a rich and fertile ground for investigating human experience, and the source of creative tensions for MBP implementers. There are robust debates in the literature about potential for compromises to the integrity of the work if MBP teachers … are naïve to the sources from which they draw."*[78]

Gemma Griffith & Karunavira

MBPs will be bound to undergo further development over the coming years, as social agendas impact on what is most needed for MBP participants, society and the wider world. There will be more versions of dedicated MBPs that join up the needs of personal *and* collective well-being, such as Mindful Climate Action[79]. Other developments will evolve finding organic approaches that thread the climate crisis (for example) into curriculum exercises, reflections and routine activities within current MBPs. A raft of creative responses and research will expand what is already happening as separate academic disciplines, such as psychological and sustainability sciences, join up and collaborate to explore many different ways of responding to current emergencies.

The group

MBPs are usually delivered in groups – and this brings a new entity into the MBP over and above the sum of the individuals present in the teaching space. Each mindfulness-based group has its own emerging character and development, unique and distinct. No two groups can ever be the same. There are very many variants, dimensions and conditions that influence the complex entity that is the group.

Mindfulness practice enables us to relate to experience in a friendly way. We might call this relational quality 'the active ingredient' of mindfulness practice. As we deepen into the immediacy of the experience of the present moment, so we recognise an opportunity to change our relationship to that which we might otherwise avoid or push away. We come closer, more often, to connecting in ways that are more open, allowing, and kindly.

The group is also relational. The process of the group represents aspects of the world coming together. This offers opportunities for MBP group members to explore new experiences as they learn about mindfulness. Much of this and many aspects of the group are mysterious. For some time the group in MBP research and teaching practice has been almost invisible, although this is now slowly changing (see chapters 3 and 4). However, for many MBP participants, the group can make or break the entire experience of learning

---

78   Griffith & Karunavira, 2021
79   Barrett *et al*, 2016

mindfulness. The relational qualities of a group sometimes have a way of coming together with the relational qualities of mindfulness to offer a space that at its best can be safe and inclusive, with the potential for MBP group members to transform their lives.

MBSR and MBCT were both designed to be delivered in a group setting, but how many need to be present in order for it to be a 'group'? There are variations between countries and curriculums. At the time of writing, the group size for MBSR is not outlined in the curriculum (2017). McCown[80] recommends groups of between 10-30 participants, so that everyone in the circle can be easily seen and heard by other members. However, we would also suggest that MBP groups of five people or less tend not to function as groups, with more exchanges mostly happening one to one between teacher and participant. A typical group size for MBSR delivery in the UK of around 10-24 participants. Original MBCT groups are recommended to be smaller with 10-12 participants[81].

The group is a container for the learning of each individual participant, and for the collective learning that is shared by group members. The experience of belonging to the group and practicing together in the group is often internalised by participants – taken away and remembered long after the programme has finished. It may no longer be possible to clearly remember the names and faces of the people who we sat with as group members, yet when the guided practice is heard or some of the oft-repeated phrases (such as 'weight going down, height going up') is remembered, the experience of sitting in the group can come again into our practice and there is a sense of how it was to belong.

The group has a clear influence on the learning that takes place in the MBP. It is this that we now explore in the rest of this book. First, we consider the evolution of theory around MBP group process and look at this in the light of the development of MBP pedagogy as a whole. This is followed by a chapter that explores research and what it tells us about MBP group processes.

Summary

This chapter has sketched out the different dimensions of the MBP, namely:

- The MBP teacher, and their different levels of teaching experience.
- The programme itself, and the model of the MBP bridge with its feet in the two interacting landmasses of ancient teachings and modern science – with some anticipation of further MBP developments that increasingly incorporate social agendas.
- The participant, and the diverse universal and specific vulnerabilities that they bring with them into the MBP.
- The group (in introduction only, at this stage).

---

80 McCown, 2010
81 Segal *et al*, 2013

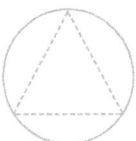

3. The evolution of pedagogical theory

How group process became important in mindfulness-based programmes

Gemma Griffith

In this chapter, we look at how the understanding of teaching MBP groups has evolved and developed. This is not an exhaustive account of the evolution of MBP pedagogy around groups (pedagogy is the method and practice of teaching), but it tracks the main themes that have arisen around group process since MBSR was first developed in the late 1970s. Group process is a key teaching skill which has gained particular momentum in the last decade as the pedagogy of MBPs has become more explicated. This helps us to understand how and why group process is one of the six key domains in the MBI:TAC[82], and has emerged as highly significant for MBP teachers. This chapter traces the development of group process from a fairly vague concept in MBP pedagogy to being regarded today as one of the key skills that needs to be cultivated by MBP teachers[83].

The foundations: was the group process explicit in early MBP texts?

Full Catastrophe Living was published in 1990 by Jon Kabat-Zinn. This brought Mindfulness-Based Stress Reduction (MBSR) to the attention of a global audience and was written for the layperson who wanted to learn more about MBSR and mindfulness. In this first book, the MBSR group process within the class was not explicitly mentioned, but then *Full Catastrophe Living* was not intended as a training manual for MBP teachers. What is

---

82 Crane *et al*, 2021

83 Ibid.

notable, however, is that themes that we now regard as underpinning group process are clearly embedded within the book. These include common humanity, attitudinal foundations of mindfulness, and the deep investigation of one's here and now awareness via experiential learning. The MBSR curriculum itself supports the group process, for example teachings on the stress-reaction cycle demonstrates how we all share the same biological bases that can lead to anxiety, depression etc. This illustrates that an understanding of shared humanity is integral to MBSR. In the preface to the second edition of *Full Catastrophe Living*[84], Kabat-Zinn wrote:

> *"Over the years, I have increasingly come to realize that mindfulness is essentially about relationality – in other words, how we are in relationship to everything, including our own minds and bodies, our thoughts and emotions, our past and what transpired to bring us still breathing, into this moment – and how we can learn to live our way into every aspect of life with integrity, with kindness towards ourselves and others, and with wisdom."*

(p. xxxvii).

The first edition of the *Mindfulness-Based Cognitive Therapy* (MBCT) manual was published in 2002[85]. Different in intention to *Full Catastrophe Living*, the manual is a curriculum guide for teachers. It carefully detailed the MBCT curriculum session-by-session, with an emphasis on the need for the teacher to have a personal mindfulness practice in order to deliver MBCT. In terms of group process, the authors wrote about the MBCT group format in relation to the cost-efficiency of teaching multiple participants together, contrasting with cognitive behaviour therapy which is usually delivered one-to-one. It is interesting to note that in the UK context in which MBCT was primarily developed, cost effectiveness was of interest to health care providers and seen as a way to meet the needs of the growing numbers of people presenting with recurrent depressive episodes[86].

Although group process was not made an explicit part of MBCT pedagogy, the authors emphasised the relationality of the teacher, the invitational aspect of the course, and the connection to common humanity through the way that minds and bodies operate. This, of course, is also shared by the teacher – the authors of MBCT emphasised how the teacher is a co-learner who explores mindfulness and its impact on vulnerability alongside their participants. The key principles set out by Segal *et al*[87] are all significant foundations for later works which explicitly foregrounded the group process.

---

84 Kabat-Zinn, 2013
85 Segal *et al*, 2002
86 Segal *et al*, 2013
87 Ibid.

Following these ground-breaking works of Kabat-Zinn[88] and Segal *et al*[89], MBP practitioners (mainly MBP training providers) developed ideas about the ways the MBP teacher can best harness the potential of the group. Of course, from the very start, MBSR and MBCT were designed to be taught in groups, but it was only later work that articulated what the key group skills are when teaching MBP groups. The section below explores the work of those practitioners who helped to shine a light on the MBP group process as a skill in itself.

The importance of group process in MBPs is made explicit

The first to overtly surface the importance of group process in the mindfulness literature was Rebecca Crane in 2009. A chapter in the first edition of the *MBCT – Distinctive Features* book, titled 'The MBCT learning environment'[90], explored the key foundations of establishing a learning environment as noted by Kabat-Zinn and Segal *et al*[91]. These included themes such as the intention of the teacher, and the relational and experiential nature of MBCT classes. It stated that the skill the teacher brings to the group process of MBCTs "is of paramount significance" (p153), as all inquiries that take place with a single participant are in the presence of the group – and one person's patterns of mind are explored in such a way as to make them familiar to others in the group (i.e. without any emphasis on the details of a story – but rather through the lens of how the participant reacted or responded to a particular event). Crane emphasised that this teaching approach – of the teacher being aware of the group process – can enhance the fundamental teachings of common humanity and be powerfully normalising for all group members. In the 2nd edition of her MBCT book[92], further emphasis was placed on group process; in fact, the chapter was renamed to 'The MBCT group learning environment' demonstrating a shift towards the importance of group process.

Soon after this, McCown *et al*[93] identified group process as one of four interrelated core skill sets of MBP teachers. They were the first to isolate group process in this way, and emphasised the manner in which the skills of group process are deeply interwoven with other skills when teaching. The first of the four core skills, which is of most interest here, is 'the stewardship of the group', which brings front and centre the way the teacher works

---

88   Kabat-Zinn, 1990
89   Segal *et al*, 2002
90   Crane, 2009
91   Kabat-Zinn, 1990; Segal *et al*, 2002
92   Crane, 2017
93   McCown *et al*, 2010

with the process of their group. McCown et al[94] wrote about how the group process is a co-creation between teacher and the individual participant, which was first described by Segal et al[95]. Co-creation here means that the teacher is not above the processes of suffering, reactivity, and mind-wandering etc., but is alongside participants as a fellow human – albeit one who may be more experienced in mindfulness practice. McCown et al[96] further developed this theme of co-creation by stating that the unique role of the MBP teacher is one of a 'catalyst', which is akin to a 'stewardship' role. The concept of stewardship is at the centre of their model. Indeed, Merriam-Webster's dictionary definition of stewardship includes "the careful and responsible management of something entrusted to one's care". When this is applied to the context of an MBP, it suggests the need for the teacher to have the capacity to hold the group 'with care' as the MBP curriculum unfolds. The diagrammatic representation of stewardship by McCown et al[97] suggests that stewardship is happening outside the circle of the group, so that when holding the class, the teacher can offer a non-hierarchal space within which the 'three treasures' can arise. See Figure 1.

Figure 1: A diagram demonstrating the link between stewardship and the group

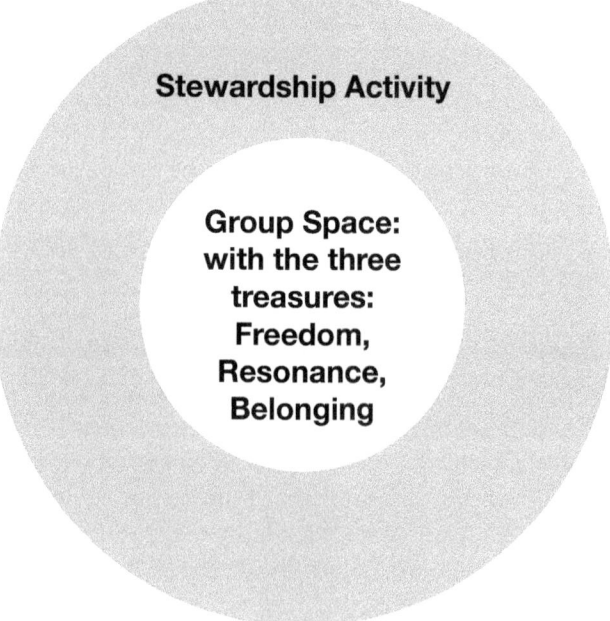

Stewardship Activity

Group Space:
with the three
treasures:
Freedom,
Resonance,
Belonging

(Based upon McCown et al's (2010) The interdependence of the group's three treasures.)

---

94   Ibid
95   Segal et al, 2002; 2013
96   McCown et al, 2010
97   McCown et al, 2010

The three treasures that facilitate learning within the group are:

1. Freedom – permission for the participant to allow themselves to be who they are in their moment-by-moment experience; moving away from what they think they should feel or do; and coming into connection with the present moment, and expressing what is happening for them during the class.

2. Belonging – participants are able to acknowledge their place in the group, both as a receiver of the care of the teacher and also from their fellow participants, and have awareness of the influence they have on others and on the group, and being accountable for that influence.

3. Resonance – the felt inter-subjective experience of the group at any one time, which can ebb and flow alongside the other two treasures of freedom and belonging.

> I found stewardship an enormously helpful concept when I was training to be an MBP teacher. I remember it helped to shift a belief that I had been holding for the first two years of my teacher training, one of 'It is my responsibility to teach something to participants' (a little bit like imparting information to students as in a typical university lecture which I was used to doing). The notion of stewardship helped me to see this previously unconscious belief clearly and helped me regard my role as much more akin to a facilitator, or indeed a steward. I could see that a core responsibility lay with creating a helpful open space within which learning can take place as the MBP curriculum is introduced.

A little after McCown et al[98], Bartley[99] published a teacher training manual for MBCT for Cancer (MBCT-Ca). This was the first time that the group process was explicitly foregrounded within a MBP teaching curriculum – indeed, the group process was regarded as "central to how our participants learn"[100]. A chapter of the book is dedicated to facilitating the learning, which, like previous works on stewardship and common humanity, regards the MBP teacher as a facilitator who cares for the process of learning[101].

This emphasis on the group that we see today partly arose out of the specific context of clinical groups, such as participants with depression or cancer. Having a diagnosis such as cancer can be a very isolating experience, and therefore meeting others in similar circumstances can offer a shared context for the experience of diagnosis and treatment. A key outcome of MBCT-Ca is one of a sense of shared humanity. This plays out in the group through participants' learning around reactivity, which often includes personal judgement and even aversion. Learning that others react in similar ways enables participants to see that their own experience is 'normal' and shared

---

98 McCown et al, 2010
99 Bartley, 2011
100 Ibid. p340
101 McCown et al, 2010; Segal et al, 2002; 2013

around the circle or on the screen. This allows them to develop a sense of common humanity with their fellow group members, which has the potential to transform patterns of reactivity. The chapter also guides MBCT-Ca teachers to work proactively with the forming, holding, and moving out beyond the 'circle' – outlining the way the group itself has a development process that needs attending to.

Shortly after these publications[102], the *Mindfulness-Based Interventions: Teaching Assessment Criteria* was published[103] (MBI:TAC). The development of the MBI:TAC arose from a practical challenge posed to university MBP teacher training organisations at the time; namely that the university environment demands that the skills being taught are academically assessed (in this case, how to be a MBP teacher). There was no assessment criteria in existence that was able to measure this at that time. Thus, a collaboration between Bangor, Oxford, and Exeter universities was born to tackle the difficult question of 'What makes a good MBP teacher, and how do we measure and assess this?'

The MBI:TAC was thus created, and continues to be an influential tool that is used internationally for the assessment of mindfulness-based teaching competence. It has been translated into seven languages to date and is used by training organisations across 14 countries. Although there have been some minor developments, the basic framework has not changed since its original publication in 2013. The MBI:TAC is central to the story of the pedagogy of MBP group process because the it placed the process of teaching the group as one of six core domains that MBP teachers are assessed on. This domain is named 'Holding the group learning environment' and focuses on how the group process offers a vehicle for connecting participants to the curriculum in a direct experiential way. This is a key point that we wish to emphasise here: that the group process is not an end in itself, but a means, a process (indeed a vehicle) to facilitate the motivation and learning of MBP participants. The domain of 'Holding the group learning environment' was divided into four key features which MBP teachers are assessed on. These are:

1. **Key Feature 1: Learning Container** – the teacher establishes a safe group environment in which active learning can take place. This includes ways of creating a space where participants feel able to voice their own experiences, even when it seems to differ from the rest of the group. Establishing the ethos of the group is important too, facilitating attitudes among participants such as listening closely and respecting all contributions, and not moving in to give advice. This key feature especially concerns the creation of safety and establishing boundaries in the group.

2. **Key Feature 2: Group Development** – the teacher shows clear management of group development processes and responds appropriately to them (see Chapter 7: Reading the group for a description of group

---

102 McCown *et al*, 2010; Bartley, 2011
103 Crane *et al*, 2013

development processes). Examples include the establishment of ground rules and group norms at the start of the course; offering more space towards the end of the course for participants to explore their own relationship to the mindfulness practices; and acknowledging the ending of the group. This key feature also includes how well the teacher works with challenging participants (i.e., anyone who may potentially undermine the teaching process, for example very dominant participants who take up a lot of the class time).

3. **Key Feature 3: Personal to Universal learning** – the teacher purposely uses the group as a vehicle to highlight common processes shared by all humans. When inquiring of one participant about their experience, the teacher consistently draws out universal themes that might relate to others whilst being sure to acknowledge the individual's experience. Moments of poignancy or distress that may arise in the group are not glossed over, but acknowledged by the teacher, for example by offering a short mindful pause. The use of horizonal inquiry relates to this key feature.

4. **Key Feature 4: Leadership style** – the teacher demonstrates authority and potency with a strong intention for the direction of learning, yet without imposing a particular view on participants. The authority of the teacher is not founded on being an expert, but conveyed through a non-hierarchical, shared human experience, which is mutually explored through mindful awareness with participants. At the same time, confidence in the process is conveyed to participants via the teacher's personhood and knowledge which participants can lean on during the MBP course. The teacher demonstrates a trust in the mindful process, one that arises from their own experience of mindfulness practice. This enables participants to learn to trust mindfulness practice also.

Around the same time as the publication of the MBI:TAC, the book *The Ethical Space Of Mindfulness* was published[104]. A core emphasis of the book was on the relational nature of MBP teaching – and what arises in the co-created teaching space through discourse and shared silences. McCown foregrounded the importance of process – the how of MBP teaching – as a helpful alternative or addition to the tendency for the pedagogy and research of MBPs to focus on the individual. Other mindfulness practitioners have since placed an emphasis on the importance of working skilfully with group process for teachers of MBPs, and consider the teacher's ability to recognise and work with group processes as a core skill. Sears[105] stated that a working knowledge of group dynamics and interventions is one of a number of key professional competencies. Brandsma[106] has a chapter on 'creating a fertile learning setting' with a section on 'the power of the circle' (p57). Woods[107] dedicated a chapter to the group process in the

---

104 McCown, 2013
105 Sears, 2015
106 Brandsma, 2017
107 Woods, 2019

MBCT program, focusing on parallels with extant psychotherapeutic literature, diversity in groups, the developmental stages of the group, and eight key teaching skills that are relevant to working with group process.

During the late 2010s, there was a lot of interest and development around group process in the pedagogical literature, and this dovetailed with the growing interest in this topic among the CMRP training team and students at Bangor University. Around 2017, Trish Bartley, Gemma Griffith, and Rebecca Crane began to draw together literature, research, and practice to work on what would become the IOG model (pronounced the i-og model)[108]. The model describes how the teacher uses inside out embodying to keep in connection with the group, alongside the three capacities of reading, holding, and befriending the group. We hope that the IOG model may also contribute to the pedagogy on the important topic of MBP groups.

Summary of the practitioner literature

The practitioner literature is broadly in agreement that how the MBP teacher facilitates group process is a key skill. This is emphasised by the inclusion of group holding as a key assessment feature for MBP teachers[109]. There are some differences in emphasis between practitioners that are worth pointing out. For example, the IOG model has the inside out embodying of the teacher at the centre, holding, reading, and befriending the group. In contrast, McCown *et al*[110] show the MBP teacher as a steward on the outside of the circle, and inside it the teacher is a co-learner in a non-hierarchical space. We suggest that while it is vital to approach the role of teacher as a co-learner (i.e., someone who shares the common humanity of having a mind and body, a stress reaction cycle, and shared reactive patterns and tendencies etc.), it is equally vital that the role of the teacher includes a sensitive leadership of the MBP group.

By consciously reflecting and bringing grounded practice into how we can best support the group process as a vehicle for teaching, we are helping to ensure that the full potential learning from the MBP curriculum is more fully available to participants, and that they have access to this learning within the context of a well held MBP group. Given that holding the group is a process, and a vehicle for learning, how can we best train MBP teachers in these skills? Group process is not something that is easily measured, yet the felt sense of the group as harmonious or fractious is felt clearly by the people in the room. There has been some research on this, and a summary is available in Chapter 4, but we have a long way to go before these questions may be answered, if indeed any clear answers exist!

---

108 Griffith *et al*, 2019

109 Crane *et al*, 2021

110 McCown, 2010; 2016

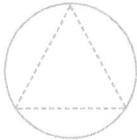

4. The research

What we know about group process in mindfulness-based programmes

Gemma Griffith

This chapter explores emerging research about how group process can influence both the way that participants learn about mindfulness, and the effects of the course on participant's well-being. For example, we might ask whether a felt cohesive group experience correlates with participants reporting greater well-being/reduced stress after the course. Very little research has investigated the MBP group process, and as McCown wrote, "The fact that we learn mindfulness *together*, that mindfulness is a relational achievement, has been obscured for decades in the scientific literature"[111]. The little research that has been done offers insights into the complexities of the group process. Before we explore what the research tells us about MBP groups, let us set the scene and explore the context around the research into groups.

Mindfulness-based programmes are complex interventions

Mindfulness-based programmes conform to specific, theory-driven processes, and can be classed as complex interventions as they have many interacting components. No two courses will be exactly the same, even when taught by the same teacher following an identical curriculum in a near identical context. If we consider the points below, we can quickly see why MBPs are such complex interventions when we appreciate the high number of factors that could influence participant outcomes[112]:

- Teachers of MBPs have complex and subtle behaviours when delivering MBPs. Participants receiving the intervention also engage in a variety of

---

111 McCown, 2016, p11
112 Craig *et al*, 2008

behaviours (variations in in-class participation, commitment to home practice etc).

- MBPs can be offered to a variety of clinical and non-clinical groups, with appropriate adaptations.

- MBPs are designed to be flexible and responsive to what emerges in the group. The inquiry process is a good example of this and means that no two classes will ever be the same.

- The vast number of ways in which MBPs can change a participant (known as participant outcomes). These include clinical outcomes such as the impact on anxiety and depression, general outcomes connected with stress, compassion, levels of mindfulness, well-being, attention, flourishing, and so on.

- There are a high number of *therapeutic factors* in MBPs that could influence participant outcomes. There are formal and informal practices both in class and outside the class; different ways of delivering the psychoeducational aspects of the course (such as 'perception' in week two of MBSR). There are also *common factors* which occur in all groups – such as group membership, therapeutic alliance, and participant expectations[113]. Common factors are key to group process research and will be explained further below.

Therapeutic and common factors

In the research literature, the factors that may influence participant outcomes can be roughly divided into *therapeutic* or *treatment* factors (in MBPs, treatment factors would include meditation practice and psychoeducation), and *common factors*. Common factors are contextual and defined as factors that are naturally present in most group therapeutic approaches, such as the relationship to the teacher, therapeutic alliance, expectancy effects, and the group process[114]. Most MBP research has been based on individual outcomes and therapeutic factors, with less attention paid to common factors. However, research into common factors is now of increasing interest in the field of MBPs[115].

There is a perspective that common factors may be more influential than has previously been assumed. Laska *et al*[116] suggest that outcomes of therapies may reflect aspects that are present in all therapies, rather than the therapeutic benefit which is supported by a particular theory. In MBPs, an example of a key mechanism of change theory relates to the way in which mindfulness practice supports the ability to decentre, or reperceive one's

---

113 Hutchinson *et al*, 2021
114 Wampold & Imel, 2015
115 Canby *et al*, 2021; Hutchinson *et al*, 2021
116 Laska *et al*, 2014

experiences[117]. There is emergent empirical support for this[118]. There is also some research that suggests that common factors are important influences on participant outcomes, for example when studies have looked at different psychological therapies to see if there are any differences in participant outcome. In some studies there is little difference that can be attributed to the type of therapy received by participants[119]. One interpretation of this is that it is not the treatment factors per se that affect participant outcomes, but rather those factors that are common to all therapies (such as being in a group, having contact with a therapist/teacher, having expectations about the therapy etc.).

Two examples of systematic reviews and meta-analyses demonstrate the complexity of working out what factors influence participant outcomes in MBPs[120]. Galente *et al* compared data from 136 randomised controlled trials (RCTs). Each RCT had an intervention arm of MBPs for adults in non-clinical settings and an intervention arm of other preventative interventions. This aimed to test if MBPs are more or less effective than other preventative interventions. A main finding, when these 136 studies were examined together, was that MBPs do have specific effects on common mental health symptoms, which may prove to be equally effective as other preventative interventions (no better and no worse). This lack of difference in outcomes between MBPs and other interventions may be supportive of common factors and the influence they may have on MBP outcomes. Galente *et al*[121] concluded that the evidence is complex and is made more so since all the RCTs they included in their study were classed as having a 'high risk of bias', which makes definitive conclusions challenging.

Van Agteren *et al*[122] took a broader approach and aimed to synthesize evidence on all psychological interventions that aim to improve well-being (for clinical and non-clinical populations). They included 393 studies in their analysis and found that mindfulness-based interventions and specific multi-component positive psychological interventions demonstrated greater efficacy compared to other interventions (e.g. cognitive behaviour therapy, expressive writing, compassion interventions). This suggests that the *type of intervention* (i.e. therapeutic factors) does influence participant outcomes. Outcomes of reviews such as these depend on what studies the authors chose to include and how they are statistically analysed. In short, we do not know what the degree of influence is of common and therapeutic factors on participant outcomes, but there is evidence supporting that both are likely to be influential in MBPs.

---

117 Segal *et al*, 2013; Shapiro *et al*, 2006
118 Segal *et al*, 2019
119 e.g. Luborsky *et al*, 2002
120 Galente *et al* 2021; van Agteren *et al*, 2021
121 Galente *et al* (2021)
122 Van Agteren *et al*, 2021

Group as a common factor: MBP research

Despite MBPs being designed to be delivered in a group setting, the MBP research literature is at the very beginning of exploring 'group' as a potential factor of influence. There are three main reasons why the group process has perhaps not been given more specific attention in MBP research:

- The MBP research field is relatively new and has focused on exploring the psychological impact of an MBP on individual participants, and what mechanisms may influence changes. We need to know *if* MBPs are helpful for particular populations before being able to pinpoint what factors *influence change*. Researchers are increasingly turning towards the question of *how* MBPs have this impact, and for whom.

- Although existing group process research (drawn from psychotherapy) has a reasonable evidence base, it does not directly link to the psychoeducational context of most MBPs – and MBPs are very different from group psychotherapy, for example. However, there appears to be many aspects that are relevant to MBPs, so careful mapping, or translation, is needed across disciplines.

- Group process is really difficult to pin down and measure (how would one 'measure' atmosphere, or resonance, or holding, for example). For this reason, the group is a highly complex process to research.

What does the research literature say about MBP groups?

The pedagogical literature written by MBP practitioners (see Chapter 3), and the literature about group process in psychotherapy (see Chapter 7) is far more developed than the research studies that specifically relate to group process in MBPs. As you will see below, the research specifically examining MBP groups is currently rather patchy. Here we offer a summary of the research studies which have examined MBP group process.

MBP participants spontaneously talk about the group process and how important it was to them

The aim of qualitative research is to gather in-depth information from participants about a lived experience. Quite a few studies of this type have been conducted by interviewing participants who completed an MBP. What is interesting about these studies is that group processes appear to be very important to participants because they mention them a lot when asked about their experience of an MBP. In five meta-syntheses of qualitative studies, which brought together 46 studies, group process emerged as a core theme in all five studies[123]. It is especially interesting that, although none of the original studies stated that they aimed to explore the group process, multiple participants talked about their fellow group participants as an important influential factor on their experience of their MBP course. However, this does not mean that the researchers did not ask participants about group process. The interview questions were not published, so we do not know either way. Across all five studies, participants broadly spoke about two key aspects of their experience of being in an MBP group.

- They spoke of how helpful it was to know that other people experienced similar processes of mind. One participant said: "I'm not a nut... I'm just an ordinary, everyday, run of the mill person who ended up in the crap for whatever reason, and so are they. So that was another thing that was a great plus"[124]. Additionally, people who attended the group together with people with similar clinical issues said that this shared experience was very helpful. Another participant said, "It is a very powerful experience sitting in a circle of people who have been affected by cancer. I find in it a very profound understanding because we all share a similar experience."[125].

- The second aspect often mentioned by participants concerned the group experience and how it helped to motivate them to establish their own practice and keep attending the course even when it was challenging: "I think if you are on your own you would quite easily walk away and give up".[126]

One qualitative study did ask their 88 participants specifically about the group process, and 76% of them spoke of the importance of group social factors and 36% spoke of instructor social factors[127]. In terms of group social factors, the following themes were identified: bonding with other members; empathy and compassion; finding it helped to know that others shared similar emotions to them; being able to safely express their emotions in the group; how the group structure helped them remain active in their mindfulness practice; and how they learned from and were encouraged by other group members in their shared experiences. Nine participants also spoke of challenges they had encountered within the group process. Two said being a significantly different age to the rest of the group "was a bit of a barrier for making friends" (p10). Some reported pressure to talk about their experience, and some felt "on the sidelines" (p10) because of this age difference, or due to more talkative members in the group.

---

123 Cairns & Murray, 2015; Malpass *et al*, 2012; Morgan *et al*, 2015; Tate *et al*, 2017; Wyatt *et al*, 2014
124 Cairns & Murray, 2013, p351
125 Tate *et al*, 2017, p7
126 Cairns & Murray, 2013, p352
127 Canby *et al*, 2021

Mindfulness-based programme groups seem to go through distinct stages of development

Cormack et al[128] proposed that an MBP group progresses through distinct stages and conceptualised this as "the group as a vessel on a shared journey" (p3). The authors used grounded theory methods to analyse interview data based upon 12 participants, six people who had attended an MBP, and six MBP teachers. They described the first stage of an MBP as 'Charting the course'. During this stage, participants spoke of their apprehensions before meeting the group, and uncertainties and anxieties experienced when they met other group members for the first time (Weeks 1 to 3). From Weeks 3 to 5, the focus shifted to participants being aware of differences and similarities in how they themselves and other group members appeared to be understanding mindfulness (named the 'spectrum stage'), with teachers encouraging all experiences to be heard. One teacher stated that Week 5 was often "a stormy session" (p7). The 'spectrum stage' was followed by what was named as 'knowing the ropes', wherein participants were more focused on the consolidation of skills within a cohesive group. Finally, the 'disembarking' stage was identified where participants mourned the course ending, and at the same time experienced camaraderie with fellow participants, were ready for the group to end, and also felt comfortable continuing their exploration of mindfulness outside of the group.

Cormack et al proposed that there are parallels with Tuckman's model (see Chapter 7), but with some key differences, particularly storming, which Tuckman's model[129] describes as a period in which participants may seek to differentiate themselves from the group and test out or rebel against the leader. In the Cormack et al model[130] however, storming is described as the participant's internal struggle with a core concept of mindfulness, that is, to turn towards difficult direct felt experiences. They suggest that storming appears to be more intrapersonal rather than interpersonal in MBPs. However, we would draw attention to this being just one study, with no other published studies looking at this theme, so we need to interpret these results with caution.

Mindfulness-based programme teachers may underestimate the importance of group process compared to their participants

Researchers from the Netherlands interviewed mindfulness teachers and their participants from an MBCT course to ask them about the role of

---

128 Cormack et al, 2018
129 Tuckman, 1965
130 Cormack et al, 2018

the MBCT teacher[131]. They found that nine out of 10 participants felt the group was very important, whereas far fewer MBP teachers (four of nine) mentioned the supportive role of the group, and in much less strong terms than the participants. A participant said, "The group gives some sort of pressure, to keep sitting and practising" and, "Recognition of the group gives trust and makes you feel at ease. You feel understood and free from prejudice from the society. So much understanding is a new experience" (p175). Teachers focused on how the group could create safety: "The group creates a safe environment for own experiences" (p175), but unlike participants, teachers did not mention the group's importance as a motivational or normalising factor. This may suggest that participants and teachers regard group processes differently – with participants seeing the group as much more important than teachers. However, it is difficult to draw such conclusions from just one small study, which was conducted over nine years ago (at the time of writing). It may be that with the increased pedagogical developments and interest in MBP groups[132] and the inclusion of groupwork skills in many teacher training courses, teachers are now much more aware of the impact of the group on participants. It is difficult therefore to know if similar results would be found if this research were to be repeated today.

We do not know whether participants have more positive outcomes in MBPs when they learn in a group or in a one-to-one setting

Some MBPs are delivered one-to-one, but most are delivered in groups. Some researchers have explored whether participants who are offered the same MBP curriculum do better in one setting over the other. We do not know whether participant outcomes are better or worse or the same in individual vs. group delivery because so little research has been done into this. We could only find three studies that directly compared individual vs group delivery and the results are mixed. Two studies reported that the type of delivery made *little difference* to participant outcomes, in both an MBCT for depression[133], and for an eight-week mindfulness course developed for non-clinical populations[134]. In contrast, Mantzios and Giannou[135] had mixed findings when they compared individual vs. group delivery in an MBP for weight loss. They reported that people lost significantly more weight if they attended the group MBP compared to the individual MBP. Cognitive-behavioural avoidance increased among participants who received the individual MBP and decreased among participants who received the MBP in a group setting. The authors posited

---

131 van Aalderen *et al*, 2012
132 e.g. Griffith *et al*, 2019; McCown *et al*, 2016
133 Schroevers *et al*, 2016
134 Matiz *et al*, 2018
135 Mantzios & Giannou, 2014

that this finding was linked to the group setting, in which the group allows participants to share experiences of 'failing' at mindfulness, and this therefore normalised perceived failure. Knowing that thoughts about failing are a typical part of the process may assist participants in turning towards moments of difficulty, thus reducing avoidance. This in turn was correlated with participant weight loss.

These mixed findings – which broadly show that there is no clear difference in participant outcomes in one-to-one vs. group courses – mirror the broader psychotherapy literature, in which there is also a lack of clear consensus of the efficacy of individual vs. group delivered psychotherapy[136]. Three studies are not enough to draw firm conclusions, although the tentative conclusion from these three studies is that there is no strong evidence that participant outcomes in group vs. individual MBPs substantially differ. Much more research is needed to explore this area further.

The MBP group itself may account for variance in participants' psychological outcomes

There are four studies that have looked at group composition or group cohesion in MBP groups, albeit with quite different approaches. Imel *et al*[137] analysed 59 MBP groups and reported that group membership accounted for 7% of the variance in change in psychological symptoms but did not account for the variability of change in medical symptoms. They could not pinpoint why group membership effected change in psychological symptoms and not medical symptoms (but they did test for and rule out teacher differences), although they suggested that psychological symptoms may be more amenable to being influenced by social factors such as group cohesion. They proposed that group membership effect was likely to be a result of the culture of a particular group having an impact on learning and practicing MBPs, with psychological outcomes influenced by non-mindfulness pathways such as group cohesion, perceived support, and expectation of change (although it is important to note that they did not measure these factors).

Group cohesion is the felt sense of the support of the group and of belonging to it (see Chapter 6), and higher cohesiveness is reported as having better positive outcomes in the psychotherapeutic literature[138]. However, in the one study that has looked at this in MBP groups[139], it was found that reported group cohesion did not affect participant outcomes (i.e. reduction in psychological distress). In a Mindfulness-Based Relapse Prevention (MBRP) research trial, researchers found that both men and women who were in groups that contained at least one-third women

136 Burlingame *et al*, 2016
137 Imel *et al*, 2008
138 Burlingame *et al*, 2018
139 Bisseling *et al*, 2019

showed increased abstinence from substance misuse at 12-month follow up[140]. The individual's gender was not itself a predictor, but the authors suggested that groups with more women encouraged group cohesion, which impacted, for example, the effectiveness of group inquiry. These three studies taken together do not offer clear answers to how group composition or felt group cohesion influence participant outcomes but offer interesting avenues for further exploration.

Common factors (including group) have effects on participant outcomes

To explore the common factor of group process, Canby *et al*[141] asked participants to rate their group after the course was complete using the therapeutic factors inventory (TFI). This measure looks at four factors to do with group process – instillation of hope, secure emotional expression, awareness of relational impact, and social learning. How participants rated their group on the TFI predicted significantly lower stress and higher mindfulness (i.e. higher ratings of their experience of the group predicted lower stress and higher mindfulness). However, when they looked at whether ratings on the TFI predicted clinical outcomes, they found that group factors did not predict outcomes in anxiety and depression.

Summary

When we look at research conducted on the group aspect of MBPs, we can see that it is in its infancy, with few research studies to draw upon. Those that have been published use different methods and have different research questions, which makes it very challenging to build up a clear picture of the influence of group teaching on participant outcomes. We need to interpret research with caution, and much more work needs to be done to determine what influence the group may have.

- There is emergent evidence that the group membership, composition, and ratings of the group process may influence participant outcomes.
- Participants often speak about the importance of the group when interviewed and may place a higher importance of the group influence than MBP teachers.
- There is mixed evidence for whether participant outcomes differ according to group vs individual delivery of MBPs. Two studies found no difference in outcomes, and one found that a group delivery improved some participant outcomes (namely weight loss and reduced avoidance).

140 Roos *et al*, 2019

141 Canby *et al*, 2021

It is always difficult to predict how a field might grow. There is a sense that more researchers are becoming interested in how the experience of the MBP group itself may influence participants. Possible directions for future research may include replication of studies to either confirm or refute current findings. We would encourage researchers to consider investigating common factors as potential mechanisms of the changes that are observed in participants, such as the felt experience of the group, to further expand this important field of research.

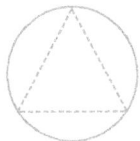

An interview with Thandi Gilder: trainee MBP teacher

How the IOG model influenced teaching the MBP group

"Hopefully what people get out of our mindfulness courses is how to be a human, with other humans."

Thandi Gilder is an experienced higher education lecturer working in psychology. At the time of this conversation, she was three years into a four-year Master's Degree at Bangor University, had taught two MBSR courses, and had recently finished a module taught by Trish Bartley in which the inside out group model was used as a teaching tool.

Here she describes how she draws on various concepts linked to the inside out model to support her MBP teaching.

Inside out embodiment

Thandi spoke of how the challenges of teaching could be supported by a sense of embodying mindfulness, in which awareness of difficult feelings, such as inadequacy as a teacher, can be folded into the awareness of what is happening. One can feel inadequate or reactive, and also have a sense of allowing this to be present as part of embodiment.

"As a teacher in a group, you are a person in the group, so things that happen in the group can irritate, or make you panic that you are a shit teacher, or kind of whatever it is. So being able to notice those … and kind of be with your humanness, and still be teaching… I certainly had

> *moments of talking about something and then, 'Oh I didn't explain that very well', and judging, and ok so now we are doing an inquiry... just the idea of inside out – this is what is happening inside and also being able to hold what is happening outside."*

This shift of perspective – from classing reactivity as being somehow outside of, or interfering with, one's otherwise felt sense that one 'should' have a serene and peaceful embodiment when teaching – to one of being able to include our reactivity and notice, and be alongside this as part of embodiment, is a radical one. The notion of inside out embodiment helped concretise this.

When the group process and learning was going well, this was described as being accompanied with a sense of embodied connection with herself and the group:

> *"It's quite magical, I think. There is something (...) about letting go of a sense of self, a sense of being a teacher, and just being in a room with these humans, who are exploring this... it's magic. Just a real sense of trusting the curriculum and the process in some way."*

When asked to recount a time when a class was not going so well and what happened internally as a result, and how that relates to inside out embodying, Thandi said:

> *"I think it is lots of racing thoughts about what do I do now. Sort of in some... there is certainly ... Trish's [Bartley] voice probably, about holding the group ... which is a real, I mean in that moment I was focused on that moment with that student, I still had a sense of the circle and so when I was, 'Oh what do I do? What do I do?' and bringing everyone in with feet on the floor, there was a sense of keeping this space. And I think in doing that, in bringing my feet to the floor, it helped me to come back. And once it had happened, to sort of let go of it a little bit and carry on with the class."*

What is interesting here is a sense of internalisation of the teaching moment – in this case from Trish – with the teacher's voice arising in moments of uncertainty, which for Thandi helped reassure and point in the direction of how to help guide the class during challenging moments. We can all probably relate to this phenomenon, of recalling key teachings when we need them. Indeed, it is a hope that we, as MBP teachers and the group, will also be internalised to some extent to help guide participants, perhaps even long after the MBP course has finished.

Reading the group

Thandi found the group development theory by Tuckman (1965) particularly useful when teaching MBPs. Having knowledge about how groups generally develop, and knowing this will likely include participants resisting mindfulness practices at some point, meant that when this happened during her classes, she had the reassurance that resistance is very unlikely to be personal or to do with her teaching:

> "… in the first 2-3 weeks when people are, like, 'I can't find time to do this practice', or coming across resistance, seeing that as a normal part of – normal is such a horrible word – but as a natural part of this process. That's really helpful to separate from, 'Oh I'm not teaching it right' to, 'Oh actually this is perfectly normal'. So, I find that useful."

Thandi described how she reads the group by deliberately looking around the room to ascertain what was going on for everyone, which also helps hold the group in awareness.

> "I look around the room, seeing what people are doing (…) as you are talking having a sense of watching people's body language, if people are doing small group work, dipping in and out to hear what they are talking about while trying not to make it obvious… So, if you've got one person who is maybe in tears or having a really strong emotion, keeping an eye on the rest of the group. Getting a sense, from body language and things when it is time to move on, fidgeting."

Befriending the self-as-teacher

A theme for Thandi is also being able to befriend the critical teaching mind, and found supervision particularly helpful for this when learning to be an MBP teacher.

> "Supervision I think really helps befriend particular critical bits. And it's really helpful to have that other perspective, because it is not always easy to befriend when we have done things we wish we had done differently. I think it is the stage I am at but it's keeping that, 'I am learning to do this' and maybe that will never go away. Even when I am qualified."

Common humanity

When asked, 'What do you think that learning mindfulness in a group gives that learning one-to-one might not?' Thandi spoke of how common humanity was a fundamental aspect of what participants gained from learning MBPs in a group:

> "Common humanity… Coming towards difficulty, coming towards anything, the teaching comes from seeing, or the learning comes from seeing, being with other people as they are learning the skills too. It's

much more than an individual pursuit, I think. The danger is that it is seen as … 'I have this anxiety and I am coming to this mindfulness course to help me with it'. But hopefully what people get out of our mindfulness courses is how to be a human, with other humans."

Part One:
Inside out embodying

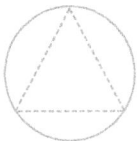

5. Inside out embodying

Trish Bartley

"We are embedded in a universe with physical and moral dimensions where every thought and action splinters into a million consequences."

Paul Broks[142]

Up to now, we have looked at some of the wider issues that underpin the teaching practice of the mindfulness-based group. These have included the different dimensions of MBP teaching (such as the teacher, the programme and the participant); the development of theory around MBP group teaching; the research into the influence and teaching of the mindfulness-based group; and the value of the MBP group, with particular consideration of current social agendas and what MBPs and the mindfulness-based group in particular might have to offer.

We turn now to consider the various aspects of the Inside Out Group[143] (IOG) model. From this point on, we are engaged in the detail of the four components of the model. We have organised the rest of the book around these four components:

Part One: Inside Out Embodying

Part Two: Reading

Part Three: Holding

Part Four: Befriending.

Within each part there are chapters that explore different aspects of Embodying, Reading, Holding and Befriending.

In this chapter, we explore the term 'embodiment' from a number of different perspectives. It is captured right in the centre of our IOG[144] model, illustrating the vital place it has in the practice of mindfulness-based programme teachers and how this relates to the mindfulness-based group.

---

142 Broks P, 2003
143 Griffith *et al*, 2019
144 Ibid.

We draw out this significance by looking at embodiment in relation to the body, attitudes and understandings, learning and insight, and in relation to intentions and the person of the teacher themselves. We also offer ideas as to how mindful embodying can be brought into teaching practice as we teach – and how this connects us to a sense of the ground that supports us, and to the planet itself.

A definition of the word 'embodiment' in many dictionaries is 'to represent a quality or an idea exactly'. The pre-fix *em-* is defined as '*bringing something into*'. From this, we can gather that embodying something is to bring it into the body. At first glance, this appears to be fairly straightforward, but we soon discover that embodying mindfulness requires a level of dedicated practice that takes time to develop. It is best to see this as a capacity to cultivate rather than a skill to acquire – and we learn over time to create the conditions that enable us to consistently embody mindfulness in our MBP teaching practice.

There is a risk that embodiment, as a term, has become a bit of a 'sacred cow' in mindfulness circles. *What does embodiment actually involve? And how do we do it?* The new version of the MBI:TAC[145] (Mindfulness-based Interventions: Teaching Assessment Criteria) addresses this. In 2021, a decision was made to change the name of the third domain from Embodiment of Mindfulness to *Embodying* Mindfulness. And there it is. Embodiment (in a mindfulness context) only makes sense when we relate it to the process of aligning *with* something (mindfulness, in this case). This change from noun to verb is helpful as it removes any suggestion that there is a final destination to be achieved – namely 'embodiment'. The verb 'embodying' captures a process that is constantly evolving. The wording of the IOG model has also been changed from inside out embodiment to inside out embodying to reflect this.

A new language?

There is much we can do to cultivate mindful embodying, yet it is difficult to articulate what it is that we are actually doing. Why is it so hard to describe? It may be partly to do with language. Capturing words that express experience tends to be challenging. The words themselves have a habit of tying things down rather than opening things up. The phase, 'We know it when we see it', does not explain it well either – though at times we can develop an intuitive sense that someone is strongly embodied. However, most education and professional bodies prioritise the acquisition of knowledge which is measurable and can be readily formulated. In contrast, experiential learning, and embodied mindfulness teaching, seem almost impossible to measure.

---

145 Crane *et al*, 2013

McCown *et al* (2011)[146] suggest that the culture of the West serves to distance us from our bodies and our embodied experience. Certainly, it is true that we are often 'in our heads', thinking and planning.

> *'We privilege cognitive understanding at the expense of the tacit; and language-based knowing at the expense of the inexpressible.'*[147]

Donald McCown, Diane Reibel & Marc Micozzi

In addition, some cultural patterns tend to view the body as an object to look upon (from outside in). Most of us may, at times, want the body to be different (thinner, taller, younger, fitter etc.), rather than seeing it as an interconnected part of us that embodies or expresses what we feel, think, relate to, and act upon.

Alongside the limitations of language, embodying mindfulness calls on us to bring awareness to the felt sense of an experience – and to use this to guide our choice of what or where to turn to next. This sensory integration aligns what is happening in the mind with what is being expressed in the body, which underlines the importance of not seeing mind and body as separate. This can seem confusing if we are new to this work and try to grasp this conceptually – and since many of us lack a natural connectedness with sensations in the body, it can be challenging to rely on the body to come back to. *Is it that we have lost this over time? Were our ancestors more embodied than we are now?*

Embodying mindfulness as practice

When we fully inhabit the body, and are aware of what is happening around us, our sense of our own internal physicality joins with the physicality of what is near us. For example, we look at blossom on the tree, and we can be fully present in the seeing, smelling, and sensing the colour, shape, and movement of the tree. Our experience can include a sense of immediacy and deep appreciation that enables us to directly relate to the tree and its blossom, almost as one being alive to another. In these moments we can connect to a sense of aliveness within and without, sharing the same air, rooted into the same earth. This links us to awareness of the interrelatedness of everything. Aspects of embodied experience connect, and we are not just aware of the experience, but we know that we are.

---

146 McCown *et al*, 2010
147 Ibid.

> There is an old story about two meditation teachers taking a walk together. The younger of the two asks the older one, "What do you teach your students? They seem to do a lot better than mine." The older teacher replies straightforwardly, "I just teach them to walk, sit, stand and lie down." The younger teacher looks puzzled "That's strange," he says, "for that is exactly what I do." "Ah," says the wise old teacher, "but when my students walk, they know they are walking, and when they sit, they know they are sitting, and when they stand or lie down, they know they are standing or lying down".

When mindfully embodied, we know our present experience intimately. This underlines the relationship between the depth of the teacher's personal mindfulness practice and their capacity to embody mindfulness as they teach. When the MBP teacher is aligned with being present and aware, there is an integrity to what they say and do. We experience them as authentic, convincing, and true to themselves and their own way of being in the world.

Embodying mindfulness is essentially a sensory practice. However, the conceptual mind often gets in the way and disconnects us from direct experience. When this happens, there is risk that we may act in ways that are at odds with our intentions. We separate from how we are actually feeling, and this tends to leak out through tell-tale body language (see Chapter 9). Eventually, we discover that the process of embodying mindfulness brings the dimensions of mind and body together into the present moment – responsive, kind and authentic. It is a noble and demanding practice.

The senses and inside out embodying

Let us now include inside out embodying to see what this adds to our understanding of embodied MBP teaching practice. As already mentioned, inside out mindful embodying is central to the MBP teacher's practice – both on a personal internal sense, and also in the way the MBP teacher relates to the space they teach in, the group members they are teaching, and the aspects of the programme being taught.

The senses are central to the practice of the MBP teacher. We might see the kinaesthetic sense of the somatic body and thinking as more *'inside'* oriented and seeing and hearing as more *'outside'* oriented. Of course, these orientations are very general. There is no real separation or division between an inside and an outside sense experience. Inside out embodying was described in our original article (Griffith *et al*, 2019) as follows:

> *"The teacher monitors the immediacy of their felt experience within the boundaries of their body – with a particular emphasis on raw sensory data arising through interoceptive (awareness of visceral stimuli originating inside of one's body) and proprioceptive capacities (awareness of the position of the body).'*[148]

---

148 Griffith *et al*, 2019: https://link.springer.com/article/10.1007/s12671-019-1093-6

The first 'inside' sense involves a felt experience of the somatic body. This can include sensations of movement in the body and also the felt experience when the body is still. Although this relates to one's own body, it is possible to simply be with these direct body sensations without 'me' getting involved (although this may not be the case with sensations that are associated with a particular narrative). It may often be helpful to pay particular attention to sensations in the trunk of the body, as they offer sensitive feeling tone feedback (awareness of pleasant or unpleasant experience). This may resonate internally with what we are seeing, hearing or sensing outside, in the group – and we can use awareness of these sensations in the body to steady into a more embodied presence – which is important in how we hold the group.

> The whole group had just re-gathered, having been in small groups in breakout rooms for a few minutes to discuss home practice. I sensed that something was not right. It was as if there was a momentary hesitation or held breath within the group. At the same time, I noticed that I was holding my breath and there was some tightness in the belly, and feelings of slight anxiety around the sternum (a familiar barometer for me). I looked around the group into the faces on the screen. "Shall we take a pause?" I suggested, and after a few moments I added, "How about bringing awareness to include your feet on the floor?" Practicing this alongside the group, I once more felt settled internally and sensed a settling in the group. I added, "Now, would you like to write in the chat with headlines or themes from your home practice discussions?" (This entire process took less than a minute or two.)

The other 'inside' sense involves the thinking mind, which is clearly an important resource in MBP teaching. However, thinking can quickly move us into mind-based conceptualising, and into believing the interpretations about what we think is happening. Thinking also has a tendency to move us away from direct experiencing (when it happens out of present awareness) and can be strongly influenced by mood and the habitual patterns of mind that then give rise to automatic reactivity.

Turning now to the so called 'outside' senses, the visual sense or the ocular, is our primary sense and tends to be overdeveloped. 'I see' is the start of how we relate to people and objects – and this can quickly move us into patterns of reactivity that result in bias and prejudice, via the perceptions and (often) implicit assumptions that we make. Whilst seeing is vital in navigating the world, we all too often create a distance from what we see on the 'outside' with what we experience on the 'inside'. There is the 'me' doing the seeing (inside) and the 'that' or the 'you' (outside) as the object being seen. This produces an immediate duality, separating our internal felt sense with what we experience around us. What we see then gets perceived in familiar ways, often taking us down well-worn tracks into the past or the future that creates even further distance.

Sometimes standing back from an experience and reflecting on what is needed can be helpful. Alternatively, in many situations, we also have the option of 'turning towards' to explore the immediacy of an embodied sense of what is here, now. Comparing these different options can help us gain insight into what is most relevant, and appropriate at different times – although there are no formulas and every moment with each group will be different and require its own mindfully embodied response.

Hearing is the last 'outside' sense to look at. When we want to hear a quiet sound, we move closer and lean in to catch the sound. There is a certain intimacy about this that makes hearing a rather different experience to seeing. It brings what is on the outside into the ear to be heard and experienced internally in a more direct way. As MBP teachers, hearing is key to how we practice, lead inquiries, guide meditations, listen to the general sounds coming from small group processes, and much more. Hearing is a vital part of the practice of mindful embodying by connecting what is outside (in the group) to what is inside (in the body) and offering an opportunity for responsive embodying from the presence of the teacher.

This brings us to the next section in which we look at the role of the body and the practice of grounded-ness as a resource to embodied MBP teaching, followed by sections on embodying attitudes and understandings, insights and learnings, and the cultivation of intention in embodying mindfulness as an MBP teacher.

Embodying mindful awareness within the body

As we have been reflecting, to embody mindfulness is to inhabit the body – to bring what we are experiencing into awareness within the dimension of the body, with awareness of the emergent physical sensations that we find there. This can appear strange and unfamiliar at first. In the early days as practitioners, there can be a tendency for some of us to 'think' the sensations in the body.

Maria had been diagnosed with a life-threatening illness. Her treatment had gone well, but she was wholly convinced she would not survive. She came to an MBP programme somewhat reluctantly and found it very difficult 'to be in the body'. Her only access to understanding what this might mean was through 'thinking' the body – and unsurprisingly this was not working for her. One evening, well over halfway through the programme, she phoned me up. "I imagine you usually get phone calls when there is a problem. Well, I wanted to share something different with you," she said. She had been digging the garden that afternoon, when she became aware of bird song. She paused to lean on her spade and saw a robin close by on the fence. She stayed very still, listening to the sound, and watching the robin intently. She felt the →

warmth of the sun on her back – and she described being washed with a deep contentment that she had never experienced before. She was still convinced she would die of her illness, she told me, but she felt so utterly content in herself and so connected with the world, that it was as if something had affected her that was deeply healing.

In those moments, Maria had undoubtedly discovered what it was to be fully 'in the body'. Her description of her experience was strongly physical and sensory. She chose to stop and stay still and in doing so was washed by the immediacy and intensity of her experience. She was so mindful, present, and absorbed that she was not troubled by thoughts, and in that space, she felt deeply content. This is an example of someone who is strongly embodying mindfulness – and through that, she then had access to embodied moments of deep contentment. Her body and mind came together, aligned in the experience. It was not that the thinking-discursive mind had disappeared entirely, but it no longer dominated her experience, or fed any negativity. It had moved into the background, due to this new experience of being primarily located and embodied in the body.

How can we square this with the demands and complexities of MBP teaching in which thinking is clearly needed? As teachers, we are involved in planning sessions, learning skills, understanding theories, and making sense of what is happening in the room or on the screen. We cannot teach MBPs without a close connection with the intellect, our values as teachers, and what is happening in the thinking mind. Our understanding lies in finding ways to align mind *and* body in the teaching role. What we teach and how we teach it does not need to get stuck in concepts or rely too much on didactic input – nor is it separate from knowing the important aspects involved in teaching, such as the central themes of the MBP sessions.

In having access to the resources of the mind whilst inhabiting the body, the MBP teacher learns to stay close to awareness of physical sensations on the 'inside' as they teach. Like all life's core capacities, this takes practice. However, as teaching experience grows, so does the MBP teacher's grounded, present moment awareness.

Grounding the body

Grounded-ness is a vital resource in cultivating this steady, holding presence. It involves an aware connection of the ground beneath the feet. So many of us spend so much time up 'in our heads', thinking, planning, and ruminating. We are buffeted by our reactions to passing experience, often only dimly aware of the impact this has on us. Once we begin to come back to direct awareness of the body – especially to the base of the body and the points of contact between the body and what is supporting us – we find we move into more balanced steadiness, no longer so much at the mercy of the impact of random thoughts. By fostering awareness of the physical contact we have with the floor beneath us, and ultimately the earth itself, we are taking an important step in cultivating the embodying of mindfulness. Without this grounded-ness, MBP teaching is inevitably less secure and less able to come from a place of balance and presence. It is more likely to rely on 'technique' and the conceptual thinking mind.

At first, when we start teaching, 'explicit' skills are at the forefront of learning. We focus on *what we teach*, in terms of the themes of the programme and the details of each session. When we have integrated these with more teaching experience, we include the 'implicit' skills, which include *how we teach* – such as embodying mindfulness and awareness of the group.

> "*How* we teach (the implicit / non instrumental) is as important – if not more so – than *what* we teach (the explicit / instrumental). A key anchor point for your teaching process is intention – what do we want the participants to learn from the session? Stephen Covey's (1989[149]) adage applies here too, how do we 'keep the main thing the main thing!'"[150]

As in other forms of learning, conceptual frameworks offer us some certainty when we are learning the 'explicit' skills of teaching MBPs. However, as best we can, we stay close to the body as we navigate the teaching of the MBP. The mind will inevitably wander and become distracted at times. This is not a problem. We learn to come back to remembering the physical sensations in the body, and the contact between the body and what is supporting the body (the chair, the floor, the ground beneath etc.) even whilst we are making decisions, solving problems, and making choices. In time, focused present moment experience becomes less polarised between one or the other (thinking mind or physical body) and we are more able to dwell within the body, as the mind is engaged.

Here is a very simple grounding practice to support mindful embodying that can be invaluable at many different points in our MBP teaching.

Feet on the floor practice[151]

Moving attention to the soles of the feet…

The points of contact between the feet and the floor: toes, balls of the feet, heels at the back…

Having a sense of the weight of the body going down, held by the feet on the floor, then shifting to a sense of the solidity of the floor beneath the feet…

Gravity pulling us closer to the earth beneath us…

Feeling a sense of being held… feet on the floor.

---

149 Covey, 1989

150 Crane *et al*, 2021

151 A recording of this practice is available at www.pavpub.com/teaching-mindfulness-based-groups-resources

This practice can take a few minutes, by moving into detailed sensations in the feet and a sense of the floor beneath – or during a teaching session, we may internally connect with feet on the floor for just a moment or two, whenever there is a need to return to grounded presence, which may be often. We may also choose to involve the whole group in a 'feet on the floor' practice, whenever it seems helpful.

It is tempting to imagine that brief practices, being so short, are simpler to guide and practice than the longer more complex ones, such as the body scan or sitting practice. However, in our experience, it can be challenging to remember to incorporate a brief practice such as 'feet on the floor' when teaching or in everyday life. If we want to have these available to support us to embody mindfulness as we are teaching, we may need to set specific intentions to practice this regularly in everyday life, many times a day for several weeks at specific times – using cues and reminders – until they are readily accessible at any time.

Here are some ideas for incorporating 'feet on the floor' practice:

Cultivate an intention to practice 'feet on the floor' whenever we:
- feel the touch of a door handle
- walk up the stairs – or walk outside on a particular path
- stand and boil the kettle
- look at the phone
- check your email

Acquiring some small, sticky peel-off dots and place one on your
- laptop
- mobile phone
- kettle
- mirror

to remind you to practice 'feet on the floor' whenever you see the sticky dot.

At any time when it occurs to you that grounding in the body may be helpful, this can include:
- standing
- walking
- sitting
- or lying on the bed (body in contact with the bed)

At times when you notice you are:
- rushing
- tense
- anxious
- distracted

In this way, after a period of time, we find that increased levels of grounded-ness become easier. Practicing 'feet on the floor' during teaching results in a stronger connection with our own experience, increases access to steadiness, and helps us to hold the group as we are teaching. It supports our capacity as teachers to embody a mindful presence. It brings us all, as MBP teachers and group members, closer to the support of the earth itself, holding us in every moment.

Embodying the attitudes and values of mindfulness

However, embodying mindfulness is more than grounding and accessing connection with a steady, balanced presence. Undoubtedly, grounded-ness is valuable and much needed – but as MBP teachers, we also need to understand how to embody the attitudes and core values that are important to this work.

What are the characteristics of the core attitudes we wish to embody within MBP teaching?

How can we cultivate ways of embodying these attitudes as we teach?

One approach is to bring to mind those teachers, mentors or peers who seem to embody qualities that we wish to bring into our teaching – qualities such as kindness, compassion, mindful presence and so on. What are they doing? How do they behave and respond to others?

> There is a photo of the Dalai Lama walking past one of his guards who is standing to attention. As he passes the guard, he touches his arm. The caption beneath reads, "My religion is kindness". What is it about the photo that has such impact? The Dalai Lama appears both casual and yet intentional in his gesture. He does not seem to look for any attention at all on himself – not even an acknowledgement from the guard. His way of connecting appears understated and respectful of the guard who is protecting him. The Dalai Lama seems to embody wholehearted appreciation and kindness in that tiny gesture.

When we meet someone who embodies a capacity like kindness, it appears effortless and natural. At best, it seems to need nothing back. It is all about the kindness, not about the person who is offering it. There is an integration within the act that involves the body, aligns with the heart, and connects with intention. In some ways, this is similar to the experience of appreciating a highly skilled craftsperson.

I remember seeing someone playing the violin when I was quite young, maybe only seven or eight years old. I was learning the violin myself by then, and even at that age I saw how easy she made it look, yet I knew from my own experience that it was far from easy. As I watched and listened to her, thrilled by the sound of the music she was making, it was as if the violin was an extension of the person playing. Her instrument was made of wood, and the young woman of flesh and bones, yet they seemed to be one entity, with the sound coming as much from the body of the woman as from the body of the violin. I imagine a teacher must have mentioned this because it would be an unusual insight for a young child – but I have never forgotten the experience – of the integration and the cohesion of violin and body, of skill and apparently effortless effort, that is born of years of practice, commitment, and natural aptitude.

In this example, the connection of skill, musicality, mind and body of instrument and player came together and were offered out to those of us present. It was powerful – and it always is when conditions combine that fully align the intention and the practice of one (on the inside) with the aware presence of other/s (on the outside).

Let us take the art of embodying curiosity as an example. Perhaps initially, as new teachers, we may have a basic grasp of what is meant by mindful curiosity. It is not entirely new to us, of course, but in the context of teaching mindfulness, we may not appreciate many of the nuances of deep listening, openness, responsiveness and so on, that we learn more about in due course. So initially, curiosity may come from an intuitive basic grasp of things. Later, in training as an MBP teacher, we have a more complete understanding and appreciation. What it is to be mindfully curious grows and deepens in us. At first, it may seem involved, conceptual and complex. Later, it becomes simpler, and we learn to bring curiosity into embodied experience[152]. When we do this, we will be interested, engaged, intentional and open. The opposite of this would be apathetic, casual, dismissive, and closed.

When we want to cultivate any of the core attitudes of kindness, compassion, curiosity or appreciation, infused as they are with embodied mindfulness, they need intentional practice. We might decide to develop a personal kindness programme over a period of time. We might choose to bring it into regular formal meditation practice each day offering kindness to ourselves and others (see Chapter 14). We can find ways to integrate kindness into everyday life though brief practices that bring us back repeatedly to embodying kindness for a few moments – perhaps as we pass a neighbour or bring someone to mind who we currently find challenging. We might teach our next MBP with a specific intention to focus on kindness. As we deepen into the experience of kindness, so we will embody it more and more in our teaching and in our lives.

---

152 Spiral learning is similar to this process – see Bruner, 1960. *The Process of Education.* Harvard University Press.

Embodying the insights and understandings of mindfulness

Having explored the role of the body in embodying mindfulness, followed by ways of embodying the attitudes and values of mindfulness, we now consider what is involved in embodying the insights and understandings of mindfulness. Christina Feldman, a well-known insight meditation and Dharma teacher, suggests that this third aspect of embodying the learning and insights of mindfulness can be described as 'living in the light of understanding'[153]. When we do this, our teaching (and living) bring together an understanding of suffering and an appreciation of how mindfulness is able to intercede.

John Teasdale and Michael Chaskalson wrote helpfully about this[154]. They emphasised the need for all MBP teachers to understand the ways that our participants are vulnerable to stress, depression, anxiety etc. and the ways that the MBP is able to make its intervention. Without understanding the two sides of this equation (the nature of suffering and the way that the MBP responds to that suffering), then what we offer in our teaching will be limited to a series of techniques. Interestingly, mindfulness is often seen (wrongly) as a technique. However, as has been evidenced through research, mindfulness practice has the potential to 'effectively transform the processes that create and sustain suffering'[155]. To teach MBPs that transforms stress and suffering requires us to be able to embody key insights of mindfulness and embed them in our teaching and practice.

The detailed intervention of the MBP maps onto the nature of the vulnerabilities that participants bring with them. The MBP group offers something extra to the process, since although each group member is individual and has their own history and personal struggles, the territory they are going through is often shared with others in the group. So, when a group member has a particular insight, they share it and open it up to everyone else, enabling learning to be consolidated in a more sure-footed, integrated, and embodied way.

Embodying the core insights and teachings of mindfulness feels like a lifelong process. However, the examples we have described of the effortlessly glorious playing of the violin, or the casually, deeply kind gesture of the Dalai Lama, offer us some clues. Both examples involve an integration of heart, body, and mind. Both have been practising their craft of music and kindness for most of their lives. As MBP teachers, we will never 'perfect' the embodying of mindfulness, however we frame and understand it. Instead, it helps if we can see this as a maturing cultivation. There are many layers involved. We start with ourselves. Personal practice, as we all know, is the vital ingredient that supports our teaching and we return to the cushion and

---

153 Personal communication 14 October 2019
154 Teasdale & Chaskalson, 2011
155 Ibid.

the mindful movement mat every day, to give time and space to be with what is there; coming back to investigate experience in the body over and over; turning towards what we want to push away and what we want to hold onto; and relating kindly, as best we can, to all the ways that we move into reactivity, especially in the consolidating of 'me' and 'mine'.

In all reputable MBP teacher training organisations, there are guidelines that require MBP teachers to attend a silent, taught, retreat every year – offered by an appropriate centre or organisation, which specialises in mindfulness. This is an opportunity to immerse ourselves in the way that mindfulness practice intervenes with the habitual patterns of mind. It is deeply personal work, coming back over and over to embodying mindfulness in the body, sitting and walking, sitting and walking, eating and sleeping. There is no better way – and we will need to sit many retreats over the years if we choose to continue MBP teaching – in order to deepen the embodying of mindfulness practice.

There are considered to be two fundamental teachings that the learning of the eight-week MBP draws upon. These are both offered as retreat themes and are widely available online and in person. The first is 'The Four Foundations of Mindfulness' (in Buddhist teachings, this is called the Satipatthana Sutta). The core of these teachings is readily recognisable within the themes of the eight weeks of the MBP. The second is 'The Four Friends for Life'[156] (see Chapter 15). In Buddhist teachings these relate to The Brahma Viharas which involve the heart practices of kindness, compassion, appreciative joy, and equanimity.

Starting with our own personal practice and attending retreats that help us learn more about the body of teachings that inform MBPs, we learn gradually to embody mindfulness more and more. This deepens over time and retreat, supervision, training, and peer mentoring all support this process.

Intention

In order to teach in a way that embodies mindfulness, as MBP teachers we start by cultivating an intention to practice this. By committing to specific intentions around what we wish to embody, we find that these qualities develop and consolidate. As MBP teachers, we may become aware of various aspects of our teaching that we find challenging. Perhaps we are finding the inquiry process challenging (this is not unusual). By cultivating an intention during inquiry to come back to a sense of grounded-ness and taking time to pause and connect with present moment awareness, we discover that we remember to include mindful embodying as a central support to our teaching. As MBP teachers, we learn to weave

---

156 van den Brink & Kostler, 2015

the helpful into the unhelpful. We disempower reactivity by removing our preoccupation with what is difficult and embodying a more present, friendly, and mindful response. This takes intention, time and patience – and even a certain leap of faith.

In earlier days of teaching MBCT to people with cancer, I was aware that I had a tendency to move in to try to fix things for participants – rather than support them to stay with what was difficult, and gently turn towards what was there. A trusted colleague (Jody Mardula) asked if she could sit in on a programme and when we had made the arrangements, she asked me what she could do to help. I knew instantly what she could offer me. With her presence in the room, I could find the courage to pause, hold, and befriend the pain and suffering that people in the classes experienced at times (and that I could feel so keenly). I shared my intention with Jody and over the course of the next eight weeks, she helped me to spot the times I was tempted to move in to rescue someone in an attempt to remove their emotional pain and make it better. I learned to recognise this urge in the body and in knowing it, could respond differently. We reflected a lot about this over those weeks. It was a turning point for me in my teaching, thanks to her support, experience, and kindness.

At first, a cultivation of some new embodied understanding may not seem to involve much sense of ease or flow. Like all new behaviours, it can feel awkward and sticky. However, as we remember our intention, and understand the steps better, we develop more confidence and trust in the practice and in our MBP teaching. It becomes more natural for us to befriend the experience rather than to move away from it. We begin to realize that what we avoid in our own practice (and life), we will be unable to embody for our participants – and what we practice through 'turning towards' will offer us insights that may directly support our group members and how we teach the MBP.

Alongside this, as MBP teachers, we cultivate an intention to be 'ourselves' as we teach, and not put on an act as if we were someone else – with a different persona to our own. We each have our own natural style. In training and through our learning as teachers, we may well find ourselves admiring some of our colleagues and tutors, and equally not be drawn to the style of others. As we start out as MBP teachers in training, we can easily become acquisitive – wanting to discover the 'right' answer to each issue; seeking to capture a phrase or remember a particular way of leading an exercise. This is so natural, but whilst there is nothing wrong in borrowing teaching approaches and being influenced by those whose teaching we appreciate, we also need to be discerning about what suits us and what supports our own way of relating and teaching MBPs. Each one of us has a personality, style, and individuality. We need to be true to who we are, because this will prove to be the best foundation from which to teach.

There is always more to learn, the path is never ending, but becoming a teacher who is embodying mindfulness inside and out requires us to trust a mode of being that is natural, authentic and genuine.

> "Embodiment starts with coming to inhabit our bodies with awareness… Like a willow tree, we can be firmly rooted in intentionality and understanding, yet bend with the wind of changing conditions. Embodiment is seamless between our values, understanding and intentions, and the ways we think, act, speak and relate. It is fundamental to teaching and learning mindfulness"[157]

Christina Feldman and Willem Kuyken

Summary

Embodying mindfulness is one of the six domains of the MBI:TAC[158], and is described as an underpinning capacity of the MBP teacher, upon which the other five domains rest. This sense of embodiment as a central feature of MBP teaching is also represented in the IOG (Inside Out Group) model[159], in which the teacher's mindful embodying is placed in the centre of the group. Both the MBI:TAC and the IOG model are pointing towards the same qualities of present-moment orientation, inside and out, that embody the key attitudinal qualities of patience, calm, non-reactivity, and accepting. The inside out focus that we present in the IOG model emphasises this embodying principle in relation to the group process.

This chapter has explored the MBP teacher's embodying of mindfulness through:

- the lens of embodying mindfulness as practice
- the senses and inside out embodying
- the role of the body and grounded-ness in MBP teaching
- the attitudes and values of mindfulness
- the insights and understandings of mindfulness
- the cultivation of an intention to embody mindfulness as an MBP teacher.

157 Feldman & Kuyken, 2019
158 Crane *et al*, 2013
159 Griffith *et al*, 2019

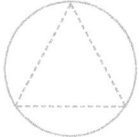

6. Launching the mindfulness-based group

Cultivating the key enablers of safety and inclusivity

Trish Bartley

"Two tasks confront members of any newly formed group. First, they must understand how to achieve their primary task. – the purpose for which they joined the group. Second, they must attend to their social relationships in the group so as to create a niche for themselves that will provide not only the comfort necessary to achieve their task but also gratification from the sheer pleasure of group membership."

Irvin D. Yalom[160]

In this chapter, we move up close to exploring some of the basic, early needs of the mindfulness-based group and how, as MBP teachers, we can understand and support those needs. The key group enablers of safety and inclusivity that we introduced in Chapter 1 have a significant influence on the depth of participants' learning and their experience of the sessions. If we want to support our participants' personal and collective well-being as best we can, we need to be able to cultivate these enablers of safety and inclusivity in order to establish and sustain a healthy mindfulness-based group process.

We start this chapter by discussing the relationship of this launching process with inside out embodying. Then we look at what we mean by launching the group and go on to draw out the details of how we can cultivate a group process that is as safe and inclusive as possible – so that we can help to build a community of mindfulness practice that best serves the learning needs of its members and of the wider society that we live in.

---

160 Yalom & Leszcz, 2005

We have included this chapter on launching the group here in Part One of the book – Inside Out Embodying – since we see the mindful embodying of the MBP teacher as fundamental to the way we are able to cultivate safety and inclusivity, using awareness from both inside (body sensations and thoughts) and outside (seeing and hearing individual group members and the group as a whole). As MBP teachers, modelling the embodying of mindfulness helps to shape group norms and helpful behaviours that support the launching of the group. Group members can then mirror these ways of cultivating grounded-ness and openness for themselves and if conditions are favourable, this contributes to their sense of safe space. Inside out embodying is central to how the MBP teacher is able to steady into their own present-moment experience, as they bring group members together for the early sessions.

However, it is important to acknowledge that we could have chosen to place this chapter within the Holding section (Section 3) as we did in the original IOG paper. Supporting the safe space of the mindfulness-based group clearly involves capacities of holding and containing. We have chosen to place launching the group here because of the vital resource that inside out embodying offers the MBP teacher and group members, especially in the context of all the apprehension that is around when joining a new group. Having the launching of the group here also serves to support a more logical sequence for you, the reader, when reflecting on the practice of teaching mindfulness-based groups.

What do we mean by launching the mindfulness-based group?

From the moment that we decide to offer an MBP, we are forming an aspiration to bring a mindfulness-based group into being. This is very different to teaching an individual participant one to one. We want to highlight the significance of the intention, the values and the capacity of the MBP teacher that are needed to support the successful launching of a new mindfulness-based group.

At the beginning of the first session there is no 'group' as such yet. Participants walk into the room or come into the online space as strangers, not knowing each other or aware in advance of who will be there. This may not be the case in some contexts, such as workplace MBPs, or if there has been a group orientation before the start of the programme. However, at the beginning of the programme, there is only a collection of participants, functioning individually. Even if some participants have been in other groups together before, while this will influence the process, it is a still a new group that needs to come into being – with a group leader (the teacher), group members (the participants), a group context (space), and a new task (learning to bring mindfulness into the lives of participants out of the experience of an MBP).

The MBP teacher is the one responsible for all the preparations involved in the actual launching of the group. Care is needed to ensure that the process is free from potential harm and that no one gets hurt. We can see this a little like the launching of a boat. The boat is a metaphor for the group and the passengers are like the group members. Imagine a traditional wooden rowing boat with several parallel plank-type seats. As people get into the boat, they may get their feet a little wet, and if unused to being in a boat they may find it quite tricky to move down and find their seat without the boat rocking alarmingly from side to side. The person who has arranged the outing and has experience of what is needed (the MBP teacher) needs to hold the boat and themselves steady whilst people get in. They may need to give advice as to where to sit, what to expect, where they are going, and what they should or should not do whilst in the boat to ensure everyone stays safe. Metaphors only take us so far, but each mindfulness-based group 'boat' eventually develops their own way of being and relating, and group members get used to how things happen – but however this unfolds, the MBP teacher has a significant and crucial role in the launching and steadying of the group, and in order to be able to do this effectively, their inside out embodying of mindful awareness will be their key resource.

Bruce Tuckman[161] described this first phase of group development as forming (see Chapter 7). We chose the term 'launching' as this highlights the significance of the MBP teachers' capacity to embody mindful steadiness and balance as they support the early beginnings of the group. Inevitably, we view this primarily as an early first stage of the development of the group. However, we also discover that the MBP group needs support in relaunching at times of transition, at the start of each session, and after upheavals (such as when a participant leaves the MBP, or if it is necessary to change the venue).

We choose to invest in bringing the mindfulness-based group into being since the group adds so much to the process of deepening practice and enabling learning, through the shared interactions, insights, relationality, and human connections that grow between group members. This also has direct benefit for connections made outside the MBP group.

---

161 Tuckman, 1965

Two group enablers: to support interrelatedness within and beyond the MBP group

As we wrote in the first chapter, there are two key enablers for the MBP teacher to facilitate, in order to bring a healthy functioning group into being:

1. **Safety** – establishing a safe process within the group.
2. **Inclusivity** – supporting respectful interconnections between group members.

And these two enablers support:

3. **Interrelatedness** – cultivating a community of practice, in ways that benefit personal and collective well-being.

Let us look at these three processes in detail in order to appreciate both the how and the why of their significance. Much of what is included may seem quite basic. However, we choose to describe these processes for the benefit of those with less groupwork experience, and by bringing awareness to what we do and why we do it, we hope to deepen our practice with MBP groups.

Safety – How to cultivate a safe space?

Safety is a basic first requirement. What does it mean to establish safety[162] in a group?

A safe space can be defined as a place where we are free from harm or hurt. This definition seems to apply to physical safety, but in the context of the MBP group it relates to psychological safety. What contributes to someone feeling more or less safe in a group will vary from one person to another. There may be all sorts of influences on participants' experiences which have a bearing on this. As MBP teachers, we may not know much about some of these influences (such as early family experience, trauma history etc.), whilst other factors may be more evident, such as the experience of discrimination through 'visible uniqueness' (gender, race/ethnicity, age, mobility, and aspects of physical appearance and so on)[163]. Our primary responsibility as MBP teachers is to respect the unique diversity that each participant brings into the group space and protect the boundaries that ensure respect and inclusivity is accorded to everyone in the group. This is not always straightforward, as everyone has a bundle of unconscious biases that influence what we say and how we act.

As we have explored in the first chapter, most of us feel apprehensive upon joining a new group. We might notice some internal rehearsing

---

162 See the chapter 1 of this book for a further discussion around safety
163 https://workthatreconnects.org/resources/about/

when group introductions start: "My name is Trish. I used to live on a mountain... My name is..." We try to find ways of soothing ourselves and feeling safe when the threat system is activated, which is what happens when we are anxious and unsure. As an MBP teacher, I have often joked with a new group that if I was being asked to introduce myself as a group member, I would probably count the number of people in the circle or on the screen, and work out the halfway point to decide when to speak! Some of us are keen to be first, perhaps to get it over with. Some of us prefer to go late, perhaps to check that we know what to do. It helps to be aware of the rituals we use and our individual patterns, so that on a good day we can hold our patterns lightly.

> "The irony is that when participants tell me how scared they are,
> I know that the room is safe!"

George Lakey[164]

Alongside our own personal feelings as a MBP teacher, there are likely to be parallel resonances with the apprehension present in the room (or on the screen if we are teaching online). As teachers and group leaders, we often 'pick up on' whatever is current for others, whether consciously aware of this or not. Resonance[165] is a good term for this – like the echo in the tunnel, or the singer's note that reverberates in the wine glass. This is true in any setting, not just in a group. We are affected by others all the time – influenced by how they are – and influencing them by how we are. This is why, as MBP teachers, our inside out embodying of grounded awareness is so central.

It can be very intimidating for some people to sit in a circle, visible to everyone else, and then be asked to talk to strangers and introduce themselves. This is especially challenging for anyone who has not had a similar experience to fall back on. The anxiety experienced by online MBP group members varies. For some people, it is easier to be online as they are usually in a familiar setting at home or at work. This is not the case for everyone, however – we are all different, and what is easier for one is not necessarily easier for another.

What can we do as teachers to support the process to be as safe as possible?

Mindfully embodying a grounded and friendly presence inside and out is probably the most helpful approach. The MBP teacher can sometimes act a bit like a conduit, 'earthing' the apprehension in the room or on the screen. Their own grounded-ness is key to how they do this. Coming back over and over to the body, the breath and the contact of the feet on the floor, offers

---

164 Lakey, 2010
165 McCown *et al*, 2010

both the teacher themselves and, through them the group, an opportunity to steady up and feel a bit safer.

We suggest there are three areas that need attention when promoting safety in the early stages of the MBP group:

- Orientation and assessment.
- Boundaries (outer and inner).
- Structure/ground rules.

Orientation and assessment

The orientation and assessment process (via a group session, online or in person, or via one-to-one meetings) helps to prepare group members to know what to expect on the MBP, and ensures it is a good time for the participant to take the programme (and that the participant is able to relate respectfully within the group).

This process takes place before the course starts and therefore before course participants come together as a mindfulness-based group. The orientation process is usually arranged individually or collectively (online or in person) with people interested in hearing more about what the MBP can offer them. The function of the orientation session is to prepare participants for all aspects of the programme, helping them commit to what is involved, and ensuring that it is a good time for them to take the course.

It can be helpful to consider the roles we need to include in the orientation process[166].

- **Information giver** – times, venue, cost, group size, other participants, home practice requirements, outline of a typical session, etc.
- **Cautioner** – can be stressful to take the course, and can sometimes involve a bit of bumpy ride.
- **Promoter** – benefits of mindfulness, headline research (this role can become overdeveloped).
- **Supporter** – what can you expect of the teacher between sessions? What other support is available?
- **Connecter** – hear the personal story/why are they considering the programme, form the beginnings of a connection that will hold participants to stay with the MBP process – especially early in the course.
- **Orientor** – the function and importance of practice, the challenges involved, and how you will manage that.

On top of these roles is the important task of 'assessment'. This ensures that it is a good time for the participant to attend the mindfulness-based programme,

---

166 The roles of MBP teacher are also discussed on page 100 in Crane *et al*, 2021

which is crucial for the participant and has an impact on the wider group. A sense of group coherence and safety will be compromised if any of the participants struggle to manage the programme and need to withdraw – or if they are unable to manage a group setting.

In the early days of teaching mindfulness to people with cancer, an overseas psychiatrist asked to sit in on the first session of a programme, during which high levels of distress were expressed by a number of the participants. It was challenging to hold so much emotion, but I was not overly concerned. I knew that some of them had experienced some very tough times, so to me it was not surprising. However, after the group had left, my visitor said how depressed she thought most of the participants were. She expressed doubt as to whether they would be able to tolerate the programme. I was surprised but unconvinced. I felt confident in the course and thought that I could support them through it. In the event, my visitor proved entirely right. Over half the group had withdrawn by the halfway point. I reflected deeply on this with colleagues and in supervision over an extended period. I came to the conclusion that my participants were not well-enough prepared for the course. As a result of thinking this through, I developed a much more rigorous pre-course orientation process. I reduced the 'promoting' role (talking about the benefit they would gain from mindfulness and encouraging them to join up) and increased the 'cautioning' role ('it can be challenging to take a mindfulness course'), whilst ensuring that participants were affirmed as adults ('whatever benefit you get from the course will be your achievement'). As a result of this, attrition rates dropped to almost zero. Group average outcome well-being scores improved significantly, and most participants mentioned how much they valued the group in their course feedback.

The assessment process also needs to ensure that each participant can relate respectfully to others and manage the experience of being in a group. This is not an issue for most people, but there are a few who may find this difficult.

In a one-to-one orientation meeting before the start of the course, I met with an older man who had had a series of illnesses that had left him feeling anxious and unsettled. He had been referred to me for a mindfulness course. We had not managed to cover much of the ground needed to prepare him for the programme – and time was passing. I noticed his tendency to interrupt and monopolise the conversation. I mentioned that the programme took place in a group context. "How do you get on in groups?", I asked him. "I can't stand them", he said. So there it was! We both agreed that the programme was not for him and instead he chose to talk things over with a counsellor who was experienced with working with people with cancer.

Boundaries: outer and inner

As MBP teachers, we also need to attend to the boundaries of the mindfulness-based group in order to cultivate safety and inclusivity. Attending to group boundaries has two aspects. The external or outer boundaries of the group relate to the membership of the group: who belongs in the group? The internal or inner boundaries convey the way group members relate within the group itself.

Clarifying the outer boundaries is an important first step

Who belongs in this group?

Our first task before anyone arrives is to ensure that we know who is coming and that we have the right number of chairs in the circle or know how many we expect to join us on the screen. Counting the chairs several times may be needed. This may sound basic, but there is nothing worse than someone arriving late to find there is no chair for them. It will reinforce a sense of not being welcome, and of being out of place, which may continue to have a bearing long after the first session. It will also impact on the rest of the group in terms of reduced safety and the risk of feeling excluded. So, if anyone is late to the first or subsequent session, we link the name of the person we are expecting to the empty chair waiting for them and make a point of pausing and welcoming them when they arrive.

Many of us teach in multi-use centres (when in-person MBPs are running)[167] and may well get interrupted by people who want something from the room or think they have booked the room at the same time. When this happens, one of our roles as teachers is to protect the safe outer boundary of the group – and actively manage the interruption, by standing up and politely encouraging whoever it is to leave, closing the door behind them. We are caring for the physical space of the group[168], which is an important part of looking after the external boundaries of the MBP. This can be quite tricky at times, so remembering to come back to inside out embodying – perhaps by pausing to notice any stream of thoughts and inner physical charge aroused by the interruptions, and pausing to tune into noticing how the event has impacted the group – and then responding to this in whatever way is helpful.

---

167 See chapter 13 Online Considerations - for relevant online teaching information

168 This is similar for an online group, although more difficult to control. We encourage participants to close the door of the room they are in – and ensure that family members respect the space, so that they do not overhear what is being said and confidentiality is protected.

I once had a class where someone in the group brought along her sister-in-law unannounced in week three. The participant was enjoying the group sessions so much that she thought her sister-in-law might enjoy them too! So along they both came. It was very tricky, and I sensed discomfort in the room (and certainly felt it within me). I welcomed the participant and the sister-in-law as best I could, held the session as usual, but I was quite careful to be as transparent as I could be to the group (about this not being an appropriate inclusion), while attempting not to embarrass the original participant or her sister-in-law. However, there was always going to be a consequence – and in this case, I never saw the original participant again. She failed to attend any further sessions, which was in some ways the best outcome for the group but not for the original participant.

This was an obvious example of the external boundaries being fractured by someone joining the session who was not expected by the group, or by me, as the MBP teacher – nor were they prepared for the session. Occasions like these are difficult to hold, but as MBP teachers, our role is to look after the safety of the whole group and to manage things as best and in as mindfully embodied a way as we can. In this situation, as in many others, it might be tempting to imagine that there are certain ways to act. This is never the case. Our challenge is to respond to what is happening in the space as best we can in the moment, rather than hold on to any preconceived ideas of what might or should be happening. These types of situations are not easy to navigate either for the MBP teacher or for the group itself. However, inside out embodying helps to bring some steadiness in, on a good day.

Timekeeping

Ensuring the session starts and finishes on time is a helpful way of holding boundaries, especially early on in the MBP. This might be difficult at the very beginning of the first session if some people have not yet arrived, but for all later sessions we might announce: "We'll be starting on time – not to worry if you are ever late, there will always be a chair for you near the door, so please come in and join us". Finishing on time is also important. A participant may have a bus to catch or some particular commitment. It is tempting to run over, to squeeze in that extra poem or finish an exercise – but in the early weeks especially, keeping to the times stated is important in building safety. This offers predictability and structure, and engenders a feeling that the teacher can be trusted to do what they say they will do. Later in the programme, it is easier to ask the group if the session can be extended by five minutes or so, and be more confident that participants will speak out if this does not suit them.

Clarifying the inner boundaries is equally important

What is expected of group members in relation to the group?

How can we, as MBP teachers, cultivate respectful ways of interacting in the group?

Looking after the internal boundaries of the group involves us, as MBP teachers, attending to the way we relate to participants, and to the way they relate to each other.

Ground rules: how can we establish structure and respect?

Ground rules help us to establish how we do things in the group. They start to create some understanding of the norms and expectations for MBP participants. Some of this will have been covered in the orientation session before the first session, but we go over this ground again, once all the participants are together at the start of the first full session of the programme.

There are many different ways of establishing the ground rules. We can facilitate a process where the participants identify ground rules themselves. This can work well with people who are used to working in experiential groups but is less helpful for those who are not. Doing it this way can also take up a fair amount of time, which is never that abundant in the first session of the MBP.

Another option is for the MBP teacher to suggest some ground rules. This keeps things clear and uncomplicated, as there is a lot to absorb in the first session. I tend to offer just two explicit ground rules with whatever group I am working with. These are *Participation* and *Confidentiality*. Both are involved with establishing and sustaining mutual respect within the group, which help to promote a sense of safety. The way we introduce these would vary according to the context, culture and population we are working with.

Offering some input about *participation* invites participants to make choices about how they will participate in the session:

> *"Participation means that you are invited to engage here in whatever way feels best for you. I may well look around the group (or across the screen) when we are having a discussion about something, and if you do not feel like saying anything – then please don't! Being mindful is all about responding in whatever way feels helpful and relevant to you in that moment. It is fine to talk and fine to choose not to talk. Self-care and making sound choices for ourselves is a large part of what we are learning here – so if you need to take a break to go to the loo or go and get some water, please do whatever you need to look after yourself."*

Confidentiality is the second ground rule we use. Most MBP teachers will include this and it helps to spell out clearly what we mean.

> *"We will be learning together – sometimes exchanging ideas and experiences in small groups and pairs, and then coming back to reconnect with the whole group. In order to keep things clear, it is best if you only share your own experience when you return to the larger group and leave others to share theirs. In this way we can feel safe in choosing what we want to share and with whom. When outside the group, it is important to respect what others have said as belonging to them. It may be best not to specifically identify other group members[169]. However, it is often helpful to share your own learning with your family and friends, if you want to. It belongs to you – of course – and reflecting on your experience of the course is one of the ways that we process learning. So by all means share what we have done and how you found it."*

In our experience, group members learn to navigate this boundary quite easily if we can outline this clearly and simply, early on. Later, we may often notice times when participants want the whole group to hear something that was said in their small group. They learn to check first with a member of their small group and ask them if it is okay to repeat it to the large group. When this happens, it is a sign that group members are embodying respect and connection and that this is developing within the group.

However, there may be times when it is necessary to intervene directly if someone behaves inappropriately, or worse, disrespectfully.

I was teaching the first session of an MBP with a small group of people with cancer. We had shared ground rules. At some point, one of the men addressed another man, who was sitting on the other side of the circle – cutting across a woman who was sharing something – by loudly asking, "What sort of cancer have you got then?" I intervened quickly, before there was a chance for the second man to reply. I then explained that asking direct personal questions in the group was not helpful and went against the ground rules that we had agreed. After the session, I had a phone call with the participant who had asked the question, and I explained the need for clear boundaries that were based on respect. He had found my intervention difficult and became rather defensive and chose to withdraw from the programme.

In these sorts of situations, it is easy to reflect on all the ways that we could have reacted differently that might have resulted in a better outcome.

Was I justified in being so direct in the session?

---

169 For example, in a MBP for people with mental health issues, or for people with cancer, it may be inappropriate to acknowledge other group members out in the community. We might discuss this in the group. "How would you feel if you bumped into someone from the group in the supermarket or at the doctors? How would you want to handle this if you were with a family member or a friend who didn't know you were going to a mindfulness course?"

Should I have let things run and left the intervention with the participant until the end of the session after everyone else had left?

This sort of situation offers many opportunities to ruminate, judge, and regret. Yet an underpinning principle as MBP teacher, and group leader, is to protect the sense of safety in the group. There may well have been gentler ways for me to achieve this. However, there are going to be times when an intervention is necessary – when, for example, something discriminatory is said. These times are invariably awkward and challenging, when it may be especially difficult to keep a consistent connection with inside out embodying. Afterwards, we may feel that we did not handle the situation well, but that is not as important as being willing to challenge discrimination, prejudice and disrespect when it appears in the group space. We always need to do what we can to protect the safety and inclusivity of group members, especially those who are often marginalised.

Inclusivity: how to cultivate respectful interconnections?

Our second group enabler – inclusivity – requires us to cultivate ways of respectfully including participants, and facilitating and sustaining helpful connections in the group.

When considering a choice of venue for the MBP, alongside the obvious physical access issues, we also need to consider the ambience and style of the venue (is it strongly middle class?), the promotional material on the walls (are the images predominantly of white people in heterosexual couples?), is the reception area appropriate for all ages, local languages, abilities etc. Orientation meetings held in the venue where the MBP will happen are valuable opportunities to ask people what they need. Can we acknowledge issues that may be relevant, such as chosen gender pronouns, chosen names, hearing challenges, language, different ages, mobility issues and so on? If we can gently open up these conversations with participants, we are enabling a way of sharing information that supports inclusivity and lets us know, as their MBP teachers, what they need from us and what might support them to feel safe and included.

Our own teaching materials, handouts, pictures, illustrations, and use of language all need careful and regular review. We have been taught to use the pronoun 'we' as we teach. It is more invitational and inclusive than separating into 'you' (participants) and 'me' (teacher). 'We' implies that, as teachers, we are still learners, humans who struggle, and practitioners who need mindfulness. However, there may well be people in the room who do not identify with those 'we' statements. For example, an MBP teacher might suggest to the group: "Perhaps we can practice 'feet on the floor' as we run up the stairs." This may be uncontentious to an able-bodied house dweller, but it may be impossible for someone in long-term chronic pain, or living in a high-rise flat, or getting old and frail – and so on. This and many other examples may inadvertently exclude some of our participants, and frame the MBP within a certain background, class, race, language and so on, however well-intentioned as MBP teachers we may be. Staying aware of the impact of what we might routinely say to a mindfulness-based group on the inside (body tightening maybe, and/or awareness of rising background rumination) and attentive to the body language of the group on the outside will help MBP teachers to pick up times when what we have said is not skillful, relevant or appropriate. And when these times happen, as they surely will, we can come back to mindful awareness with a guided pause, or brief practice that involves the breath and/or the body, which will support teacher and group alike.

Welcome and introductions

A welcome is all about receiving someone warmly into the teaching space. It is such a widely used term that we forget how important it is. It requires our embodied presence – our present moment aware presence – in order to authentically and kindly welcome another into a space for the first time. It has an immediate impact. We notice the genuineness of the welcome we receive. It registers internally, immediately. Smiling helps, but an overly sweet first engagement is not necessarily authentic. Our intention might be to offer a warm, grounded and appropriate connection to each participant as they arrive.

Introductions follow, once the session has got going and participants have found their seats. Names will be shared and perhaps something about what they are hoping for. We may choose to share something about ourselves as MBP teachers, enough to instill confidence in our capacity to teach the group but not so much that participants feel intimidated. Depending on the size of the group, we may invite people to talk in pairs (or perhaps threes, if online) before introducing themselves to the whole group. It is easier to talk first with one or two people than opening up to speak to the whole room – but there may be a risk of sharing too much too soon. This early process needs gentle but secure inside out embodied holding. Anxiety is reduced when there is sufficient structure, so participants need to know what we are asking of them. However, a lot depends on the context, the people in the room or on the screen, their levels of experience, and what feels comfortable and relevant. As in other situations, there are no formulae – except to be sensitively aware and mindfully embodied as best we can be. This may be the best support we can find for these early MBP moments.

Grounding helps the teacher to welcome participants, facilitate introductions, suggest ground rules – and so on. Maybe an eyes open, light introduction to 'feet on the floor' practice is also a good choice of brief practice here.

Small group work

We want participants to feel that there is a place for them to belong in the group. Forming early connections with others in the group can help a lot. As teachers, we facilitate this by inviting exchanges in pairs, threes, and larger small groups, in person or through the use of online 'breakout' rooms. Even in an overall MBP group of only five or six, we can still break into twos and threes for introductions, discussing topics, sharing ideas, exploring home practice experience and so on.

When setting up a small group process, we need to be mindfully embodied and really clear about the question we are asking the group to discuss. Writing it on a flipchart or whiteboard works well, or posting it in broadcast if we are online. There is likely to be a lot of internal mental chatter at the start of the course as people get used to ways of working – so group members may have less available attention to take in what is being said. Repeating the discussion question or task can be helpful – and when we do, we need to ensure that we use the same question! This may seem obvious, but faced with blank expressions from participants, I often find it tempting to reframe the question – or add a second question to the first in the (forlorn) hope of making things clearer. This does not help! Having small group tasks that are succinctly described promotes safety. Participants then know what they are being asked to talk about and are free to connect with their fellow group members, without worrying about remembering what they are meant to be doing.

We find that it is probably helpful to include at least one small group process in every session – and more if we can. This is especially true for the first session whilst launching the group. These small group processes do not need to take long. Six or seven minutes might be enough to share ideas and gain a sense of connection. One teacher trainee fed back that they did not have the time on the MBP to include small groups. We explained that it does not need extra time. It is just a way of bringing the learning into the heart of the group instead of teaching didactically or opening things to a full group discussion (which in the early stages when launching a group is likely to be unproductive).

Smaller groups (of, say, two or three) have the potential to create more intimate and personal connections. Larger small groups (of, say, five or six) offer broader perspectives. Changing the size of the groups keep the process fresh and widens the opportunity of connecting with different people, which is so important. At the beginning of an online course, break out rooms of threes work well. The teacher is not able to see how things are going, so twos are more of a gamble online, before the group is settled, and we know how group members are relating. Pairs work well for in person courses, with the teacher in the room, and later in an online MBP when group members know one another better. It is well worth considering what size group best fits the task at hand.

With online breakout rooms, the random allocations systems on the platform usually ensures that participants get mixed up every time. When inviting 'in person' small groups, this needs a little more intervention on the part of the MBP teacher to ensure that participants are not in the same small group each time. It can help to establish this 'mixing' as a norm from the very first session of the MBP. One way is to stand up, invite everyone else to stand as well, and then suggest they, "look around the circle and see whose name you don't know, or who you haven't yet spoken to, and walk towards them to form a small group". If we have someone in the group who has difficulty in moving comfortably, we can invite them to stay in their chair and ask others to make a group around them. In this way, we are ensuring a mix of participants into the small groups, so that as soon as possible everyone has spoken to everybody else.

It is worth conducting this process fairly actively as it is quite natural for group members to be drawn to stay in the same chair or part of the room that they first sat in. This is a way of creating personal safety, but it soon becomes unhelpful when small groups form with the folk who are nearest. If this continues over the weeks, there will be minimal mixing and similar small group compositions every time. So, standing up and inviting everyone in the group to stand up too, serves two purposes – it facilitates inclusivity and interconnecting, and by encouraging participants to move we are also increasing levels of grounded-ness and establishing ways of working in the group that serve us well later on the MBP. In time, there is an ongoing shift of people sitting in different chairs throughout the session – and if we choose, we can bring attention to this and ask how it feels to keep moving, as a way of highlighting the natural pull we have of wanting things to stay the same.

When participants come back after a small group process, we need to gather some brief themes so that discussions are joined up (to some extent). This seems like a functional task – "Tell us what you were talking about" – but it has more to do with re-investing and regathering the process of the whole group. There are many ways of doing this, but as with other early processes, repetition early on helps participants get used to what is involved. We might use a device to help the group synthesize their small group discussion by asking for a few 'little nuggets' from their discussions – "by sharing the essence of what really interested and engaged you".

Without this sort of guidance, small groups will tend to offer a longer, more comprehensive restating of their discussion. All we want are the headlines, so that each group has an opportunity to hear a little from the others, to reassure them that they were in line with the other groups and re-connect as a whole group. These small group/online break-out room discussions facilitate a sense of inclusivity and support the opportunity for exchanges to flow back and be integrated into the learning of the large group.

Inclusivity and inquiry

Early inquiry processes also offer opportunities to support the beginnings of the group by joining up experiences and including the whole group. Here is an example that will be familiar to MBP teachers.

> During an inquiry following a practice, a member of the group shares that they felt agitated at one point and places a hand on their belly as they refer to this. The MBP teacher gently invites an exploring of this, and as the participant moves closer to their experience, they become distressed. By inviting everyone to move attention to their feet on the floor, and place a hand on their belly, if this feels ok, the teacher enables the whole group to be involved in holding the agitation and distress of their group member – and since some members of the group may also be feeling agitated, and/ or be affected by the distress, the group steps up to mutually hold itself and all its members, beyond just the original person who first felt it. Not only is agitation and distress shared around the group, but so are grounding, compassion and care.

Experiences such as these will build confidence and interconnection in the group and in mindfulness practice itself. They can be quite new ways of relating to experience for many people – and even though distress has been present, some people will be left with a stronger sense of belonging and feeling part of the group. The MBP teacher gives special attention to their own inside out mindful embodying at these times.

Interrelatedness: to support the group to become a community of mindfulness practice

How do we build a Practice Community?

This is the third and last process to explore in relation to launching the group. In some ways this can be seen as an outcome to the way we have already cultivated safety and inclusivity within the MBP group. In other ways, this is an ongoing and slightly different element that supports the launching of the group

The MBP course structure itself facilitates this. As we know, guided practices are embedded into every session. They cultivate growing awareness of physical sensations in the body, and gradually develop the practice of befriending patterns of mind. Engaging in a shared practice, whether online or in the room, creates a collective field that connects practitioners and their experience together, inside and out. During the inquiry process, as participants reflect on their experience, a sense of mutuality develops as they learn that their experience was similar – or, which can also be connecting, that it is ok to be different.

As well as the more formal, longer practices, we can also thread brief practices into the sessions, maybe just for a few seconds at a time. We may wisely choose to establish this from the very beginning of the course. Not so long ago, a short practice was assumed to be a Three Step Breathing Space. Whilst these are valuable tools in the mindfulness-based practice repertoire, they can be difficult to remember at critical moments of anxiety, anger or threat of overwhelm. Brief practices, such as Feet on the Floor, The Pause, and Coming to the Breath etc. are short, simple and accessible in the moment, if established regularly. They can be employed in class and practiced at home and are invaluable in fostering the value of everyday moments of reconnection and grounding. They are also vital in supporting the inside out mindful embodying of the MBP teacher as they build a practice community within the mindfulness-based group.

Interrelatedness in the horizontal inquiry

We look at horizontal inquiry in more detail later in Chapter 12, but we want to mention it here to connect inquiry to the role it has in building a community of practice and supporting the group in its early launching, interconnection and interrelatedness. Horizontal inquiry, as the name suggests, is a way of exploring the experience of mindfulness practice in the group – not so much focusing on one participant only (vertical inquiry), but weaving shared experiences horizontally across and around the group. We include an example of this in the box below.

As the inquiry process takes place immediately after a guided practice, its function is to help participants explore their experience and draw out the learning from the practice, probably linked to the themes of the session. It can take a little time for group members to get used to, and for MBP teachers, inquiry is widely experienced as the most challenging aspect of learning to teach. In early inquiries, there is a risk that new teachers may be tempted to go 'vertical' in our inquiries, which may be too deep, too soon. Instead, using a more horizontal approach, we can join up similar responses from individual participants to others around the circle or across the screen.

Horizontal inquiry

Someone shares that they fell asleep during the body scan. The MBP teacher acknowledges this gently and then widens out to others in the group. "Did anyone else feel sleepy?", and looking around the circle, or scanning across the screen, they deliberately open out to link one participant's individual experience with others who might have felt something similar. The teacher then acknowledges any nods, or murmurs of agreement that signify similar experiences. By doing this, the MBP teacher is linking a personal narrative (of an experience within a body scan) with other personal narratives and joining them into the universal: "Yes, we quite often feel sleepy during a body scan, don't we?"

Why is this so helpful in relation to the interrelatedness of the group?

Feeling sleepy during a practice may well activate judging critical thoughts such as "I shouldn't have felt sleepy. I am the only one who felt sleepy. I am hopeless at mindfulness" and so on. Learning that others also feel sleepy is 'normalising' their experience. There is relief on hearing that others do this too. This opens up the possibility of relating more kindly to the experience (of feeling sleepy and judging oneself for feeling sleepy). It is also helpful in including different types of experience. If appropriate, we might follow this example with: "Did anyone feel something different?" and then normalise that too by inviting others to acknowledge their similar experience. And even if no one does – we affirm that "we have lots of different experiences throughout a practice. They are all completely normal and valid."

Inquiring in this way, using a light touch, also has the function of gently warming up the group and enables those who feel more tentative to join in with just a nod or a murmur of agreement. We cannot overestimate the value of this process with a new group (and with more experienced ones too). Normalising helps to establish bonds of connection, inclusivity, safety and relationship.

Conclusion

It is human nature to connect – so it is not difficult for people to come together as the group is launching. When group members share a common purpose (to bring mindfulness into their lives) and engage in a shared process (to learn how to practice mindfulness), significant obstacles would have to be in place for the group not to come into being and for interconnectedness to come about. If, as MBP teachers, with inside out embodying, we can invest in the mindfulness-based group enablers of safety and inclusivity, we are supporting the interrelatedness in the group within a community of mindfulness practice. By resourcing the MBP group in this way, we are helping to lay the foundations to support well-being for individual group members in ways that offer skills and resources that can be taken and used outside the MBP group to benefit the wider society.

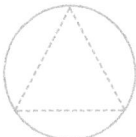

An interview with Dave McCormack

Dave describes himself as an accidental adult educator, having migrated from secondary school teaching to community development and adult education over three decades ago. He works in a university-based Department of Adult and Community Education, where he is course leader for a suite of courses in the field of Adult Guidance Counselling. He is also a husband and father. He says that he continues to live with an intention to learn from his daily lived experience of family and work – and how to live more skillfully and wisely.

The complexity of the group in mindfulness

Humans are relational beings. We are formed in relationship to others, so when the group is harnessed well within an MBP class, it can be potentially transformative.

> *There isn't really an individual who is not formed through relationship. I think what the group does is that it opens things up, it offers a possibility of being able to see the world in a different way (…) And so groups are very, very, deeply challenging. But they're also deeply confirming.*

Dave spoke of the infinite complexity of what goes on in a mindfulness group, and the importance of the mindfulness teacher understanding this, and being able to ground the group in a strong learning container.

> [With a meditation practice] *you become aware of the complexity of your own subjectivity. And the ways in which your mind just unbearably has endless, endless, possibilities. And craziness – as you know. Off your mind goes wherever it wants to go. When I say I have a sense of the complexity of my own subjectivity, and it feels infinite*

(that complexity). When you put that together with another 16, or 17 or 18 people, you really have infinite possibilities of reactions and actions and responses and the group just takes on a life of its own, in a way that has meaning. [The teacher needs] to make sure it's safe. And needs to be embodied and grounded. And that you're not following every whim, in the same way that you don't follow every whim of your own mind. You don't follow every single possibility in the snow globe self.

(The idea of being able to watch your own perspective.)

How to teach groups: similarities between adult education literature and mindfulness pedagogy

There are many parallels between the adult education literature and the pedagogy of mindfulness – one of these is being aware of what we as mindfulness teachers bring to the space.

You're never neutral. Your action as an educator is always politically significant. I mean, you're either liberating or you're furthering entrapping, you're never neutral.

Drawing upon the adult education literature, Dave draws comparisons as to how this dovetails with the way we approach teaching mindfulness in groups, such as facilitating learning through dialogue (the inquiry) rather than from the stance of being an expert.

Edward Lindemann was one of the earliest adult education thinkers. He was writing in the 1920s in the States. He talks about our lives as living textbooks. An adult educator wasn't necessarily somebody in a classroom. We are all adult learners. We are all on a journey of learning in living our lives. An adult educator is somebody who facilitates that learning. Malcolm Knowles (…) talks about learning emerging through dialogue – not through an expert teacher.

Creating a space in which present-moment experience can be explored is key to how Dave approaches teaching an MBP class.

The first step for me is always about creating the learning community. When I begin with groups, I really try to create a space that is different from normal interaction. So it's like creating a strange space for people where the norms of, you know, everyday conversation don't have to be handled; where it is okay to be in the here and now. But also it's okay to be in the here and now with a narrative.

Salzberger-Wittenberg's work has been influential in how Dave approaches and thinks about groups, and about the role of the leader and the value of their awareness of their internal, emotional process as they teach, and how he relies on this to help hold and read the group.

I think [Salzberger-Wittenberg's book (2013)] *could be a very valuable resource for mindfulness teachers, because she comes from a psychoanalytic viewpoint. And so she talks about the importance of beginnings and the importance of endings and also transitions and resistance to learning and how an educator can use their own emotional processes to give them information about working with a group.*

Mezirow's theories of how adult learning takes place demonstrate how important it is for the mindfulness teacher to create a space in which people feel safe to be vulnerable.

Mezirow writes that adult learning emerges from a disorienting dilemma. We learn from the challenges that life gives us. When we get disorientated, our sense of internal harmony is disturbed. This offers us an opportunity to look at our own frames of reference and watch how they need to be expanded or changed. In terms of learning groups, we are therefore encouraging people to come together out of their vulnerability and disorientation. We create a container for their vulnerability, where people can think with it and through it.

Jarvis is another influence for Dave in how he makes sense of his role with groups in adult education.

I also like Jarvis' idea of 'disjuncture'. He writes about what happens when our 'homeostasis' (balance) is disturbed, and we find ourselves at the limits of our repertoire of skills and resources – and this results in us finding the motivation to reach out for new learning.

Similarly, the work of Linden West is also key to thinking about how a carefully managed group process can facilitate both intellectual and emotional learning.

Linden West talks about the border country of adult learning as sort of a messy place where your solid identities are gone. In this disorientation, we lose a sense of who we are. Our solid identities go when we're vulnerable – and that is a learning opportunity. Adult education at its best creates the space for that to be held, contained. And to be able to be thought about and talked about, not only in an intellectual way, but also in an emotional way.

The potential learning from groups

Dave feels that the aspiration for what individuals might learn from being a member of an MBP group can be wide-ranging, from creating a space to learn to approach one's own experience in a new way, to influencing active change in the world.

> *This is exactly what mindfulness groups are seeking to do – to create a space for people to challenge their perspectives, and for the vulnerability of ordinary adult life to be talked about and thought about in a grounded, supported and contained way.*

> *Kabat-Zinn* [comes from an] *individual psychological way, and he seems to see that as a kind of an accumulation … some sort of bringing together and if there are enough people like that, then maybe the world will change. Whereas Paulo Freire is much closer to a form of political empowerment and active change. But I think both are saying the same thing – which is that if we're in as full a possession as we can be of our faculties and our potentials, we have a right to have that full capacity. And we will be if we have those… We will be gigantic, potent, democratic beings.*

Part Two:
Reading
the group

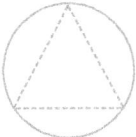

7. Reading the mindfulness-based group

Gemma Griffith

Reading is one of the three teaching capacities in the IOG model, in which it means the teacher's capacity to 'read' the group as they are teaching (i.e. to have a fairly consistent awareness of what is going on in the group, and drawing upon key group theories to interpret the group process). Reading the group intuitively – such as knowing when an activity is causing members in the group to grow restless or tired etc. – is a skill that we probably all have to a greater or lesser extent. It is possible to develop this skill further by learning about key group development theories and being in and leading groups ourselves. Here we present selected theories and models about group process which have clear links to MBPs. Although there are multiple models of group development available, here, for the sake of clarity, we have chosen to describe Tuckman[170], and key group development factors by Yalom and Lesez[171]. Additionally, we briefly outline two theories about participant factors that may influence how participants relate to the group and teacher, the first is 'the group imago'[172] and the second is attachment theory[173].

Although this chapter may seem daunting at first – particularly if group process theory is new to you – we hope that you will find in time that the theories presented in this chapter will start to form a part of how you naturally read the group as you teach. Some theories may appeal to you more than others, and none are perfect, but the ideas contained within them can be very helpful to the MBP teacher. You may have access to other group theories that you have used in other contexts, which may be equally useful to you and may well compliment with the theories that are presented here.

It is important to clarify that although there are several theories about group process that we will introduce in this chapter, we are not suggesting

---

170 Tuckman, 1965
171 Yalom and Lesez, 2008
172 Berne, 1963
173 Cassidy & Shaver, 2002

that learning how to read the group is purely about learning and applying theories in some abstract way. Instead, the intention is to enhance the skills you already have and to help relate those skills to group process theories. The key is to have a knowledge of key group process theories as you teach, but always making sure you teach the group that is in front of you rather than applying ideas from theory about what 'should' be happening. As Carl Jung once wrote, "Learn your theories as well as you can, but put them aside when you touch the miracle of the living soul"[174].

Group development theory

Tuckman originally published his four-stage group development theory as a team development model for the workplace[175]. It is a theory that is still used and relevant to group process six decades later. There are other group development models available, but Tuckman's group development theory is a helpful model for MBP teachers, as it describes typical stages in group development, and points towards what the group might need from the MBP teacher at each stage. If we understand the stage our group is at, we can adapt our teaching style and respond to offer the group what it needs as the MBP course progresses.

Below we outline Tuckman's theory, with comments about how using it can be helpful when teaching MBPs. According to Tuckman[176] the four stages are:

1. Forming
2. Storming
3. Norming
4. Performing.

Later, a fifth stage was added, known as Adjourning or Mourning. Although the five stages are described as neat and separate, we need to bear in mind that group development can be much more complex and a lot less linear than how this model appears. Groups may move back and forth between the stages, and cycle back to the beginning (forming) perhaps even after touching into a very highly developed stage (performing). However, there is largely an agreement that groups do develop in predictable ways[177].

Forming is the first stage of Tuckman's model[178] and describes how individuals meet and start to form and identify as a member of the group. In an MBP group, there is often uncertainty in the room during Week 1, with participants unsure of what is expected of them. At this early stage, they usually do not

---

174 Jung *et al*, 1953, p73
175 Tuckman, 1965
176 Tuckman, 1965; 1977
177 Bonebright, 2010
178 Tuckman, 1965

know anyone else in the group, and therefore tend to be more dependent on the guidance from the teacher. Some participants may test the waters in terms of the teacher and other participants in the room. During this forming stage, it is helpful for teachers to have a directive style, and to establish strong boundaries so that participants have a clear sense of what is expected. This includes:

- Having the practical arrangements clearly in place.
- Outlining 'group rules' of behaviour and confidentiality, and ensuring that the group has understood them.
- Encouraging participant-to-participant connections by using pairs and or small group work frequently throughout the first MBP sessions. This allows participants to meet and get to know each other which can help the group to form.

How long forming takes depends on the group. For some, it may come together after only one or two MBP classes. For other groups (particularly if there is a lot of absent group members) it may take longer and even overlap with other stages.

Storming is the second stage[179], when group members establish themselves in the group in relation to the teacher and other participants. In this stage participants have more clarity about the purpose of the group, but some uncertainty still exists. Tuckman posited that cliques may form which could lead to power struggles, and some participants may test their interactions with the teacher and with fellow participants. Here, we define this type of storming as *Interpersonal* storming, as it takes place between the group members (including the teacher). As Tuckman's model was developed with teams in the workplace, which are very different to MBP groups, it is unclear how common storming is during a typical MBP class. In our experience, storming in an MBP group tends to be more subtle than the way it is described by Tuckman (for example, a participant being consistently late to class, or small groups that carry on talking after the teacher has asked them to return to the big group). In the practitioner literature, Woods[180] wrote that storming in MBP classes seems to manifest more often in the *intrapersonal* (within the participant) rather than *interpersonal* (between participants and the teacher). Both types of storming will be explored below.

Interpersonal storming

Tuckman[181] originally wrote about interpersonal storming, and although in our experience it occurs less often than intrapersonal storming, knowledge about interpersonal storming can be enormously helpful for mindfulness teachers for those occasions when it does happen. Interpersonal storming

---

179 Tuckman, 1965
180 Woods, 2019
181 Tuckman, 1965

can include how participants might test the boundaries of the group as they establish themselves as members. This can manifest in ways such as a participant appearing annoyed and asking lots of direct question which challenges the teacher. An example of how having some knowledge about storming helped me (GG) to understand and navigate a challenging moment in the MBP classroom follows:

In a group I taught some years ago, in week one of an MBSR class, after I had explained the bodyscan and options for postures (including sitting), participants had settled on their mats for their first bodyscan practice. I was a minute or so into leading the practice, when a woman lifted her head to look at me, and in a slightly accusatory tone called out, "Why are we lying down rather than sitting?" I saw straight away that this had disturbed the group, and caused other participants to shift their bodies slightly and some of them lifted their heads to look at me and the participant. This comment was a challenge to what I had invited the group to do, and I recall feeling at a loss as to how to respond. I immediately felt that I must have done something wrong. However, I was lucky enough in my teacher training to have already been taught about storming; indeed this was from being a student in a module that Trish was teaching! So this initial uncertainty quickly merged into suspecting that this was example of 'storming'. I responded something along the lines of, "There are a few options of different postures we can use when meditating, including lying down or sitting, and if you would prefer to sit for this one, then do feel free to move to a chair". She nodded, seeming satisfied and settled back into a lying down posture as I resumed leading the bodyscan.

My knowledge of storming helped me to understand this incident from a wider perspective. My usual habit-mind took me immediately into self-criticism 'What have I done wrong here?' and yet, at the same time, I recognised that this might be storming and therefore need not be taken as personally as it had first felt. It also helped me later when I took some time to reflect on this incident. I was able to identify interpersonal storming as a fairly natural part of the group process – and this had a positive impact on my confidence and courage in responding. This is not to say that I had no responsibility here. I might have needed to emphasise the choices around posture more clearly, as they did not appear to have been heard in this instance (indeed I now take greater care in class to underline all the possible postures we can choose before starting the first bodyscan practice). Storming can be very challenging to experience as teachers and it helps for us to support ourselves when storming is encountered – either through supervision, or by using the reflective tool for MBP teachers, the TLC, which has a section in it on how we can reflect on a challenging teaching incident[182], which may be particularly useful if interpersonal storming has occurred during a MBP session.

---

182 Griffith *et al*, 2021

Intrapersonal storming

Intrapersonal storming is what happens internally in participants as they work with challenges in their experience of the MBP – such as those inherent in developing a regular mindfulness meditation practice. This is a more common type of storming in our experience and indeed Woods[183] noted that storming in MBP classes is more likely to manifest *intrapersonally* than interpersonally. Woods[184] also drew helpful parallels between intrapersonal storming, where participants experience difficulty with meditation practice, and the five hindrances – which are the classic struggles with meditation practice as described by traditional contemplative teachings (these are: restlessness, sloth and torpor, doubt, desire, and aversion). Intrapersonal storming is therefore what participants typically experience in meditation practices (e.g., with the bodyscan, participants often experience sleepiness or restlessness). This can lead to participants thinking they are 'getting it wrong' and struggling with practice.

One research study supports the idea of intrapersonal storming. The authors mapped out the developmental stages of an MBP group based on interviews with MBP participants and teachers[185]. They reported that in the early to mid-stages of the group (Weeks thee to five) participant's grapple with trying to understand mindfulness and start to test out and compare their understanding and felt personal development in comparison to other participants in the group. One teacher in the study described week five as "A stormy session" (p7). This points to intrapersonal storming as being a key process of both group and individual process. Therefore, intrapersonal storming may be a helpful concept for MBP teachers to be aware of. When participants first engage with meditation and report to the MBP teacher experiences such as busy mind, sleepiness, annoyance etc – these common experiences are an excellent sign to MBP teachers that individuals in the group are sincerely engaging with the practices and that experiential learning is taking place. In fact, it would be concerning if this type of intrapersonal challenge and storming did not occur, as it would point to a lack of engagement or indifference towards the course and the practice. We have known some early-stage MBP teachers who have thought that if participants report difficulties with practice, this is a sign of their poor teaching. This is far from the case and instead, intrapersonal storming is likely to be a sign of engagement with mindfulness practices. When we recognise this is occurring in an MBP class, as a teacher, we can emphasise to our participants that it is simply part and parcel of how we develop a sincere mindfulness practice, and further, that it is a universal experience[186]. This is a key point to emphasise when we read that this form of intrapersonal storming is

---

183 Woods, 2019
184 Ibid.
185 Cormack *et al*, 2018
186 Woods, 2019

taking place – particularly if we notice that it causes participants to start to negatively judge themselves about how 'good' or otherwise they are at mindfulness practice.

Norming is the next stage and Tuckman[187] described this as when participants become used to their roles as participants and have established protocols for ways of doing things. Within an MBP class this might include familiarity with dropping into a short meditation practice, pair work, inquiry etc. Norming is also the stage in group development when participants respond well to the teacher, have a sense of their place and role in the group, when there is a shared commitment to the work of the MBP, and the teacher is respected by the group. In general, we can say that we can read norming when the group is cohesive and they work well together. The role of the MBP teacher shifts from the directive role which was necessary during the forming (and any storming) stage, to a more facilitative and enabling role. This may involve a lighter touch when teaching – for example, perhaps noticing relevant themes that may emerge naturally from the group and giving time to explore these.

Performing is the last of Tuckman's original group development stages[188]. This stage is reached when group members are clear about why they are doing what they are doing and have coherent intentions that align with the group as a whole. Group members have formed strong connections among themselves and are able to work collaboratively, and with more autonomy. Participants look after each other and support each other in their discoveries of mindfulness practice with a deepening capacity for reflection. This performing stage is often a joy to witness as a teacher, when the group is focused and on-task, shows care for all group members, and needs minimal 'holding' from the teacher (beyond the curriculum-led input that is necessary). Inspiration and care seem evident in the group. The process appears almost effortless and is characterised by a sense of flow and ease.

Adjourning, sometimes also known as mourning, was a stage added by Tuckman about a decade after the original model was published[189]. It is highly relevant to MBP groups as the eight-week course is a time-limited group, and therefore inevitably has an end point. Adjourning is not so much about the group development process itself, but is a reminder that endings need to be acknowledged and the well-being of members considered as the programme comes to an end. In MBP groups, people have sometimes allowed themselves to be vulnerable by sharing their discoveries about mindfulness in the context of their present-day challenges. They may have witnessed the vulnerability of others and the group can feel closely bonded. For some people, it may be difficult to acknowledge the ending of the group. We can help prepare participants throughout the course – for example, in the

---

187 Tuckman, 1965
188 Ibid.
189 Tuckman & Jenson, 1977

'half-way review' which is embedded in the MBSR curricula in week five, participants are invited to consider what they have learned so far, and what their intentions are for the rest of the course. It can be helpful to include resources from week six onwards that help participants continue to practice after the course has ended. This may include apps, audio guides, and any suitable online or local meditation groups. This gives participants a chance to engage with these materials/resources during the course, which may mean there is less of a gap in support for their personal mindfulness practice after the eight-week course ends.

Yalom's therapeutic factors

Having explored Tuckman's contribution to our understanding of the stages of group development, we now turn to Irvin D Yalom, widely considered a pre-eminent theorist and innovator within group psychotherapy practice. Yalom described 11 therapeutic factors which represent the way therapeutic change may be influenced by the enormously complicated interplay of human experience. As these 11 factors come from group psychological therapy, not all of them are directly relevant to MBPs. Here, we outline four of the 11 factors that seem to be most relevant to MBPs, and describe how they overlap with the MBP pedagogical literature. The four factors we will be exploring are: universality, imparting information, imitative behaviour, and group cohesiveness.

Therapeutic factors: universality

Universality is described as the "disconfirmation of a client's feelings of uniqueness"[190], and how this discovery that we are not alone in feeling the way that we do can lead to a sense of relief. Yalom and Lesez[191] wrote of an exercise in which people in the group were asked to write anonymously the one thing they would not want to share in a group. The most common response was the 'secret' of feeling a basic lack of competence, and that "one bluffs one's way through life" (p7). Knowing that this overall sense of 'lack' and bluffing through life is a natural human experience can offer a feeling of being part of the common human tapestry.

Mindfulness-based programmes include universality within the curriculum, where it is termed 'general vulnerability' and is defined as 'traits shared by all humans'[192], with an explicit focus on the biological underpinnings of these traits. This includes our capacity for language and thought (which can separate us from our direct experience and instead focus on the past or the future), automatic pilot, and the stress-reaction cycle. The message is that these biological underpinnings are not our fault. We will inevitably get

---

190 Yalom & Lesez, 2008
191 Ibid.
192 Crane, 2017, p69

caught up in ruminating on the past or the future, get stressed, anxious, sad, bored etc. MBPs do not attempt to change this – indeed they are not able to directly, but they draw attention to the fact that these biological processes exist. They are something that we all share as humans, and thus this awareness of the universality of shared vulnerabilities facilitates participants' exploration how they are *in relationship* to their stress, anxiety etc. Participants come to an MBP class with different levels of knowledge about these shared traits, and through the shared discovery of closely examining the *process* of the interconnectedness of mind, thought emotions, and body – we discover together that we are all shaped by these human traits.

Therapeutic factors: imparting information

Within therapeutic groups, the therapist often imparts information about the mechanisms around mental health and other information that is relevant to participants. This may happen implicitly, with information being offered by the therapist as an emergent part of the group process. It can also happen explicitly, with direct instructions about various psychological processes – known as psychoeducation[193]. Teachers of MBPs impart information in both explicit and implicit ways. In the original MBCT curriculum, for example, participants are didactically taught how to identify their depressive relapse signature, and how to link their moods with their activities[194]. A lot of information is also shared through implicit experiential learning and inquiry in MBPs[195].

Therapeutic factors: imitative behaviour

In psychotherapeutic group literature – imitative behaviour points to the phenomenon of how the therapist's behaviour influences how participants behave and communicate with each other[196]. For example, if a therapist is calm and kind in their interactions with participants, participants see the impact this has on themselves and others and can learn from this observation. Participants also learn from other group members – particularly if they observe a group member grapple with an issue that is similar to an issue they are also grappling with.

There is some evidence that mindfulness teachers underestimate the influence of the group[197], likewise, therapists may underestimate the influence of imitative behaviour in group psychotherapy[198].

---

193 Yalom & Lesez, 2008
194 Segal *et al*, 2013
195 Crane *et al*, 2021
196 Yalom & Lesez, 2008
197 van Aalderen *et al*, 2012
198 Yalom & Lesez, 2008

In MBP groups, the concept of imitative behaviour has strong parallels with inside out embodying[199]. In the MBP pedagogy, there is an emphasis on training around embodying mindfulness, and it is one of six domains in the MBI:TAC upon which MBP teachers skill is assessed (Crane *et al*, 2021). The embodying of mindfulness and other core qualities and insights not only helps the teacher when teaching, but also communicates this embodying – the practice of being in touch with one's own experience moment by moment – to the group through their very being and behaviour. Looking at others and seeing what mindfulness practice can facilitate can be a powerful motivator for also 'trying on' mindfulness. This does not mean that we have everything going smoothly in a class, indeed the opposite can sometimes be true.

At the start of lockdown in March 2020, we had to switch our entire mindfulness master's course at Bangor University to online delivery with only two days' notice. I (GG) and some colleagues ran our first session online and were beset by several technical hitches which I found rather stressful. However, we managed it as best we could, and we got back on track. At the end of the session, a participant told us that, for the first time, they had understood what embodiment actually means. They elaborated that this insight happened while they witnessed our teamwork as we managed the challenges of the technical hitches in a non-reactive and collaborative way. The lesson here is, by being mindfulness practitioners ourselves we were able to hold the session and the group with a degree of patience and calm whilst things were not going smoothly, and although this was not an intended part of the teaching, really helped a participant understand what embodying mindfulness means. This example shows the importance of imitative behaviour, or how walking the walk and embodying our practice as teachers can have a powerful influence on participants.

Therapeutic factors: group cohesiveness

Group cohesiveness is difficult to define, but most of us have experienced how being a member of a discordant or disinterested group feels very different from a harmonious, engaged one. The psychotherapeutic literature defines group cohesiveness as covering all relationships in the group: teacher to participants, participants to each other, and to the group as a whole. Yalom and Lesez[200] defined it as:

> "*the result of all the forces acting on all the members such that they remain in the group, or, more simply, the attractiveness of the group for its members. Members of a cohesive group feel warmth and comfort in the group and a sense of belongingness; they value the group and feel in turn that they are valued, accepted, and supported by other members.*" (p55)

199 Griffith *et al*, 2019
200 Yalom & Lesez, 2008

High group cohesiveness and an attendant sense of safety[201] and belonging allows people to take risks – so it is an underpinning factor which allows other positive factors to emerge. It is not helpful to see this as a fixed state, as group cohesion can fluctuate during the life of the group. In psychotherapy groups, it is consistently reported across the literature that there is a significant correlation between participant reported cohesion and psychotherapeutic outcomes[202].

For MBP groups, there is very little research on group cohesiveness[203]. We found just two studies that looked at this. Bisseling *et al*, 2019, reported that felt group cohesion within an MBCT course for cancer patients did not affect participant outcomes (i.e., a reduction in psychological distress). On a 12-week mindfulness and acceptance-based course for participants with social anxiety disorder, group cohesion was not found to differ between the MBP and a comparative 12-week CBT course[204].

We want to emphasise, however, that the lack of evidence about the influence of group cohesion in MBPs does not mean that this fundamental factor is not relevant. Indeed, the pedagogical literature implies that the relationality of the MBP group is important to the process of teaching MBPs – and to the participants themselves[205]. We have very little research which attempts to measure group cohesiveness within MBPs from which to draw.

Another factor in the mix is the therapeutic alliance or therapeutic relationship – which describes the way that individual participants relate to and engage with the healthcare professional – or in the context of MBPs, to the MBP teacher. As research is still emergent, and since MBP groups vary widely, we do not know to what extent the therapeutic alliance may impact on group process or on participant outcomes in MBPs. In the MBP pedagogical literature, the relationality of the teacher and the stewardship of the group is deemed as important[206]. Yalom & Lesez[207] suggested that group cohesiveness may depend more on the individual relationship with the teacher in structured groups (which MBPs would be – since they are time-limited, structured groups where the teacher generally follows a programme curriculum). They wrote: "For some clients and some groups (especially highly structured groups) the relationship with the leader may be the essential factor"[208].

---

201 See chapter 6 for an exploration of launching the group to establish safety and inclusivity
202 Burlingame *et al*, 2016
203 Hutchinson *et al*, 2021
204 Kocovski *et al*, 2013
205 Crane *et al*, 2021
206 Crane *et al*, 2021; McCown *et al*, 2016
207 Yalom & Lesez, 2008
208 Ibid.

Participant factors

The patterns that people bring with them into the group

Having looked at some of Yalom's therapeutic factors, we now consider the impact the individual participant has on the group process, in terms of what they bring with them into the group. We all have particular patterns, often drawn from early experiences, that influence how we relate to peers and to teachers. These can affect whether we speak often or hardly at all in group settings, and how we might be drawn to or repelled from other participants etc. These deep patterns can sometimes be brought to the surface with participants on an MBP, either unconsciously (how they naturally relate to the teacher), or consciously (realising and working with some deeply held patterns that surface during the MBP).

If we turn again to more established psychotherapeutic literature when thinking about participant factors in MBPs, we find that most research has focused on participant demographic variables, attachment style, readiness to change, and expectancy[209]. In this section, we will highlight some key theoretical concepts that may be useful when thinking about how to work with personal patterns that may manifest within the group (including our own as teachers). We will explore two ways of thinking about participant factors – the Group Imago theory and attachment theory. Note that these theories do not explicitly bring in systemic social factors as being influential, but there is an increased awareness of the importance of these[210]. The theories presented here can reassure us that groups are highly complex, and that as MBP teachers we are not in control of what people bring into the room. We can only work with people as sensitively and wisely as possible. This can offer us some relief! We are not and cannot be responsible for individual patterning that often comes from influences in childhood. All we can do is be aware of this and respond as wisely as we can as we teach.

The group imago

The group imago[211] refers to how an individual views the group in their own idiosyncratic way. This differs between people – the relationship with the teacher, participants' relationships with each other and how they envision the relationships between other people in the group. This personal group imago may not be held in conscious awareness but can powerfully influence our actions. In a group of 12 MBP participants and

---

209 Hutchinson *et al*, 2021

210 Crane *et al*, 2021

211 Berne, 1963

one teacher, there are 13 group imagos – i.e., 13 different perspectives of the group – all happening simultaneously and all changing as the group changes. The group imago is therefore subjective and has five stages (the last one was added later in 2015 by Hay) – provisional, adapted, operative, attached, and absent.

The provisional group imago:

This is the vision of the group that an individual holds before the group has even met. They may have a sense of the MBP teacher (depending on the orientation process) but are unlikely to have much sense of any other group members – who at this stage will be an undifferentiated 'other' in the mind. This is a useful concept for MBP teachers as we can then appreciate the differing expectations of group members and their own place within it. Some may enter the MBP group feeling that everyone else knows more than they do. Some may enter feeling they know it all already. One of the teacher's tasks in the first few sessions is to help to break down the undifferentiated other imago to help form connections between individuals in the group. This can be facilitated using frequent pair and small group work.

The adapted group imago:

After the group has met for the first time, the participants' group imago adapts to the reality of having met certain members of the group, but there may still be some who the participant does not have a clear sense of. They may begin to know a few others in the group by name and superficial details – and the rest of the group may remain as an undifferentiated group, for example, 'those that sat on the other side of the room and I didn't get to speak to'. This process will be happening in the first week of the MBP when perhaps expectations are confirmed or confronted. An awareness of this process that is teaming underneath week one can help the MBP teacher to skilfully navigate this sensitive time. They may be aware of some aspects of the group (such as the pairs introduction process) coming together nicely and at other times the process in the room feeling quite sticky and awkward.

The operative group imago:

This moves us on to when participants are able to see how they and how others fit with their sense of the *teacher's* group imago. According to this theory, this is a key process by which participants decide how to behave towards other members of the group and the teacher. Do we adapt to the leader and other members of the group or not? The teacher is looked to as a guide for how to work with fellow group members. How we as MBP teachers respond to each group member is consciously or unconsciously noted by the participants and helps create the ethos of the group. This links to one of the factors by Yalom and Lesez[212], that of 'imitative behaviour'. Inside out embodying is also key to this, which allows MBP participants to experience directly how mindfulness practice manifests in the teacher. Teachers adhering to the group rules created in the first session, such as respect, listening, confidentiality etc. is also part of creating and maintaining this ethos.

Attached group imago:

At this stage, participants have developed a clear sense of all individual members of the group, including those they feel drawn to and want to work with, and those that they may want to avoid or minimise contact with. The way they relate to the leader has also settled. In an MBP class, it is helpful to continue to foster relationships between participants by giving time for pair or small group work.

Absent group imago:

This stage was added later by Hay[213]. This group imago forms after the group has ended. The theory suggests that it is possible to hold onto a sense of a group even after it was left long ago. If the participant felt supported within the group, and gained a sense of belonging, the memory of that group can remain as a helpful resource. In MBPs, participants often report that their continued mindfulness practice is greatly supported by bringing the group to mind and practicing as if they are still sitting within the group.

You may notice that some aspects of these theories overlap and intertwine. For example, it can be useful to think of the group imago in relation to Tuckman's group process theory[214]. They complement each other and address both issues of group development[215] and a sense of the individual's development through the group[216]. The group imago is grounded in psychotherapy, but there are useful extractions for MBP teachers. In the context of MBPs, the group imago model speaks volumes about the need to orientate, assess and prepare participants for how it might be to be a member of a group. The model also is an encouragement to MBP teachers to cultivate awareness and compassion for group behaviours that arise. Berne's group imago[217] is a way of acknowledging and concretising this. It suggests ways in which the group leader can support and make sense of the development of the group, without needing to know the detail of the group members' backgrounds.

---

212 Yalom & Lesez, 2008
213 Hay, 2015
214 Tuckman, 1965
215 Ibid.
216 Berne, 1963
217 Ibid.

Attachment Theory

It might also be fruitful for us to bring attachment theories to mind when looking at the factors that influence what participants bring with them into MBP groups. Broadly speaking, these are childhood experiences of attachment that can be drivers for social and personality development theory, which was developed by Bowlby and Ainsworth in the 1950s and 60s[218]. According to the theory, our attachment styles as adults are usually based upon the attachment relationship with a parental figure during childhood, and are broadly split into four categories (Secure, dismissive-avoidant, anxious-preoccupied, and fearful avoidant). Recent research which followed children into adulthood found that child security or insecurity (as measured by the Strange Situation test), predicts the degree of 'stability' in adulthood at age 32[219].

This is a complex subject area. However, in relation to teaching MBPs, we know that participants may have various attachment styles which may (or may not) become apparent and serve them well or be something of an obstacle in terms of how they relate within the MBP group. The centrality of 'holding' – a Winnicottian term – is emphasised by some MBP practitioners[220] and echoes the concept of attachment with the group and the teacher in particular, as the secure base that is needed from which to explore. If the base is insecure, then exploration and learning may be more difficult. Insecurity may be fuelled by the participant, the group, the teacher, the curriculum, or an interaction between them. Enabling a secure base (that includes establishing group ground rules, a culture of grounded-ness and a warm welcoming environment) allows the participant to explore their experience of mindfulness. This may prove to be a key resource, whatever they bring with them into the group.

Summary

In this chapter, key theories that can enable the MBP teacher to read and understand group processes were outlined along with their relevance to MBPs and the IOG model (Griffith *et al*, 2019). Understanding the processes that happen beneath the surface of the group and the knowledge to perhaps label what is happening (particularly with inter or intrapersonal storming) can support MBP teaching.

---

218 Bretherton, 1992; Cassidy & Shaver, 2002
219 Young *et al*, 2019
220 Bartley, 2012; Santorelli, 2010

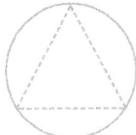

8. Reading: the impact of personal histories and social constructs

What do group members bring with them into the mindfulness-based group?

Trish Bartley

> *"Make space for the deeply personal. We can nurture our need for connection and relationship by creating an empathetic bond with future generations across the timescape… (by) seeing ourselves as part of the bigger picture."*

Roman Krznaric[221]

In this chapter, we explore the various influences that participants may bring with them into the mindfulness-based programme (MBP) group, from early personal histories, social and cultural constructs, and the impact of traumatic experiences. We look at the implications of this in relation to reading the group and what MBP teachers can do to support group members to grow together as a practice community. This material builds from the theory around groups that was shared in the previous chapter, Reading the Group

As we are discovering, groups are complex and can be a bit of a mystery. MBP teachers are responsible for many aspects of the development and containment of the group, but it might be a mistake for us to see ourselves as wholly instrumental to their success or failure. We can certainly contribute a lot, but the key ingredient, after the programme itself, are the group members, our participants.

---

221 Krznaric, R. (2020)

Why is one group so different from the next?

As we described earlier, we may find ourselves teaching two different groups, the same MBP, in the same venue, in the same week, and yet the feeling of being with one group, and the discussions, progress, and experience that arise, are quite distinct from each other. There are many factors to the different conditions that make up each group. However, the connections between participants with their different histories, identities, patterns, personalities, and intentions contribute a lot to the launching, connecting, and ways the group learns together.

Personal histories

We suggest that we might usefully explore the influence of personal history on group membership through our own personal experience, by looking at the early influences that have shaped our own patterns around how we are as members of groups. This is not an exercise that we would facilitate with our MBP participants, but it is helpful to us, as MBP teachers, in offering insights into group membership patterns and how this may play out in the MBP group. These influences come from our first families, early school groups, neighbourhoods, and workplace teams, indeed, any past experience in groups that may have some bearing on how we relate to being a member of a group now.

Family Atom Exercise

The Family Atom Exercise[222] helps us explore these early influences. We have often offered this during mindfulness-based teacher trainings and our trainees find it significant and insightful, both personally for themselves, and also in relation to understanding their MBP group members' behaviour within the group and towards them, as their teachers.

If, as you read the description of the process, you have an immediate reaction that this is not something you want to do, there is no need for you to engage with it. Sometimes, even contemplating this sort of exercise may stir up some unwelcome reactions and memories. The exercise in itself is quite safe, but it is important to respect your immediate response and perhaps do a grounding anchoring practice or engage in something quite different until or if you feel you want to engage with it.

---

222 In some contexts, this may be referred to as family constellation work, although the way we explore this here is with the use of a very light touch.

Preparation

We suggest that you find a colleague or friend to do this with, either online or in person. It is also possible to do it on your own, but the process works better when it is held as a reflective dialogue with someone else. There is no need to go into things in great depth. Ten minutes each is probably plenty of time.

Materials

If you are doing this in person, you will need a few dried beans or buttons, or some small objects, such as little stones or pebbles. You also need a sheet of plain paper or a napkin to place your objects on. If you are connecting with someone online, it probably works best to draw your 'family atom' using a thick flipchart pen and a piece of plain paper. You can hold your drawing up to the camera to show your partner and then discuss things together.

Method

Thinking of you when you were around three or four years of age, how many small objects do you need to represent your family 'atom' at that time? (parents, step-parents, caregivers, grandparents, siblings, and anyone else living with you). Remember to include yourself!

I shall demonstrate this by using my own family as an example. I need six little objects since there was me, two parents and three siblings. So here is a picture of them:

The family atom

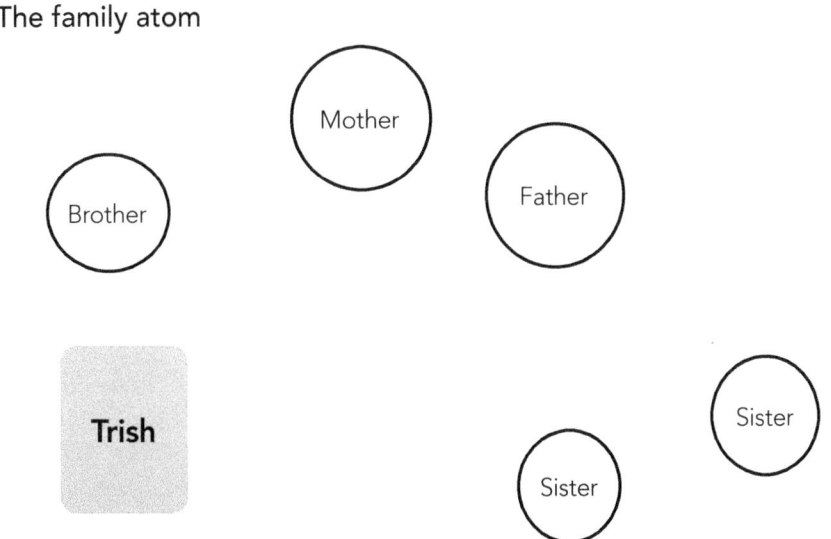

I have arranged my 'buttons' in relation to how I see the connections in my family when I was very young. I place my brother close to my mother and myself close to him. My sisters are slightly to one side because they were a fair bit older.

If I was doing this with a partner, we might first agree how long we might spend on this, and then ensure we share the time equally. We would then take turns to ask each other some questions to draw out a little more detail. It is tempting to turn this into a personal biography session, which may divert us from the purpose of the exercise, so staying with patterns that are represented by the objects is probably most helpful. At some point, when you have both done enough, you can reflect on the following question: *How do these family patterns influence how you are in groups, if at all?*

You are now ready to reflect on this question with your partner, or on your own, from the perspective of being a group member, not as an MBP teacher or group leader. If you are doing this on your own, you may choose to use a journal to capture some of your ideas. This has the effect of facilitating a bit more reflection (almost as if you are bringing another person, the journal, into the process).

Here are some further questions to help you draw out your ideas:

■ How do early relationships with your siblings influence, or even replicate, what happens for you in groups? Do you become competitive / feel superior to / feel inferior to / feel protective of other group members / feel included / feel excluded?

■ Are there any roles that you play in groups that are similar to how you were in your first family? Rebellious / adaptive / eager to please / withdrawn / caregiving / rescuing / critical / etc.

■ How does your relationship with your mother / father / parental figure when you were young play out in groups, in relation to you and the male / female group leader/s? Trusting / lacking trust / confident / admiring / critical / fearful / doubting / putting on a pedestal etc.

If at any point, you notice any strong emotion rising, come to a brief practice such as Feet on the Floor or a brief breath practice. This will help you to hold whatever is there. Standing up may also be helpful, perhaps moving away from the images and stories for a moment or two, and moving into the body to offer a bit more grounding and anchoring. We can find that reflective processes involving our first family feel tender. This is a reason for doing this exercise with someone else, as it offers support and can be more fruitful, learning wise.

Once you've explored things enough, coming to a wider question that moves us from the personal to a more general understanding of people in groups. We now apply our personal learning to what may play out in our participants.

What does this exercise offer our understanding of what our participants bring with them into groups? Let us draw out some of the possible influences:

We may discover that early sibling relationships influence the ways that participants connect with other group members. Those with generally happy family backgrounds, with siblings they felt close to, may find it fairly easy to make connections in groups. On the other hand, those who have grown up in more isolated or fractured family contexts may find it more challenging. These two examples are clearly very over-general. Few families are consistently one or the other, but they illustrate the spectrum of different and usually quite complex sets of conditions that influence how we manage various social contexts, including groups.

We may also find parallels from the patterns of relationships that were made with parents or parental figures. These may resonate with how participants connect with teachers and group leaders. Those who come from older families or from cultures where parenting patterns were more traditional, may feel more comfortable with structured programmes and more directive styles of leadership. They may like to look up to their teachers as experts. Most participants feel safer initially if they have a sense that the teacher approves of them. This often plays out in the early days of a group when group members want to get things right. It helps them feel more secure. At the other extreme, there are group members who tend to move into the role of challenger, doubter, or of withdrawing. Others might automatically take a position of assuming that the group leader will not be much good[223]. A lot rests on the personal attachment patterns that were formed in early life, unless personal inner work has taken place later that contributes to repairing these inner patterns. Again, these examples are very overgeneralised, but we hope they are of some use in sowing seeds that cultivate further reflection.

As MBP teachers, it is helpful for us to be aware of the wide range of factors that may go back to early childhood which have a bearing on how people connect in groups. We might remind ourselves of this, especially when we have a participant who has difficulty in connecting with others in the group. It is easy to assume that this is a personal judgement on us, as their MBP teachers, and our skill in teaching. This is not usually the case, and it can be very helpful not to take things personally when a participant reacts in a way that we may find challenging. Our practice, as MBP teachers, is to hold true to what is required of us in offering the MBP, staying grounded, embodying mindfulness, and cultivating empathy and compassion for all our group members, especially those we struggle to find connection with. The participant may adjust and settle in time, with mindfulness practice and skilful holding, and a chance to connect with fellow group members. We rarely know what lies behind the reactions of a group member, but it is still

---

223 See Imago Group Model in Reading theory section chapter 7 and also Paula Sonrisa Sturmer's interview on page 149

possible as MBP teachers to practice grounded-ness, friendly openness and patience that is authentic and genuine. This may help the participant more than we can imagine, and might be a new experience to how people usually relate to them.

It can be especially helpful to remember that participants may bring many different personal, historical and social influences with them into the group when we encounter an example of 'storming'[224] during an MBP. Storming (as described in Chapter 7) is often a necessary function in the development of the MBP group. It serves to test out the boundaries and establish whether the group is a safe space to belong to. This tends to be acted out at an unconscious level, either internally or overtly externally, especially by those who have not experienced much safe holding in the groups they have been in before. Until the capacity of the MBP teacher and group leader is tested and found to be adequate in maintaining a safe reliable space, it may not be possible for some participants to fully engage in the MBP group process, and this will inevitably impact on their experience of learning mindfulness.

The influence of school groups and the experience of early work-based teams may also have a bearing on the way some group members relate to authority (and the MBP teacher). The examples that we have drawn out, and the influences that we have explored, are fairly unsubtle ones and relate to the impact of personal histories. You may well want to go into this a bit more deeply, perhaps in your own experience, and by reflecting on the participants you have taught in your own MBP groups. Remembering that not taking things personally as an MBP teacher is a helpful response, whilst embodying compassion and a grounded mindful presence.

The impact of social constructs

In exploring what participants bring with them into groups, another important area of influence is the systemic social constructs that society imposes on individuals and their personal identities. We would need to make a long list (in no particular order) that includes race, gender identity, cultural heritage/s, class and socioeconomic background, sexuality, mobility, age, religion, and body image. These and more affect the ways that power, influence and a sense of inclusion (or the opposite) can play out in groups. Some forms of diversity are overtly visible and evident; some much less so. All impact in different ways, some powerfully and systemically affect the places and opportunities open to different individuals, and the way the world presents itself through automatic and often implicit assumptions of power, status, and privilege.

It is vital for us, as MBP teachers, to become more aware of the ways that these systems play out in our groups (and wider in the world). Where is the

---

224 Tuckman, 1965

power amongst the group members? What assumptions are being made? Who speaks first in discussions? Are there occasions when some group members talk over others? This is not about judging or condemning, but it is about being aware of the implicit bias that often exists unconsciously, that leave some people feeling less welcome or included than others. Our work as MBP teachers needs us to find ways of working to support our groups to be inclusive safe spaces. This requires us to become aware of all the ways that result in some group members not feeling fully included and how, as teachers, we might be contributing to that. The spaces we create in our groups are not neutral or free of bias[225]. They reflect the system and culture that we teach in and come from.

This was brought home to me strongly some years ago, when I was living and working in South Africa, in a rural area impoverished and historically excluded by Apartheid. I was there for an extended period, engaged in participatory development/action research with local people, exploring ways to enabling them to develop their villages (such as access to clean water, women's leadership and pre-school resources)[226]. Some months into the project, I remember my discomfort when a group of white, male European donors came to the village with a view to considering granting some much needed development funding. The European men behaved in a way that I can only describe as 'colonialist'. They spoke and acted with apparent assurance of power, authority and superiority. They seemed to be unaware of the impact of their presence on local people and what had been involved in terms of the time, cost, and effort that the villagers had put into making them welcome and giving them refreshment. I felt deeply ashamed and embarrassed of being white like them. It left me reflecting painfully on whether I too made assumptions and behaved in ways that disempowered the people I was working with.

I felt that we shared a sense of connection and I cared about their lives, and was thoughtful about the work we did together, and the processes we had developed as Afrocentric rather than Eurocentric, and especially ensuring there was space given to the women's voices. Yet now, looking back, I realise that however well-meaning, my attempts to facilitate ways of working that were empowering to the villagers were inevitably underlined by my white privilege. How could it not be otherwise?

I offer this reflection in order to highlight the way that culture is reinforced through the unwritten norms and systems framed by the mainstream (in the example above by the group of European funders and by me as their development worker) that are 'unconscious' until challenged or brought into awareness. Societies in the West are deeply rooted in racist and colonial history, which plays out in countless ways systemically.

It is a huge task to challenge inequality, yet every one of us, as MBP teachers, can uncover our own personal examples of the implicit bias that

---

225 See Chapter 6: Launching the group
226 Bartley, 2003

inevitably lurks under the covers of awareness. When asked about next steps, a black colleague encourages us, as MBP teachers, to keep opening up conversations about social inequalities so we can educate ourselves and uncover the unconscious attitudes and mainstream influences we may be perpetuating. One of our key tasks as MBP teachers and group leaders is to raise awareness and find opportunities to include the voices of those groups and populations not yet seen or heard much in mindfulness circles. The MBP group is a place where we can hone awareness of those 'on the margins', whose voices are often not heard, and where we can change the usual norms and co-create others that are more inclusive, mutual, respectful, and kind.

An exercise for MBP teachers

We have another exercise that we invite you to explore, preferably alongside a colleague, that may offer some insights into this area of inclusion and exclusion in groups. You don't need any particular materials. However, you might want to read the paragraph that follows first before you engage in the exercise. Then having read it, you can take the ideas suggested and go for a slow gentle stroll around your room, or outside, reflecting on what you remember and how it felt, and what was needed in the situation.

Method

Start by walking mindfully around the room (or it is fine to sit if you prefer), feeling your feet making contact with the floor, ground or carpet, with awareness of the colours, pictures, and objects in the room.

When you feel fairly settled and grounded:

- Bring to mind a time when you did not feel included in a group. You felt on your own and 'out of it' in some way, whilst everyone else seemed to belong.
- Can you connect with how this felt to you 'inside' the body? (And if you do not remember, become aware of how it feels now, as you bring this experience to mind.)
- Can you connect with how it affected you in the group? (How did you relate to others in the group? How did you view the group leader, if there was one, or those who had status in the group? How did this affect your involvement in what the group was doing?)
- What was happening that resulted in you being left out? Remember how you felt and what your thoughts were about this situation.

After a few minutes, let those memories fade somewhat and bring your attention back to your feet, your breath, and your mindful walking.

Reflection

It would be helpful to have a colleague to reflect on this with you, but if that is not possible, using a journal might be the next best option.

What general sense did you have during each of those question sections? You probably found that some aspects were easier to connect with than others, which is understandable.

We engage in this exercise in order to touch into a felt sense of how it might be to inhabit the margins of an MBP group. We can never fully know, of course, unless we have had this experience ourselves. However, we can intentionally cultivate awareness to understand the different ways that we in society marginalise groups and individuals, and we can stay vigilant around noticing these patterns within the groups that we work with. Our intention in writing this section is to support every MBP teacher to do what they can to enable their groups to be as inclusive as possible. In time, we see that our group spaces are never 'neutral' (in terms of socially constructed identities). As Paula Sonrisa Sturmer says in her interview, "You can see how the system plays out and … the ways in which you can actively dismantle it. But this won't happen through denial or presuming neutrality."

An MBP teacher colleague, when reflecting on her capacity to feel into the experience of her hospice patients, remarked that she could easily connect with those who came from disadvantaged backgrounds as she had experienced poverty herself when growing up. However, she said that she could not imagine how it would feel to be so compromised by brain injury that speech and movement were slowed right down. She just knew that the person concerned needed to not be rushed and to have plenty of time to communicate. She had learned how to build this into the groups that she was teaching in a way that involved the whole group in supporting the person affected to take her time.

Trauma

Our last section, looking at what group members bring with them into the MBP group, involves trauma and traumatic experiences [227]. These are events, such as abuse, violence, life threatening experiences, sudden bereavement or loss, that have strong impact on the individual participant and may well show up in how that individual connects with others in the group. Trauma can happen as a result of a one-off or a series of events, being directly harmed, seeing or being told about someone being harmed, living or working in a violent and traumatic atmosphere, and being affected by trauma in a family or in your community. Trauma can also be developmental, happening early in life, perhaps through neglect, abuse, or some deep childhood harm that continues to impact long into adulthood.

---

[227] We recommend Eluned Gold's chapter in Essential Resources book for a succinct and helpful overview of trauma in the context of MBP teaching. See Gold. E (2021)

Thankfully, as MBP teachers, due in large part to the work of David Treleaven[228] and others, we are now much more aware of the widespread prevalence of trauma and how we can be sensitive to the impact of trauma in ways that are safe and grounded, and which offer choice.

> "*Trauma refers to any threatening, overwhelming experiences that we cannot integrate... After such experiences, we are often left with a diminished sense of security with others, and in the world, and a sense of feeling unsafe inside our own skin.*"[229]

This is an area that we need to be vigilant around in orientation sessions when preparing people for an MBP. However, in view of the fact that many of us will have had a range of traumatic experiences, we need to assume that there will be participants in every MBP group that have been affected, as we, as MBP teachers, may well have been too. Realising the widespread prevalence of trauma and recognising it in the mindfulness-based group space are vital steps to responding sensitively.

Trauma can get triggered in MBPs, as they can elsewhere. The impact of trauma is expressed through the body and can be accompanied by memories and emotions that can be hard to manage and process. This impact is sometimes evident or sometimes hidden, staying internal. These can trigger one of the three reactions of flight, fight and freeze, or a sequence of them. The social context we were brought up in, and now live in, is a significant factor in our exposure to trauma. Any traumatic experience is challenging and can be personally tragic and life changing, and the areas where we live, levels of income, race and gender, and even, for instance, if we use a wheelchair, all have an impact on the ongoing risk of being exposed to trauma. Trauma is not just personal. It also has a strong social and political context. This is true in the West, and markedly so in countries and communities where there is widespread violence, war, unsafe work, and high levels of abuse. All these can result in pervasive exposure to trauma. For some, it almost becomes the water they swim in and the air they breathe.

Trauma impacts individuals and groups of individuals. When a participant who has been affected by trauma joins an MBP group, the connections they make with other group members will be impacted by their personal sense of safety in the group space; the relationship they have with their bodies; the potential for having overwhelming emotions, or experiencing a shut down and withdrawn response; or whether they may have a strong urge to leave. These will all impact on what they need within the MBP group and how easy or challenging it is to participate. However, trauma is much helped by the experience of being included in a safe practice community space.

---

228 Treleaven, 2018
229 Ogden, 2015

This is not the place to look at the detail of mindfulness in the context of trauma. However, we always seek to support the safety and inclusivity of the MBP group as far as possible, with teaching invitations that emphasise choice, kindness, and groundedness. This will be helpful to a participant who has a history of traumatic experience. We emphasise the importance of offering appropriate orientations, where trauma is included as a consideration around whether it is a good time to take an MBP, or whether other support might be better first. Embodying mindfulness is key. Plenty of brief practices woven into our sessions help us, as teachers, to stay grounded and steady, and help our participants to learn to regulate strong feelings in themselves and in the group when they arise.

> *"Given the prevalence of trauma in our societies, as MBP teachers we must also acknowledge our own trauma histories and the implicit biases that cloud or alter our perception... The ethos of MBPs begins with a sense of the innate integrity and wholeness of a human being, no matter what may be happening that seems otherwise... What might arise in an MBP teaching space is a natural longing to live from that wholeness ... the steady frame of the MBP practice, can be a primary resource for healing and growth."*[230]

Our Baggage Comes with Us

We might call them 'the fractures of childhood',
or maybe worse, much worse....

It is as if we have these trailers, heavy with life's junk
which we are forced to drag behind

Only until we join with others,
through the listening and speaking,
the heartfelt knowing and connecting,
can we stop and release some of that history,
upcycling pieces into something better,
something kinder.

Like producing an orchestra out of a slag heap
full of the world's rubbish,
thoughtlessly cast off by some.
Transformed, valued
and made quite wonderful by others.

Let us pause and see.
Let us include and hear,
lest we pass through one another like blowing snow.

---

230 Gold, 2021

Summary

There are many and varied influences that impact of what group members bring with them into the MBP, and how this affects the way they relate to other participants, the group as a whole and the MBP teacher within the group.

Some awareness of these influences may offer us, as MBP teachers, opportunities to read the mindfulness-based group and understand a bit better some of what is happening within the group.

These influences can be drawn from three key areas:

■ Early personal history. This influences patterns of sibling/peer relationships and affects the way group members may relate to the MBP teacher/parental figure.

■ Social and cultural systems. These play out through the different levels of power and status held by MBP group members, and patterns of implicit bias and discrimination that influence what is said and done (by group members and the MBP teacher). This can result in the majority (who hold privilege in society) occupying the mainstream position in the group and some in a minority left out in the margins.

■ Past traumatic experiences. These can impact on feelings of safety, and therefore affect capacities to connect in the group and engage with the learning.

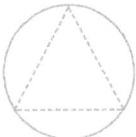

9. Reading body language

Signs and signals in the mindfulness-based group

Trish Bartley

"How frequently a touch by the shoulder, a handshake, or a look tells us more than can be expected in a long monologue. Not because our speech is not accurate enough. Just the contrary. It is precisely its accuracy and definiteness that makes speech unsuited for expressing what is too complex, changeful, and ambiguous."[231]

Group development theory and the established understandings from psychotherapeutic, adult learning and organizational contexts help us to develop ideas about how we might read the group at different points, and in different moments[232]. Integrating group theory into teaching practice enables us to do this with more skill and understanding. In the previous chapter, we learned more about the various influences that affect what group members bring with them into the group[233]. In this chapter we reflect on what we understand from the body language of group members. This helps us develop awareness of how safe group members are feeling and how they are connecting with others and with us, as their MBP teachers. Towards the end of this chapter, we introduce an exercise that we call 'The Group Animal', which brings all these different ways of reading the group into a simple reflective exercise.

Research suggests that we are constantly interpreting the non-verbal signs and signals from the body language of others[234] and this is thought to represent a very significant proportion of the feelings and attitudes that we communicate and infer from one to another. We are well aware that feelings can be conveyed in a single glance, but we grasp clues in many other ways

---

231 Rotenberg & Arhavsky
232 See chapter 7
233 See chapter 8
234 Mehrabian, 2007

as well, and these tend to be assimilated and interpreted automatically, out of conscious awareness. This is happening all the time from one person to another in the MBP group, especially across the circle[235] between group members, from the teacher to the group, and the group to the teacher. It is useful to explore the premise that whatever is expressed by group participants verbally or non-verbally is probably expressing something for the whole group. We can obviously take this too far, but as a general principle it is a reflection worth consideration, and might offer us some clues into understanding the complexity of the group a little better.

The body of the group

Body language is a type of a non-verbal communication in which physical behaviours, as opposed to words, express or convey attitudes, moods and information. This includes facial expressions, body posture, gestures, eye movement, touch, and the use of space. We are all expressing and picking things up in this way all the time, from the very moment that someone walks into a room and we greet each other. This is not about forming judgements, or suggesting it is a good or bad thing, but simply to raise awareness that we are naturally reading and unconsciously interpreting all sorts of subtle signs and movements from others all the time, as they are from us. There are a lot of complex ways in which we move our bodies as we express ourselves. We imagine that words are more important than body language but actually the two go together.

Participants are therefore giving and receiving messages and signals constantly between them within the group. Some of this is happening on a conscious level, perhaps with a welcoming smile, or on an unconscious level, perhaps when a participant crosses their legs and looks away. These conscious and unconscious behaviours are important and easy to misinterpret.

Group members are also picking up a whole range of attitudes, forms of attention, moods and emotions (and more), from us, as their MBP teachers. These inevitably 'leak' out of us. The group will be aware of who amongst them is favoured and is getting the most attention from the teacher, who is missed out and is experienced as challenging. This plays out all too obviously in the body language of the MBP teacher and needs diligent awareness if we are genuine in wanting our groups to be inclusive. This is not to suggest that we learn to mask our body language, not at all, but it is vital, as MBP teachers, that we develop learning resources that build awareness of our conditioning, implicit bias, and unconscious prejudice that will show up in the ways that we communicate non-verbally (and verbally) with others. As MBP teachers, we may discover that we

---

235 Body language is not so apparent in online MBPs as so much less of the body is in view, although facial gestures may be even more significant.

can sometimes perpetuate forms of discrimination, albeit inadvertently. In becoming more aware, we can learn to respond differently and be more mindful, sensitive, and ethical in how we work with different forms of diversity, staying true to an intention to authentically widen our circles of inclusion, understanding and respect.

The group too has a 'body' which we can get clues from. It can show itself at times in the resonance and natural 'co-creation'[236] as the group develops. As MBP teachers, we seek to keep some of our awareness 'out' in the group, so that we can read the signals. These are many and varied, and may include where people sit, how they sit, how they move, and what they do with their eyes, and the eye contact that they make. The group body language is not a simple aggregate of the participants' individual body language but comes through in some of the patterns that we can notice in different parts of the group. Perhaps there is a general sense of restlessness in the group (or parts of the group), or some disengagement during an inquiry or an exercise, or maybe some ripples of emotion that move from one group member to affect others in the group. It can be discovered, often through hunch and by trying out different hypotheses that with experience, can help us to read what is happening and what is needed from us, as their MBP teachers.

What to look for in the details of body language

We might start by looking at how close or how distant we choose to position ourselves to another, and how others position themselves in relation to us, or in relation to others. Facial expression and eye movements are important messengers of emotion. We communicate a lot through eye contact, or lack of thereof. Body movement, stillness or tightness demonstrate ranges of restlessness or steadiness, agitation or calm. We also convey moods and emotion through breathing rates, sweating, pulse rate, blood pressure, flushing, blushing, and so on. Some people are very expressive with their hands, perhaps directing them towards or away from some part of the body. These are all available for us to pick up in the inquiry process, both in relation to an individual participant but also to the group as a whole. We can get a sense of how fully the group is engaged when an inquiry is happening, and what the group seems to be experiencing, to some extent. Awareness of our own experience as MBP teachers also gives us clues into what is happening, through a parallel process with the individual participant involved and through a wider group resonance.

This transmission and interpretation can sometimes be quite different from the spoken word. Words can infer one thing, whilst at the same time

---

236 McCown *et al*, 2016

body language is suggesting something quite different. An example of a discrepancy between words and body language is one that frequently happens in the group inquiry.

> We are engaged with a participant who is describing something that holds some sensitivity. We would like to explore a little deeper but are not sure whether it would be wise. Perhaps we say to the participant, "Is it okay if I ask you some more about this?" The participant will invariably say, "Yes, it's fine", whilst looking flushed in the face, pulling back, and with their eyes widening. The body language of the participant is clearly at odds with what is being said.

However, if we are too literal with this, we may misinterpret what we think we are seeing. The clues that we are noticing need to join up and make sense in the current context. For instance, it is widely considered that crossing the arms represents defensiveness, but it may be a sign of feeling cold, or of self-soothing. We only know or can guess when we bring other factors into account as well. What is the temperature of the room? What is happening in the group? How have they responded to the course thus far? Do they often move or behave like this? And so on.

It is interesting to reflect that language alone is quite limited. This is especially true with emotion, and body sensations. We don't have a vocabulary that adequately expresses what we are feeling at any one time. It is one of the reasons that poetry can be so powerful, with its use of metaphor and imagery that move us closer to a deeper sense of personal meaning. The intonation, pitch, pace, and volume of the speaking voice is not strictly speaking considered to be part of body language (termed non-verbal communication), but nevertheless it offers significant and often unconscious signals.

> An example of this occurred when a teaching colleague was attending a class I was teaching. She was sitting in on the session to give me feedback on my teaching. It was the first class of a new course. As I opened the door to welcome in the group, I apparently spoke very fast, in quite a high tone and rather loudly. I was aware that I was feeling nervous with her there, but I had no awareness that I was speaking so loudly and differently at the time!

This example demonstrates the value of inviting a colleague into a session, to give us feedback on our teaching. Video recording an MBP session is another option to help reflect on our own body language that we may not be aware of. We can also share parts of it with our supervisor for feedback.

Body language is especially important on first meeting someone. We tend to form lasting impressions in just a few moments, which are based more on what we see and feel than on what is said. This may result in a strong view about someone before they even say a word, and highlights yet again the implicit personal biases that are often unconscious and under the surface of awareness. These may relate to people who… and the words that follow the 'who' can be many and various, including style, voice, body size, race, gender, politics, background, sexuality, identity … the list is long.

In an MBP context, the impact of that first meeting holds true as much from the participants towards the teacher, as it does from the teacher towards the participants. This two-way effect continues throughout the life of the group, although as mindfulness practice is cultivated and embedded, and group members and teachers get to know each other better, there is growing awareness of thoughts and reactions, and it becomes more possible to relate with immediacy and openness rather than moving into more reactive and habitual ways of interacting.

When someone is speaking, they will invariably gesture with their hands and have a variety of facial expressions as they describe their experience. Our task as teachers is to be aware of this as we listen and connect. Sometimes, it is almost as if the experience is being acted out through the movements of the body and the expressions on the face, and this will often ripple into the group.

I had an example of this recently when a member of the group was engaged in an inquiry. They spoke of heaviness in their chest, and as they mentioned this, they moved their hands away from their body, from the chest with palms out, saying, "I'm not having that. I don't want it." It was clear from their body language and the tone of their voice that they felt strongly. Their reaction was active, and they vigorously 'pushed' the heaviness away. Following this, a number of other members of the group later described various forms of resistance and experiences that they did not want. This pattern was not immediately obvious. It did not shout, 'This group is embodying resistance'. However, reflecting afterwards, it was clear that the first participant's resistance had opened the door for others to share something similar. Eventually, in the event, this proved to be a growing edge for the development of the group that enabled them to be more open, authentic and honest.

As new MBP teachers, we might assume that the verbal language we use is more significant than the body, in guiding practices, leading inquiries and in the way we communicate in general. Yet as the quote at the beginning of this section suggests, words can be quite limited. When we communicate, we bring together what is being said with a whole multitude of different signs and signals that we absorb in subtle and complex ways.

As MBP teachers, in the group context, we deliberately cultivate awareness of each participant and the group as a whole, through observing and interpreting all the layers of verbal and non-verbal communication that take place throughout the session. It might be especially important to bring awareness to particular group members who seem tentative, monopolising, on their own (only man, only person of colour, only older/younger person etc.) or a group member who is communicating something that is a bit out of step to the rest of the group.

Reflective questions might help to tease this out:

- How is Wesley doing in this third session?
- Are there any signs that they are beginning to get a little bit more comfortable?
- How are they in the small groups?
- How are others with them?

We take care of individuals with the intention of seeing what they need, so that they can get as much as possible from the course. We also look at 'Wesley' in the context of the whole group, and the whole group in the context of 'Wesley'. We seek to read the behavioural clues from individual participants, between participants, with the group in its own right, and between us, as teacher, the group, and individual participants. There is a lot to reflect on! However, it is important that we hold this in the service of increasing awareness of how we support the safety, inclusivity, and interrelatedness of the MBP group.

The Group Animal

We now share the 'Group Animal' as a light-hearted but useful exercise to help us further in reading the group. Metaphors are widely used to help to offer fresh new ways of perceiving something. *If this was a plant or tree or animal, what would it be?* Using this tool, we now introduce an exercise that can often help to tease out the patterns of the MBP group or the developmental stage it may have reached.

Think of a MBP group that you've recently taught, or one that was especially memorable in some way.

What animal comes to mind that might represent your group?

All groups change as the MBP progresses, what animal might represent your group at the start? How big is it? How fast does it move? What is its style and character?

Some examples that I've come across as answers to these questions include:

- A flock of sparrows: 'happy and excitable, not very grounded and tending to flit from one thing to another' (an early group, maybe not yet a launched group).
- A meerkat: A small mammal that lives underground and stands up on two legs to look for danger and then disappears fast whenever anything is spotted, suggesting a group that is anxious, unsettled and in threat mode.

Later in the MBP, what animal might represent your group at, say, week 4?

The group will have hopefully launched by then, so 'the flock of sparrows' may have become a bit steadier and more grounded. Perhaps it has developed into a four-legged animal such as:

- a curious domestic cat, sometimes as if at a mousehole (were they storming a little?)
- a cow chewing the cud (perhaps not yet fully engaged, but reflective and peaceful).

By the end of the programme, and possibly much earlier at times, when the group is able to move into its optimal potential as a group, and there is coherence, connection and rich exchanges around the circle, we may find the group animal grows into animals such as:

- a lioness, keeping an eye on her cubs, able to rest, yet also respond fast when needed.
- a stag standing on the mountain in its prime, strong, dignified, present, looking out over the landscape.

This tool gives us the chance to move away from our inevitable pre-occupation with how individual participants are doing, even though they need considering, and move into more of a focus on the group as an entity in its own right, and how it is developing. We use the group animal to remind us of this, by looking to identify a single animal, usually, that might represent the group as a whole. As already mentioned, groups develop over time. So the group animal also changes from session to session (or even within a session). Our reflections relating to the group animal is not something we would share with the group itself, but it might be a valuable reflection on the way home after the session, or when reflecting on the online session soon after it has finished, or within a supervision session, especially if we have any concerns about the group.

Working with a group, there was a participant who had a strong influence but who was erratic in terms of time keeping and personal boundaries. When reflecting on this with a colleague, they asked me what the group animal might be. I replied that I thought it would be a big cat of some sort (as it was a very able and strong group) but one that had a twitchy back leg. It was if the group was being held up by this one participant. This helped me see quite clearly what was happening, both with the individual participant and in terms of the group. As the sessions continued, I asked the participant how they were getting on, and whether there was anything that they needed from me to help them get more from the programme. Soon after this they settled, and I sensed a much smoother flow of connection with them and within the group as a whole. In time, they really came into their own in the group, and as a result the group really blossomed. It was as if when the back leg 'released', the big cat could move into its full potential, and realise its power and grace.

If this sounds useful to you, you might include it as part of your post session reflection. →

If the group was an animal, what would it have been in this session?

And then reflecting:

What does the group need from me as teacher, to grow and move and eventually find its optimal potential?

Summary

We learn to read the group in and out of the sessions in a more reflective way, by bringing together awareness and understanding of all the ways that we communicate verbally through words and non-verbally through the many forms of body language. By cultivating this awareness, we are more able to interpret what is happening in the group and what the group needs to support safety and inclusivity.

We bring this awareness alongside other reading tools such as:

- group development theories
- the influences on group members through personal history, systemic social and cultural constructs, and past traumatic experiences
- the signs and symbols such as body language within the group
- metaphor, such as the group animal, to help us read the group.

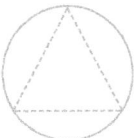

An interview with Paula Sonrisa Sturmer

Paula is the co-organiser of the Mindfulness and Social Change Network – an international collective exploring the potential and barriers for the secular mindfulness movement to contribute to more sustainable and socially just societies. Paula is also a mindfulness teacher and offers training and facilitation within social and environmental justice movements around issues of identity, power, collaboration and regenerative practices.

This interview focused on how we might acknowledge the 'inside' of embodiment in the context of what we bring into the room as teachers, including our demographic characteristics. It is important to acknowledge that this interview is grounded from the viewpoint of how those who are mostly in the mainstream of MBP teaching – meaning not necessarily the majority, but the ones that set the tone, communication-style and behavioural norms (often unconsciously) – can usefully be made much more aware of issues of inclusivity.

Paula is interested in exploring areas around the influence of power and rank (the power we have relative to one another in relationships, groups, communities and the world, which can be earned and unearned) and the importance for teachers to have at least a basic grasp of this in order to support the creation of truly inclusive spaces. This issue dovetails the social justice and social change work that Paula is deeply engaged in.

What we bring into the room with us

Paula spoke of how the first step towards greater inclusivity is the MBP teacher's inner work in understanding their social identity and how this influences how we see others, how we are seen and how we 'show up' in spaces. Paula emphasised the importance of recognising that we are not 'neutral' as teachers – all of us walk through what she called 'social smoke' from which we inhale messaging about our socially constructed identities and their relationship to others, with all the biases and prejudices that come with that. These are not always conscious but are pervasive and ever-present. Awareness of this is vital in supporting inclusivity in MBP classes.

Paula describes how important it is for her to acknowledge that her background influences how she behaves and how she is perceived when she walks into a room, and that this affects how 'safe' or vulnerable she feels and how comfortable she feels to express herself.

> "[I am] white for example … I [am a] women. I'm heterosexual… I'm middle class… these are elements of my identity, and I bring them into the space. I bring them as a group member, but I also bring them as a teacher. And everybody that comes into the room is coming with socially constructed identities and these will be having an influence on the group space."

Inner work is vital

Recognising that we are not neutral is the start of engaging with the work of inclusivity. If we want to go deeper in this work, Paula speaks of how closely examining the 'social smoke' that we move through can help us to understand how the spaces we create are likely to be exclusive to some people, unless we make express efforts to change that.

> "I've spent the last year doing work on whiteness, understanding what my white privilege looks like. And it is really, really difficult. Because you start to realize that you are part of the system of racism – you have absorbed bias and prejudice – you reinforce racism through white silence, or fragility, or tone policing and it's very uncomfortable to see it… but it's also very liberating. You can see how the system plays out and you can see the ways in which you can actively dismantle it. But this won't happen through denial or presuming 'neutrality'."

Paula has learned through her work that: "to my horror, I become silent when racism is mentioned, because I didn't know what to do. And my concern around making things worse meant that I said nothing." That silence is "just as much a part of the system of oppression as saying something outright, because the silence is basically not addressing the racism in the space." From this, it follows that an intention by individuals or organisations to become more inclusive is not enough – we have to be prepared to educate ourselves, face the difficult reality of how we are part of creating and maintaining spaces which are exclusive, and be prepared to shift power.

> "I think we need to be careful … that if we say we're going to create safe spaces for everyone, actually, that does take a certain amount of work for it to really be safe and inclusive … which I do feel that we have the responsibility to do."

Paula spoke of the need to acknowledge what we come in with as MBP teachers – our own perceptions and biases towards ourselves and to others; if we are not prepared to see this then they will unconsciously drive our behaviour in socially patterned ways, reinforcing power dynamics that prioritise the safety and comfort of some people over others.

> *"What's arising for the teacher in relation to different individuals in the group and different dynamics within the group? If we are white, how are we showing up to people in the room who are people of colour? If we are women, how are we showing up to men and vice versa? How are we showing up as a particular age to people who are older or younger and so forth, you know, really to gain a bit more understanding of whose voices are being heard and who is being silenced, which behaviours are being validated and which are marginalised, whose 'comfort' are we, as teachers, protecting and who is having to accommodate as a result."*

How exclusion can play out in the mindfulness context

Paula spoke of how those with privilege tend to not notice that they have it, particularly when power comes from having a higher 'social' rank[237] (the power that we have due to our social and cultural standing as part of a dominant group in society). This lack of awareness can prevent a group from thriving and/or fuel inner conflict or conflict in the group, as those setting norms are getting their needs met while others are not. On the other hand, we tend to notice straight away when we find ourselves to be in the margins and are much more likely to see how power dynamics are playing out in the space.

Paula's view is that all of this affects our thoughts, feeling and behaviours – and yet in mindfulness settings we don't explore how these group dynamics are affecting us and the group – even though we value our present moment experience and, in particular, alleviating suffering. Yet, it is important for us, as teachers, to be attuned to these realities and actively working with participants to bring our mindfulness practice into creating inclusive spaces so that everyone in the group – and not just some – can thrive. Key to this is our experience of connection – with our own experience, and our sense of connection (or disconnection) with others.

> *"Let's say for example, someone in the group is gay … and the teacher is heterosexual. Throughout the course, every reference to relationships that the teacher gives – verbally or in handouts – only reflects heterosexual relationships… It's likely that this is not the first*

---

237 http://rhizome.coop/wp-content/uploads/2018/10/intro-rank.pdf

time that this has happened to the participant, and it could trigger historical and current pain about how it is to live in a heteronormative culture. Even in a mindfulness space, which is where we are hoping to help relieve people's stress and improve well-being, can trigger pain and be exclusive when we are not aware of how social norms and biases influence the spaces, we, as teacher, create.

Practical changes to MBP teaching

Paula named a simple yet powerful example of how her work with inclusivity had led her to change her teaching practice:

"Nowadays when I teach at my centre in Spain, the first thing we do when we go around is we ask people to say their gender pronouns. So we say, tell us your name, where you come from, and the gender pronoun you wish to be named by. And we do that because we know that a lot of people who come on the courses that we teach do not identify in a binary gender... So right from the beginning we're recognizing that part of feeling safe in space is to have your identity acknowledged and valued and for the facilitator to help make sure that no one is misgendered."

She challenged the concern that asking about pronouns might alienate those who are unaware of the variations of gender identity and find the notion a challenging one. She challenges us to acknowledge that we can't commit to creating inclusive spaces if we are only prepared to do that as long as we don't 'upset' the mainstream. It is not true inclusion when those from marginalised identities – whether that be people of colour, people from the LGBTQI community, or those with a disability – are expected to fit in and assimilate into white, heterosexual, able-bodied spaces.

"The fear that the rest of the group might be 'put out' by having to say their gender is an example of how the mainstream maintains power in the sense that their behaviours and values around binary gender norms kind of get set as what's valued."

She suggests that there are many ways that we can consider creating equitable, diverse and inclusive spaces before courses even start. We could, on the application form, ask people to state their preferred gender pronouns for example, so that then right then from the beginning you're acknowledging that there are different genders.

Paula concluded by highlighting that all of this points towards the central reality that we are beings that exist and are shaped by our social, cultural and historical realities. Mindfulness is a powerful tool to help us to notice what impact this has on us and others, how this shapes and affects the spaces we create. It helps us to have more choice over what we perpetuate and what we choose to dismantle for the well-being of all of us. Being mindfulness teachers doesn't make us neutral or separate us from social dynamics. It can, however, help us grow in our resilience, commitment and skilfulness in creating truly liberating spaces and practices, which can only come from tending to the collective as well as the individual.

Part Three:
Holding the group

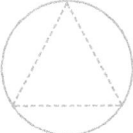

10. Holding the mindfulness-based group

Trish Bartley

"Usually, people work hard to make things happen. Yet it might be that things happen by themselves... The working of the universe goes on constantly like hands finding other hand."[238]

Holding the group is the second of our three capacities within the Inside Out Group[239] model. Holding follows on from Reading, as now that we are better able to interpret what is happening in the group we can, as MBP teachers, take care of the safety and learning of the MBP group. We learn to interpret what is needed to enable group members to explore their experiences, both pleasant and unpleasant, in the context of a safe, well-held and inclusive mindfulness-based group.

In this chapter, we start by looking at the different components involved in the MBP teacher's inside out holding practice, including the holding needs of the individual participant, the MBP teacher, and the group as a whole. We include some reflective exercises that help us explore these different components and underline the importance of intention in how we hold the MBP group. We then tease out a framework for understanding the development of the holding process. Finally, we link this to leadership styles as they relate to holding the mindfulness-based group.

Holding can be considered as providing a container for the group. Whilst 'containing' sounds more restrictive and 'holding' suggests more of a sense of care and responsiveness, both terms have their uses and are theoretically similar, relating back to early mother/child development theory[240]. Containing focuses more on the nature of individual

---

238 Tarrant, 2008

239 Griffith *et al*, 2019: https://link.springer.com/article/10.1007/s12671-019-1093-6

240 Winnicott, 1971

relationships in the group 'making (the)... experience 'containable'[241]. We choose to use the term 'holding' for this context, since arguably it gives the group as a whole a stronger focus.

The different components of inside out holding

The holding of a group involves the MBP teacher retaining awareness of several different elements happening at the same time, namely:

- the individual participants
- our own process as MBP teachers
- the MBP group 'circle'.

This takes intentional practice until eventually it becomes more intuitive, honed over time.

Holding individual participants

Some participants come to the MBP with specific goals, perhaps to recover from a life event or soothe a period of heightened anxiety. Something will have prompted their decision to take a mindfulness-based course, and it is likely to involve some levels of physical or emotional pain and suffering in some form. As MBP teachers, we may be aware of some of our participants' stories, but we are unlikely to know much detail, nor do we need to, beyond ensuring that it is a good time for them to attend the course.

However we manage the process of orientation, crucial to supporting the launching of the group[242] is our responsibility to enable each participant to learn to bring mindfulness into their life. As MBP teachers, we seek to stay in touch with a sense of how each participant is doing as the course progresses, perhaps finding time to briefly reflect on each one individually after each session. This helps us to identify who needs more attention and how we might best do that.

By including the group in awareness, we still remain aware of the needs of the individual. The two are not incompatible. Often, individual participants need some specific holding at certain points during the course. As MBP teachers, we are frequently scanning around the group during sessions, to remain in contact with everyone in the circle or on the screen. As we do this, we are bound to pick up different levels of engagement. There may be some participants who we have concerns about. We might discuss these in a supervision session. We may bring one of our participants 'onto the cushion'

---

241 Bion, 1967
242 See Chapter 6: Launching the group

by including them at the beginning or end of a personal sitting practice. Or perhaps we choose to make contact with the participant outside the group (if this has been agreed before the start of the MBP) to find out how things are going. One or all these approaches will help us to gain new perspectives, cultivate more compassion, and explore our own reactivity.

There is no conflict between holding the individual and holding the MBP group. Both are needed, and if all is going well the group itself contributes a great deal to holding its members.

Holding our own process as an MBP teacher

Inevitably, there will be times when we react to events as they unfold in the room, or on the screen. We might well wish this was not the case, but authentic MBP teachers are human! We are committed to continuing to learn and practice throughout the full span of our MBP teaching, however there may well be times when we say things that we wish we had expressed differently. We may forget something or someone, have a moment of irritation, or even internal panic, and then try to cover up the moment.

> In training MBP teachers over a number of years, some of the richest learning came for trainees when at some point I needed to stop the training process, rewind what had just happened, and investigate my own reactivity in discussion with the trainee group. This always proved empowering to the trainees, some of whom would comment at the end of the year that those moments had been the most helpful of all. Slowing down and being transparent about moments of automatic reactivity can be hard to do, and extremely uncomfortable at times, but they are needed to make real what it is to be fully human.

MBP teaching is not about being perfect. It is about being generous, genuine, authentic, and present with things as they happen, which may need a moment of acknowledging, "I'm not sure where I was going with that" or "Let us come back and take a pause here". Then, choosing to invite everyone to take a pause and come back to present moment awareness. These impromptu moments of pausing are so valuable in holding us personally in our teaching role, and in holding the group, when we lose our way, or if something tricky has happened. As teachers, we wisely stay in touch with the body and mind to inform our own personal experience on the inside, and a sense of the group in the room on the outside. We cultivate an intention to remember to hold it all, by coming back to a grounded embodied presence as best we can, using the contact of feet on the floor, body on the seat, the breath or some other anchor to steady us many, many times in a teaching session.

The MBP teacher is a bit like the conductor of an orchestra (the MBP group), listening carefully to the solo tunes, whilst keeping an eye and an ear on the harmonic balance of the whole, and what the composer originally intended. Really skilful conductors facilitate the joining of one instrument to another, inviting a listening here, a gentle quietening there, and with a sense of who needs to speak and be heard, and who has a quieter, more subtle, supportive voice that needs to come through. The music score created by the composer (the MBP) sets the shape, tempo and content for the orchestra to interpret. The conductor is not in charge as such, but is facilitating the orchestra to connect and listen and make the music. There are then some rare moments when musicians go beyond collaboration and technical brilliance, to share with us a vision of true community, present in the world.

Holding the group circle

After the individual participants and the MBP teacher, the group is the other entity in the room, mysteriously developing and changing over the weeks, rarely predictable, often surprising, and sometimes deeply connecting. There are occasionally some precious times when the group comes into an alignment that holds its members, and others when there is confusion and uncertainty over what on earth is happening in the depths of the group. Our task, as MBP teachers, is to use our understanding of group theory and our mindfulness practice of embodied intention to help us hold the group process as best we can, trusting that a well held group process will serve its members, and remembering that groups are generally much healthier than we may realize. Once the group launches and things begin to settle, individual boundaries can seem to soften, so that there is a joining up of felt experience around the circle (or on the screen). This is not about losing a sense of self (although some people fear that when they join a group), but about a coming and going of individual and group boundaries.

If the MBP is happening 'in person', we sit together in a circle with everyone visible to each other. There is a certain power and agency in this, that some may find intimidating if it is new for them. However, the circle offers a natural equality, with everyone equidistant from the centre. Nature is full of curves. It has few straight lines. The circle in MBPs facilitates the 'secret life of the group' enabling participants to exchange glances and communicate subtly without words, often away from the awareness of the MBP teacher. This can add a natural richness and helps to dilute some of the power and influence of the teacher. Circles are often used in traditional forms of community gathering, sitting around an open fire, with each person accessing the warmth and light equally, where all are included.

As MBP teachers, where we choose to sit in the room has much to do with personal preference and the layout of the teaching space. One guiding principle is to avoid sitting in front of a window, especially one that has lots of light coming though. It will be very difficult for group members, and your co-teacher if you have one, to see your eyes and therefore connect with you.

Most rooms have a focal point. We find that if the teacher sits there (you might call this the top of the room), it can be helpful in supporting a strong holding role when the group is new, or when there is a need to bring a more directive leadership style, and more structured holding into the space. However, when the MBP process is well underway, as teachers we might choose to sit at the diagonals of the circle, rather than 'in charge' at the top. It may be worth experimenting to see how different positions feel, and what they offer at different points in the MBP.

> On a training retreat many years ago, one of the trainees seemed to be struggling. Concern was heightened when the trainee failed to show at one of the practice sessions and some of their belongings were found on the grass near the lake. The teacher, sitting at the top of the room, shared news of this situation with us and suggested that we sit together in a fairly close circle to meditate for the safety of the trainee. I chose to sit opposite the teacher. This was not a considered move on my part, but an almost intuitive one, feeling the need to help to hold what felt like a very troubling moment. (It was later discovered that the trainee was safe and had gone home without telling anyone.)

If we are teaching online, there is much less visibility and no circle, just a screen that only shows the head and (sometimes shoulders) of the person. However, the screen group can still form, and be held as a group, often quite richly but in different ways to in person groups[243]. Online groups are strongly influenced by the connections that happen in the breakout rooms (small group processes). These take place away from the eyes of the teacher, and arguably may mean that online groups are more independent.

With sufficient experience, we can come to trust the group to take up the roles that are needed or may be missing for some reason. This may prove to be part of the way the group is held.

> I was snowed in for one of the teaching weekends for mindfulness masters' students. Some students had managed to fly in from Europe, but living on a mountain, only 30 miles away, I had no way of getting in. This was long before we were familiar with online teaching, and there was no access to larger screens, I 'taught' the 18 strong members of the group using Skype via a small 13" laptop on a chair within the circle. This was the third of five teaching weekends and up to that point, slightly surprisingly, the student group had not quite found itself. The teaching day changed all that, for the group came together powerfully, sharing leadership roles, collaborating creatively, and with everyone (including me) learning a huge amount. What appeared to be a significant problem proved to be a real turning point for the group. They went on to have some of the highest marks of that module for some years and produce a tranche of very fine teachers.

---

243 see Chapter 13: Online considerations

As this example shows, it is easy for us to assume that things fall part if it were not for us, the MBP teachers. We might be wise to question this, and notice all the ways that the group shares in the holding of its members, especially during the later stages of the MBP, when the group is sufficiently mature to work more independently. It is evident that when fellow group members say something kind or helpful to another group member, it comes over loudly almost as if via a loudspeaker. Any of us who have experienced this will recollect how much more powerful the learning and connection is when it comes from within the circle.

> Some years ago, I attended an experiential workshop with seven others, all unknown to me. It was facilitated by someone who was clearly skilled and experienced. As the workshop got going, everyone's comments were acknowledged, added to the flipchart, or verbally noted in some way, except mine. At first, I wondered if I was imagining things. Was he really ignoring me? But as it became more and more obvious, one or more of the group would smile across at me whenever this happened. This helped me to carry on contributing, as there was a tangible and really enjoyable sense of connection in the group, albeit in the context of a decidedly odd process. Surprisingly, I learnt a lot on this workshop (and even remember some of the material to this day, decades later). Afterwards I reflected on whether he was aware of what he was doing, or maybe he was deliberately waiting for one of us to challenge him. I even wondered if I reminded him of someone he wanted to forget! As it was, though not ideal, I came to no harm and I learnt how powerfully groups can hold their members, even when some crucial part of group practice is missing.

Mindfulness practice offers us a unique opportunity to influence a helpful and wholesome group culture. Through cultivating a kindly approach, we can foster ways for the group to relate that are nourishing and affirming, authentic and kind. Participants enjoy being in an environment where support and encouragement is felt amongst fellow group members. This widens the benefits of holding, out around the circle and onto the screen group too. This also offers skills, appreciation and interrelatedness that can be taken out by participants beyond the MBP after the sessions have finished.

What culture do you cultivate in your MBP groups?

The eight-week MBP itself has a structure that supports and holds the learning. The process has a certain rhythm and predictability. However, there can be potential for a competitive culture to emerge, particularly in workplace settings, where rivalry and blame is sometimes endemic. In the early days of the group, there may a tendency to vie for the attention of the teacher, of wanting to get it right or needing to know the 'answers'. If we stay close to the practice, and reflect on what the group needs, we can find ways of cultivating a kindly, tolerant culture that holds all group members and develops ways of practicing and learning that support well-being and empathic relating.

Each of these three dimensions – the individual participant; the MBP teacher; and the group itself – all have a role to play in the holding process and in the culture of the group.

To explore this experientially, we now invite you to engage in an exercise that we call Aikido Walking[244], to enable us to look further at what is involved in 'holding the group'. If you prefer not to try this out at this time, perhaps you can imagine that you are… If you have a colleague that you can do this with (online can work well), then maybe arrange to do this together so that you can jointly reflect on it afterwards.

Aikido walking exercise

Imagine we are in a large room with ten or more other people. We are invited to walk across the room in three different ways.

Choose a destination on the other side of the room and walk towards it with a sense of purpose. You might imagine that you have a train to catch, and time is passing.

Once you have arrived at your spot, you turn around and repeat the walk, choosing a new destination and walking there quickly with purpose. You do this four or five times, as does everyone else in the room. There is a sense of fast-moving bodies crisscrossing the space.

Then we stop and pause, you may notice you are a little out of breath. You become aware of sensations in your body having walked in this way, and of standing with the contact of your feet on the floor.

On the second walk, the instructions are the same with an added ingredient. As you walk with purpose to your chosen spot, you include (or imagine you include) awareness of the people around you and notice the colours and shapes of the room you are in. You might make eye contact if you want, and you may choose to smile at others as you walk past. Repeat this, four or five times.

Then we stop and take another pause, to notice the breath, the body and a general sense of how you are feeling, coming back to your feet on the floor.

Different modes of engagement: What did you notice on each walk?

1. With the first walk, many people report that they feel pressured. It all seems rather rushed and busy. Getting to the chosen destination is all that matters. However, a few people find that they rather like having a definite goal. They find it stimulating and exciting.

2. When they move to the second walk (with more awareness of the others in the room), many people notice that they find themselves slowing down. It feels more spacious, and they find they make allowances for

---

244 Much appreciation to See True Mindfulness Training in The Netherlands https://www.mindfulness-trainingen.nl/ (and Franca Warmenhoven in particular) for their contribution in creating this exercise

others in ways that they did not on the first walk. They also have more awareness of the room they are in.

3. On the final walk, there is less overall uniform experience. Some enjoy pausing and connecting with what they see happening in front of them. A few mention that they feel warmly towards everything that is held in awareness. Others say they felt uncertain and even confused, 'What am I meant to be doing?!'

This exercise mirrors some of the different ways that we can react. In the first, there is only the individual and their experience. The others in the group are almost an inconvenience, in the way, and sometimes even heading for where the individual wants to go! This is how we are in automatic pilot, striving to get what we want, unaware of the bigger picture, and careering towards driven doing mode.

In the second, we bring others into more mindful awareness. We find ways to accommodate them, shifting direction or even compromising our chosen destination so that they can go where they want. The goal seems less important. This eases out the pace and can even open up a sense of spaciousness, though there is just as much movement. We begin to connect to other individuals and even a sense of everyone moving.

Then we come to the final part of the exercise. What is this about? The instructions are less straightforward to understand. We open to include a wider visual focus and take in the space of the whole room, the full context and all the people moving in front of us. We stand pausing, with awareness of feet on the floor and body standing, holding the whole scene in view, no longer so aware of individuals, in the wider focus of the whole. This can be a connecting experience, in fact it can be immensely satisfying, to offer a befriending gaze to the whole group. However, it is also amorphous, unclear, impossible to perfect, difficult even to articulate.

We now move to apply some of the learning from this exercise to the practice of the MBP teacher and what is involved in holding the group.

Intention to hold the group

A way of looking at this exercise is to consider it as a somewhat crude analogy of the different stages of MBP teacher development. At we start out as teachers, we are much occupied with the goal of delivering the programme as best we can, with a focus on the content of each week. As experience develops, we begin to give more attention to our individual participants, notice how they are doing, and start looking out for the ones we feel connected to, or concerned about. In the final version, there is a much wider focus of attention. This joins with an intention of taking in the flow of the group, as another entity in the room or on the screen.

This correctly implies that it is almost impossible to hold everything in awareness from the outset. It is too complex and there is just too much to be aware of. We cultivate different qualities and skills as we go. These depend quite a bit on the depth of our personal mindfulness practice, the training and supervision we have had/are having, and the particular sets of skills that we bring with us into this work.

So notwithstanding all of that, **what is the practice that helps us to hold the group?**

INTENTION is key.

I like the metaphor of a finger post when I am reflecting on intention. The sign shows the way to head for. It does not identify the actual destination but guides a general direction, and as we set out, we find a path to follow that is aligned to the direction of the sign. Others have been there before.

As MBP teachers, we may need to frame an intention that includes a focus on remembering the group as an entity in its own right, in the room or on the screen, which includes all group members, who we hold with kindly awareness. Without this intention, we will tend to move into default mode of giving the majority of attention to those individuals who we feel drawn to, apprehensive of, who dominate the group, or who we feel concerned about. As we learn to read the group, we develop the experience to know what is needed in key moments. Over time, as this building of holding capacity happens, we can sometimes come to be aware of an almost visceral felt sense of the group and what it needs. Often, this more intuitive holding does not involve many words, for as resonance develops, the group 'field' matures. When this takes place, the MBP teacher and the members of the group find ways of connecting that seem to seed kindly awareness into the group circle. Then, when uncertainty, fear or distress emerge, there is courage and intention to turn towards, holding it and being with the experience as best we all can.

Holding the group when co-teaching

It may be helpful to explore how two or more MBP teachers (co-teachers) hold the group when they are teaching together.

When co-teaching an MBP, it might be tempting to have a bit of a rest when your colleague is teaching or leading an inquiry. However, we find it incredibly useful to actively share the group holding. This means that when something unfolds that is challenging for an individual participant that affects the group as a whole, the teacher not leading the inquiry or actively teaching at the time, is able to scan the group and see what is happening around the circle or on the screen. This needs sensitivity, but it may be possible to catch the glance of someone who looks affected by a fellow participant's inquiry, and gently stay in touch with them, so they know you are there. However, when someone in the group is strongly affected, they may well sit with the head down, as if trying to hide their distress. In that case, whilst monitoring how they are doing, we might seek to catch the eye of our co-teacher and show them subtly with a glance who amongst the participants is distressed. This may sound easy, but it takes trust and familiarity of working with someone to be able to communicate in this way. However, in time, it is remarkable what we can develop in co-teaching, and at times we can find that we can hold the group together robustly, safely, kindly and in a way that aligns the MBP teachers with the group and each other.

It may be obvious from what we have just explored that when co-teachers sit opposite each other in the circle (or if there are three teachers at equal points around the group), they are more able to communicate non-verbally with each other and have a better chance to hold the group. In some MBP teaching traditions, teachers choose to sit next to each other, so that they can talk easily, and indeed this may well be advantageous. However, in terms of the group process, we find that sitting opposite works better. Amongst issues already mentioned, this enables the co-teacher (not leading the inquiry or actively teaching) to be able to pay particular attention to their colleague's 'wings' (the people sitting either side of the one who is actively teaching). It is always more difficult to see those sitting next to, or close by, in their peripheral vision, when they are engaged across the circle. This is especially the case when the teacher is holding an inquiry with someone sitting immediately to one side of them, since as they turn round towards them, their back is towards people on the other side behind them. This means they have no contact with those participants behind them at all. Co-teachers used to working together can cover this effectively, to ensure there is some holding of the whole group at all times.

Understanding holding

We start this section with a well-used and helpful metaphor that enables us to appreciate the MBP teacher's role of holding the group. We will use the example of a mother and her son to make it possible to distinguish the different roles between the two. However, it could just as likely be a father, grandmother or other caregiver and a child.

A mother takes her child to the play park. They have been there many times before, and she knows what he can manage and where he needs help. She sits on the bench, and he leaves her to go off and explore. She keeps half an eye on what he is doing, so that when some much older lads arrive, charging up the steps of the slide that he is about to go down, she can quickly move in to help him. When he was younger, there was no sitting on the bench with her phone. She needed to stay close, often holding his hand or lifting him up to reach the higher equipment. Over time, she has learnt to intervene only when he needs it, to let him discover more for himself. Her older daughter now at school, was more adventurous at the same age. She loved taking risks and pushing things to their limits. She would swing as high as she could; and want to be spun fast round the roundabout. The mother has learnt to adapt to her two children, the styles and stages in their development, and what support they need from her at different times.

And so it is with groups. Whilst not suggesting we need to 'mother' our MBP groups, or that they behave like children, this metaphor helps us to appreciate the different styles, stages, needs and characteristics of different groups. In time, we learn what each group needs and how to hold it appropriately. At the beginning when launching, all groups need some hand holding. Later, we discover what might work best. Is this a group that enjoys going quite fast? Or is this one that needs careful steady explaining? As an MBP teacher and group leader, we learn to find ways of teaching and holding that suit the group's phase of development and ways of learning, knowing when to intervene, perhaps with a brief grounding practice, when to leave more space for the group to find its own way, and when to bring in some humour and include a lighter touch. Early on, we focus on building trust to keep things safe. Later, we choose to invite more challenge, perhaps leaving longer gaps when guiding practices, and turning questions back to the group to answer for themselves. All this is in the service of enabling the group to become a learning community that holds them close to their practice and includes their hearts.

> **A participant's group experience on an MBP**
>
> 'I was amazed at how much any awkwardness was diffused in the first session. The group was lovely; I felt invested in their future, not needing chapter and verse of their lives, but with a huge sense of wishing them well. Listening to the voice on the practice CDs always recalls the warmth and the positivity of the sessions.'

Leadership styles

We each have different approaches to the way we hold MBP groups and their learning. Some notions around these three leadership styles[245] are worth reflecting on, especially in relation to what the MBP group might need at different stages of their development.

Autocratic leadership

In the early days of the MBP group, there is a need for structure. Having a certain clarity of direction is helpful, while the group forms and gets used to how things happen on the MBP. This is a time for the MBP teacher to step up and hold the group in a way that is perhaps more autocratic and direct. This may not be a natural style for some of us. We might naturally favour a more facilitative or democratic style. But in the early days of an MBP, when participants feel uncertain and there is a general nervousness, and a lack of a felt sense of safety, a clear structure (what we do next and how we will do it) is more holding, as long as care and kindness is also threaded in. The combination of the two, directive and kindly, can be very reassuring to a new MBP group as it launches.

Democratic leadership

Most MBP teachers will probably employ a facilitative style most of the time (see the facilitation section Chapter 12). Once the group has launched, and there is more confidence in understanding how things are done, then as MBP teachers, we are looking to find ways of maximising the involvement of the group and including everyone, especially amongst those who experience discrimination and are often excluded from other groups and networks.

But then something may occur that disrupts the flow in the moment, and it may be necessary to move to establish more direction again, or perhaps to interrupt a discussion that is heading in an unhelpful direction. A democratic leadership style requires embodying equanimity on the part of the teacher. This is not just steadiness, although that is certainly needed,

---

245 Lewin *et al*, 1938

but a way of leading and facilitating the group that is characterised by equalness towards all. This involves mindful enabling so that everyone can contribute in a way that best suits them. Some will contribute verbally, others through body language, perhaps with a nod or a smile.

Laissez faire leadership

The third leadership style is known as laissez faire. This can be interpreted as an unwillingness to get involved. It suggests passivity and inaction on the part of the leader. This style rightly has a bad press in management circles, as laissez faire behaviour in leaders can result in ignoring aspects of team or group behaviour, such as bullying, racism, sexism or another form of discrimination against others.

It has limited use in an MBP, except perhaps right at the end of the programme when it may be skilful and appropriate for us to step back and offer a lighter and more flexible touch with the group. These are the moments when we let the group decide, perhaps a date for a follow-up session, or arranging car sharing for the Day of Practice, or setting up an online group amongst group members. We leave it to them. There is little structure and perhaps even facilitation is not much needed as the group are able to manage themselves. However, through most of the programme, a laissez faire leadership style would be unskilful and even unsafe. There might be a muddle between this style and a more democratic way of holding the group. However, when as MBP teachers, we hold the group there is always a focus on process and an understanding of what is needed in that moment or at that stage. This understanding involves active reflexivity, and highlights the difference between a democratic leader and one that behaves in a more laissez faire way. The first is responsive and present. The second is passive, and invariably not very present.

Different leadership styles are needed at different stages

Although every group has its own character and development, we can probably draw out some general patterns over the life of the MBP group. In weeks one and two, as the group is launching, we need to hold the group with more structure, grounding, and clarity of task. This is closest to an autocratic style. In weeks four to six, when there may be more emotion and challenge, the group may show signs of storming[246,247] and may need holding in ways that allow for feelings of distress to be expressed where group boundaries are secure. Up to now, the primary responsibility for maintaining safety and inclusive holding lies with the MBP teacher, but

---

246 Tuckman, 1965
247 see Chapter 7: Reading the group

increasingly the group contributes to holding. This emerges over the life of the group (in some MBP groups more than others). In weeks seven and eight, as we move towards the end of the group, the teacher may take a step back and if the group is functioning well, there is less need to actively intervene, beyond keeping the programme on track. This gives the group a chance to explore and experiment; allows group members to discover their own way of adapting mindfulness practices; and enables them to be free to make meaning in ways that best applies to them and their lives. This may be the time when mindfulness-based group members may make connections between their practice of mindfulness, their learning relationships in the group and what is happening in the wider world.

These broad suggestions are only pointers to look out for. They are not fixed or rigid. One MBP group can be very different to the next, and the needs of each group reflect that.

Do you know your own 'natural' leadership style?

Some ways of holding are influenced by our own personal leadership style. It may help for each of us to have a sense of what that might be. This is an exercise that can offer insight into our own styles of leading. You might choose to reflect on this exercise yourself or share it with a colleague to discuss together.

Leadership exercise

Imagine you are with others in a spacious room. The large group is divided into a number of smaller groups each consisting of five or six people. Your task is to lead your little group safely into an opposite corner of the room, keeping them together but avoiding the pillars in the centre of the room, and ensuring that your group does not collide with any of the other small groups. Everyone has their eyes closed except you (and the other group leaders). You can use words and touch to guide your group. (You can also bring some imaginary guardians into the room to keep a look out for everyone!)

How can you keep your group safe while successfully guiding it across the room to the opposite corner?

Before you read on, perhaps you might close your eyes for a few seconds to decide how you might manage this task.

Will you ask your group to stand in a line with each person holding onto the shoulder of the one in front, and then guiding the first in the line across the room to the other side, avoiding any obstacles as you go? Perhaps you will arrange your group in a circle, in touch with each other, with space in the middle, and then move them to the left or to the right as needed as they remain in circle formation? Or maybe you will have them stand in a clump, touching each other, so they are all together moving in one close unit?

There are no right ways of doing this. This exercise can be fun, or sometimes slightly alarming depending on the awareness of the leader.

Having done this a few times, some common tendencies that seem to emerge include:

■ Some leaders are only focused on the front of the group and forget to look at what is happening at the back, which means that people at the back can sometimes bump into the obstacles and may not feel safe or included.

■ Some move their groups too quickly, which does not allow enough time for adjustments to be made to avoid the pillars or the other groups. The result produces an exciting ride for some, and a scary one for others.

■ Some leaders are over cautious, going extremely slowly, with lots of detailed directions. This tends to be quite irritating, as there is too much structure and not enough exploration.

■ Some leaders are so consumed with the goal of getting to the other side of the room, that they forget to attend to the way they manage to get there and what their group is experiencing. This can result in all sorts of confusions and lacks awareness of boundaries, which compromises the safety of the group.

These are interesting analogies for various ways of holding groups. Can you recognize your own tendencies?

Do you tend to concentrate on those participants who are quite vocal and demanding, perhaps forgetting about those 'at the back' who don't say much?

Do you have a habit of keeping things 'too' safe, detailed and steady, perhaps resulting in a rather sedentary process that may be a bit dull and under engaging? Do you take things at quite a lick, perhaps not pausing enough to give attention to see if this suits your group, nor allowing participants enough space to contribute and learn? Or are you so focused on the content of the MBP that you are not much aware of the group process, and how the group is needing to be held?

You may not recognize your particular style from the examples above, and inevitably these are exaggerated in form. However, it might be worth reflecting on this in supervision or with a colleague. Recording and then watching your own teaching, though challenging at first, is very helpful in teasing out some of the 'invisible' ways that we hold our MBP groups. 'Invisible' since it is hard for us to spot, as we inevitably see and experience things out of a personal perspective, through our own eyes.

The other relevant factor here is that all groups are different. We cannot emphasise that enough. There are so many different influences on each group, even beyond what each individual participant brings. This can be a challenge at times, but is more likely to bring joy into the mindfulness-based group. Skilful embodied holding from the teacher and from within the group itself can produce rich learning and cultivate an environment where connections and well-being can flow.

"Only through communication can human life hold meaning." [248]

Summary

We have explored aspects of holding the MBP group through the different perspectives of the individual participant, the MBP teacher, and the whole group as an entity in its own right. In drawing out some ways to shed light on the role of holding, we have emphasised the uniqueness of each mindfulness-based group. There are no short cuts or formulae for developing the capacity of holding the group. It comes gradually with experience, reflection, insight and practice. In some moments, a felt sense of what is needed may intuitively come clear.

We have included several MBP teaching examples and a number of reflective exercises that we hope will offer ways of understanding holding, that as teachers we will often already be doing. Kind intention and mindfully embodied awareness are our key practice capacities. They enable us in time to bring the holding of the mindfulness-based group as a fascinating and rewarding aspect of our MBP teaching.

---

248 Freire, 1970

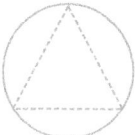

11. Holding: inside out practice guiding

Trish Bartley

This brief chapter explores some aspects of how MBP teachers guide mindfulness-based practices, and what helps us to practice inside out guiding[249]. We have placed this chapter next to the Inside Out Inquiry and Facilitation chapter as they naturally go together. However, it is worth emphasising that whilst guiding, inquiry, and facilitation are all key features of holding the group, they also rely on our first capacity of Inside Out Embodying.

We have included a recorded practice that relates to this inside out holding guiding, which we hope will help with this. It can be downloaded at www.pavpub.com/teaching-mindfulness-based-groups-resources

When we start out as MBP teachers in guiding mindfulness-based practices, we may find it quite difficult to hold awareness of both the inside (the teacher's own internal experience of the practice) and the outside (the experience of the group and individuals in the group) at the same time. There are evident advantages in learning to guide in this way. We are more able to mindfully embody the practice if the process of guiding is informed and held by our own personal awareness as MBP teachers (on the inside). We are also more able to connect and respond to the group and the individuals within it if we are aware of what is happening (on the outside).

It helps to practice this a bit like sitting on a rocking chair, moving back and forth, back and forth. Starting with attention on the 'inside' (in the body of the MBP teacher), we may choose to move 'out' at the end of the phrase. Once 'out there', perhaps we pause and breathe, whilst opening an intention to connect with and hold a sense of the group. This is a little like listening to the subtle 'sounds' within the body of the group and opening to them. Then we come back to bring attention to the 'inside', including awareness of the body of the teacher, to see what phrase is needed that comes directly out of our own experience of the practice.

---

249 For a fuller exploration of guiding mindfulness-based practices see Crane *et al*, 2021

In time it becomes more possible to hold both dimensions together (or almost together), at the same time. However, there will always be times when, as MBP teachers, we need to bring a particular emphasis to the inside or the outside – perhaps when our attention wanders, or when we have a sense of the group's attention wandering, which is probably a cue that more anchoring is needed. In my experience, the two often happen together. I might notice in the inquiry that follows the practice, some descriptions of mind wandering at moments that I can remember when my mind had wandered. As MBP teachers, we may often discover that when the attention wanders, group members' attention drifts too, and when this happens the group and the MBP teacher together need to bring things back to present moment awareness.

As MBP teachers, we are bound to teach in ways that mirror our own personal patterns. Are we more focused on our own experience or that of others? In relation to guiding 'inside out', we probably either veer towards 'going in', to give most attention to our internal experience, or we privilege 'going out', to focus predominantly on what is on the outside in the group. Both have their pitfalls. Too much focus on the inside, will clearly limit connection and awareness of the group, which will affect our capacity to hold the group, and respond to what they need. Too much focus on the outside will compromise mindful embodying, authenticity and direct personal experience of the practice. This may result in a more automatic practice 'script' and a reduced capacity to guide out of our own experience. The ideal is to combine both.

We can start practicing inside out guiding (probably with the eyes closed, if that is how we usually practice) as soon as we are familiar enough with the shape, the language, and a sense of rooted embodying of the practice itself. There are bound to be times when there are ripples of disturbance in the group – perhaps a sound outside reaches the room or is audible from those on the screens; perhaps there is a movement suggesting restlessness, or someone shifting position in the group; or maybe we discern a pattern of breathing that suggests that someone is upset. When this happens, we may naturally choose to open the eyes to see how the group is doing. This enables us to respond within the guiding, perhaps with a renewed emphasis on grounding and posture which is the best support we can offer the group. Indeed, our groundedness and embodying of mindfulness in our own practice as we guide may be more effective than any collection of words that we use. It also seems that the phrases that are most anchoring for the group are invariably the ones that connect us, as MBP teachers, most powerfully to our own present-moment embodying. This confirms a sense of alignment from group to MBP teacher, and teacher to group, and validates the growing pedagogical MBP teaching literature that we hold the group in a number of ways, which includes the MBP teacher's own mindful embodying.

In conversation, a colleague shared with me that the only way they could feel a genuine sense of 'arriving' at the start of each session was to stand up and practice 'Standing in Mountain'. Their current group of participants were quite challenging to teach. They were health and care professional staff, highly stressed and quite ambivalent about mindfulness and taking the programme. As we reflected on things, it became clear that if this is what this MBP teacher needed to support their confidence and teaching practice, then it was important to fold this into the opening of each session. Once they found an authentic way of doing this, the benefits in helping them to settle became evident, both for them and for the group.

We can assume that increased confidence, groundedness and embodying of present moment awareness on the part of the MBP teacher enabled them to hold the group more effectively, despite the ambivalence in the group.

We start guiding mindfulness-based practices with attention to the posture of the body – whether sitting, lying, walking or standing. This is true for body scan, mindful movement practice, sitting practice, and even with the brief and the short practices. How much attention we give to this depends on personal preference. However, in relation to the practice of inside out holding, there seems to be much value in lingering longer on this arriving practice at the base of the body. We might choose to spend some time at these foundations until there is an experience of 'landing' within the teacher's own experience – contact of the feet on the floor, seat of the body with the seat of the chair, weight going down, and the solid beneath the body – holding.

It is tempting when we start to guide mindfulness practices to rely on scripts, but we soon discover that this has the disadvantage of limiting the teachers own mindful embodiment. We inevitably focus on the words rather than the experience of the practice inside the body and outside, as it is being received by the group. The volume of our guiding is important in how we hold the group, as the voice tends to get quieter as we become more settled and 'internal', and we need to connect and be able to hold participants wherever they are sitting in the room. It can be enriching for MBP group members to be guided in a practice and held by someone who is embodied and present; who plays with words and phrases as they emerge freshly out of the experience of the practice.

Summary

Holding the group as we guide a mindfulness practice requires an embodied and grounded presence on the inside of the MBP teacher, and kindly aware attention of the group on the outside. This balance of inside out mindfulness helps us to remember to guide the practice out of our own experience, rather than depending on or remembering an internal script.

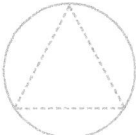

12. Holding: inside out inquiry and facilitation

Trish Bartley

"The whole stance toward, or relationship with, experience that the instructor embodies in the inquiry dialogue will be a major factor in helping participants themselves embody a new way of relating to experience .... Taking part in the 8-week program increases participants' kindness and compassion towards themselves.... The inquiry process is probably the main arena in which the instructor has opportunity after opportunity to embody these qualities as participants report experiences they regard as failures, weaknesses, or mistakes."[250]

John Teasdale

Having looked at inside out practice guiding, we now move on to explore inside out inquiry with a particular focus on involving the mindfulness-based group and what this asks of us, as MBP teachers. We follow this with a section that looks at facilitation practice, the way we involve group members in discussions, curriculum exercises and so forth, in order to increase participation and deepen the learning potential across the group. Finally, we consider key ways of supporting the mindfulness-based teacher in their holding of the MBP group.

Inside out inquiry

Most beginning MBP teachers, and even those of us with more experience, find the inquiry can produce the most anxiety out of all the teaching skills. Yet it is also a process that can be hugely rich in learning for group members and MBP teachers alike. In some ways, it is a continuation of the practice, offering participants another way of bringing mindful awareness to their experience. It can also serve to connect the group, through a sense of shared vulnerability, from which learning can emerge. As with the previous chapter

250 Segal *et al*, 2013

on inside out guiding, it is helpful to remember that all aspects of MBP teaching practice rely on embodying mindfulness, coming back over and over to present, kindly awareness, inside and out.

The inquiry 'dialogue' or 'conversation' is facilitated by the MBP teacher with group members, in order to explore the mindfulness practice that has just taken place.

Three layers of inquiry

The inquiry process[251] is led by drawing out:

- Direct experience of sensations in the body, and emotions and thoughts in the mind.
- The relationship to those experiences (feeling tone).
- Any learning or meaning that evolves from the patterns of those experiences that links to the themes of the MBP.

These three layers are central to MBP inquiry teacher training[252] and are helpful in making sense of mapping the inquiry process. However, when as MBP teachers, we are first learning the skills of inquiry, these three layers risk becoming goals to achieve. When this happens, connection is lost between the inside awareness of the MBP teacher and the outside awareness of what is happening in the group of the individual group member (being inquired of). Instead, there may be a tendency to try to lead a 'good' inquiry. How to manage this? It can be helpful to notice the internal pull to 'do' the inquiry well, and maybe pause and come back to a sense of contact with the body (feet on the floor perhaps) and then pick up where the inquiry has been left or start another thread.

When we are beginning to teach MBPs, there can also be a pull to bring through a teaching and learning point (layer three) and we may be tempted to squeeze one in, even if there was little connection with what emerged in the inquiry. This is understandable but with a bit more experience, we discover that it can work well to stay with inquiring into layers one and two (the direct experience and the relationship to the experience), reassuring ourselves that we do not need to bring out teaching points every time.

We suggest that inside out inquiry includes an explicit intention to keep the whole group in view, even whilst the primary focus might be on an individual group member. As best we can, as MBP teachers, we seek to practice with embodied awareness of what is emerging on the inside, whilst staying in contact with the group as a whole, and individual group members, and

---

251 Ibid. See Chapter 12
252 Ibid.

what is evolving on the outside. The two directions of awareness, inside and out, are finely tuned and emerge together, since, with experience, what is happening in the group often resonates in forms of sensations inside the body of the MBP teacher. Using horizontal and vertical approaches to inquiry, and a flow between them, can add to the collaborative learning of the whole group and contribute to a sense of shared humanity between group members. We now explore horizontal and vertical inquiry in more detail.

Horizontal inquiry

Horizontal inquiry is a way of relating the experience of the practice that has just happened to the group as a whole, by inviting brief responses across the group rather than focusing predominantly on one participant at a time.

We might start an inquiry 'horizontally' with a question such as, "What was going on for you in that practice? Can you share a word or a phrase, so that we can explore what was there in the room/group?". As each word is individually offered, we acknowledge it and then scan the circle with another question to thread the experience around the group, "Anyone else like that?"

Let us imagine that you are the MBP teacher, and you have just guided a body scan.

Somebody offers the phrase, "I felt restless". Gently acknowledging that first offering, maybe with a thank you and following it immediately with, "Anyone else felt restless?" And as you look around the full circle in the room (or all the faces on the screen) you might notice some nods, which you acknowledge with, "So there was restlessness in the group, yes, thank you. That can happen at times for us all. What else was there? What else did you notice?" Someone might say, "I felt quite sleepy". And again, you acknowledge that in your own way and then look around the group with the question, "Anyone else felt sleepy?" If the group seems ready for some humour and very gentle teasing, you might add "Really? Surely not!", with another scan around the circle, so that your gaze passes across every person in the group. Maybe you make eye contact with those who are nodding and smiling. The group is learning to play a little. Then perhaps someone is brave enough to say, "I was afraid I snored!"– followed by shared laughter and knowing glances across the group. "So, a number of you felt sleepy, and some of you felt restless AND sleepy. That's interesting, isn't it? We have lots of different experiences at different times." When we have words from the group that appear quite similar (e.g., calm, settled, pleasurable, relaxed etc), we might deliberately invite in words that offer some contrast. "How about a different type of experience? Perhaps not so calm and relaxed?" This invites a range of colour onto the palette of the group experience. It demonstrates that it is ok not have to have similar or 'positive' experiences. We hope that the group is realising that this can be a place where they can try out exploring experience as it is.

It is important to add that this example is not a formula of how to lead an inquiry, horizontal or otherwise. Each of us develops our own style, and we soon come to realize that the inquiry process is best guided by what is happening in the group, the individual participant and within the MBP teacher. Inquiry skills are cultivated by being responsive, flexible and intuitive, so that the process emerges out of the moment. Sometimes, it might be just the moment to bring in some humour or playfulness, but if it is planned rather than emerging spontaneously out of the moment, it can feel out of place.

Having emphasised this, we want to draw out some pointers and possible rationales around horizontal and vertical styles of inquiry, with special attention to 'inside out' and to the presence of the MBP group.

Why is horizontal inquiry helpful? And why is it relevant to holding the group?

Horizontal inquiry can have the effect of making an experience 'normal' when it is shared with others around the MBP group. As MBP teachers, we embrace this potential in our willingness to hold the group process, knowing how healing and transformative normalising can prove to be for group members. This in turn may also impact on widening a sense of inclusivity in the group. Group members may tend to assume that they were, say, the only one who felt restless in a body scan or bored in a sitting practice. Following on from that assumption comes all sorts of reactive thoughts, "I'm no good at this," "I'm different to the others in the group," "Everyone else is calm except me," and so on. Horizontal inquiry can help to reduce these myths by seeing the nods, smiles and audible murmurs of agreement from others in the group, and having them specifically acknowledged by the MBP teacher. This can be helpful at any time in the group, especially at the start of the MBP when participants may be keen to get it right (and concerned not to get it wrong). Realising that others also feel restless/sleepy and so on is reassuring. A participant might admire someone in the group. "They look clever", they think. Then in the horizontal inquiry, the same person admits to feeling sleepy, or restless, or whatever, which not only helps to dissolve the projection, but also empowers the participant to realize that their own experience is normal and quite okay.

Horizontal inquiry also brings a gentleness into the way which we, as MBP teachers, approach inquiry. In the early days of the group, it can be unhelpful to go too deep, too quick, which is a risk with the more traditional vertical inquiry. With a more horizontal approach, going around the group, we have a chance to 'warm up' the process and the group members, easing them into getting used to sharing aspects of their experience quite minimally at first. For most of them, all that is involved is a nod or a smile or a murmur of agreement, which is very different to how we normally exchange. New groups need to learn the ropes gradually, which they will do quite quickly if they feel safe in the group, and they have a sense that they are being included.

At first, horizontal inquiry may need some practice for the mindfulness-based group to get used to. Generally, people say much more than one word or phrase when sharing an experience. We want to recount the whole story! In horizontal inquiry, group members learn to share a small part of the whole. They also learn that it is fine to have different experiences. We might feel sleepy, and we might feel restless. That is how it is. It becomes possible to see that there is no right way, and this is as true for one participant as it for the whole group. This way of starting an inquiry engages all group members whether they share a word or not. Some may step in with just the smallest nod in response to a shared word (or even agree internally and silently), and by doing so, they start to feel that they can belong and are included.

The MBP teacher is modelling that everything that arises in a practice is holdable, the whole gamut of experience is okay. So, whatever is brought into the inquiry process can be held by the MBP teacher with practice, on the inside and out (as long as basic ground rules are respected). In a practical sense, horizontal inquiry is not only effective in including subtly even the quietest group member, but it also does this in a way that takes much less time than vertical inquiry, which may be helpful if time is a factor in the session.

Popcorn

Horizontal inquiry can be confused with another group process, often used in inquiry, which we will call the 'popcorn' method here. Popcorn generates a list of experiences, which seems to start in the same way as horizontal inquiry, with an invitation from the MBP teacher to share an aspect of the practice experience with one word. This can be a useful thing to do, but it does not offer the same opportunities to normalise experience nor include group members in as effective a way. In terms of group process, popcorn can seem a bit flat and lacks the potential to go much further. It might help to be clear about the difference between the two, as they can easily be muddled and seem like the same process. In popcorn, what tends to follow is that a number of members of the group will 'pop out' their words, sleepy, restless, wandering mind, pain, and so on. And in that flurry there is no opportunity to thread the words around the group one by one with, "Does anyone else feel like that?" There are too many to follow up on. So, although popcorn gives a sense of the different range of experiences in the group, it does not offer the same potential to normalise one participants' experience alongside another, or add an inclusive aspect to the process in the way that horizontal inquiry can.

How can we to manage to stay with horizontal inquiry process and avoid moving into popcorn? We simply stop and then slow down the process with: "Hang on, let's have one word at a time. Let's take yours Maria, 'restless'. Anyone else felt restless?"… and so on.

Vertical inquiry

At some point we may choose to explore a group member's experience a bit further. We call this vertical inquiry, which is the 'normal' or traditional approach to inquiry. Usually, a moment arises when there is an opening to go deeper, perhaps something that was offered in the horizontal process needs more exploring, or maybe this seems a good moment to gently engage someone further. This will often register inside the MBP teacher perhaps through a stirring of curiosity to want to know more, and a sense of connection available with the participant.

Vertical inquiry appears to focus on an individual participant and their experience. All the questions about the practice are directed to that one person, unlike horizontal inquiry, where we thread the questions and responses around the whole group. In horizontal, we seem to be working at a more generalised level. In vertical inquiry, we invite an exploring of direct and more detailed personal experience of the practice. It is important to be aware that going deeper into vertical type inquiry can be much more exposing for the participant and needs gentle holding. However, during vertical inquiry, we also find it is vital to keep the group engaged and to continue to hold the whole group process. This enables every inquiry to be an opportunity for the whole group to learn, be engaged and feel included.

Staying in contact with other members of the group during a vertical inquiry is important, but it can be challenging at times. As MBP teachers, we naturally want to maintain eye contact with the person we are inquiring of, since this is how we hold them and help them to stay connected to us and their experience. However, we also want to know how the group is responding to the inquiry, as this is one of the ways that as MBP teacher, we decide whether to remain, deepen or close the process with this group member. To resolve this, it may be possible at a suitable moment to 'leave' the participant briefly, by breaking eye contact, and scanning around the group, we can see and feel into how the inquiry is being received and experienced.

Inquiry in the midst of intensity or with managing challenging situations

If one person in the MBP group is feeling emotional, these feelings are likely to ripple around the group and affect others too, especially in groups that are becoming strongly interconnected. This might be a moment to hold the whole group, including the person engaged in the inquiry. We might invite them and everyone in the group to all pause and practice 'feet on the floor'. This invites embodied grounding as ballast to what is unfolding and supports the MBP teacher themselves to hold the moment.

> In week five, following a sitting practice, one of the participants became visibly upset. They described moving up close to an area in the body that held pain and they were anxious about what it might mean. Were they ill? Their father had recently died of cancer. The way they described this experience was vivid and very affecting. There was almost a sense of the air changing in the room, as if everyone at that moment was holding their breath. Guided by my own internal response and what I felt in the room, I suggested we take a pause, and gently come to the breath with eyes open. This produced a tangible release in me, and the participant involved looked steadier. On firmer ground, we then continued with the inquiry, acknowledging how powerful an experience can be, in a way that affects us all.

Sometimes we have a participant who at the start of many inquiries, steps forward first. If this seems habitual, we need to find out how the group finds this. There may be some impatience or irritation, or (most likely) some body language of the group that suggests 'switching off', almost with an internal "Not them again!" We may notice a similar reaction in ourselves, as MBP teachers. How to manage this? It helps to understand that some people need to speak and be heard in the group to feel safe and included, yet this pattern can sometimes link to aspects of assumed power and status in the group. It may need some intervention on the part of the MBP teacher depending on their interpretation of what lies behind the pattern.

Horizontal inquiry might be useful here. There may be an opportunity to interrupt, in a firm but kind way, perhaps with an acknowledgement of, "I'm going to interrupt you…", and then maybe, "Let's take a pause here. I'm keen to hear, is there anyone else who experienced something similar to what Zara was mentioning?"

We then have a choice after involving the group and pausing the narrative. We can return to 'Zara' to close that particular dialogue by thanking her and then moving on to the next exercise, or perhaps to another vertical inquiry with someone else.

So, to recap, it is important to stay aware of the group during vertical inquiry. If at any point the group engagement drops, or there seems to be some reactivity in the group, we find it is helpful to find some way of holding it all so that each inquiry, whether vertical or horizontal, connects the whole group to a potential to learn and practice mindfulness. If as MBP teachers we can include an ongoing and consistent awareness of what is happening inside in the body, this becomes a valuable resource that helps us decide on the choices we might make next. Pausing and including a Feet on the Floor practice is always an option, not just when some intensity is being expressed, as this helps to hold and reconnect the group as a whole and reinforces the value of brief practice threaded into everyday life.

Inside out facilitation: the mindfulness-based teacher as facilitator

Mindfulness-based programmes involve participants in learning experientially rather than through theory (although that too has its place). This happens through questions, discussions, small group process, inquiry, exercises and scenarios, sometimes with the use of a flip chart, whiteboard, online presentations or equivalent.

Facilitation is both an approach and a skill that is central to experiential learning. It implies a process that makes things easier ('facile' is French for 'easy'). A facilitator is someone who enables a group of people to share their experience collaboratively, rather than on their own. It is a positive and optimistic process, often referred to as 'bottom up', which ideally seeks to include and involve all group members especially those who may be marginalised, and not often heard in the group or out in society. At best, a facilitation process empowers and encourages connection and collective learning. The teacher and participants are all learners, and in fact they simultaneously teach and learn. In a mindfulness context, this involves us as MBP teachers to step into the same shoes as our group participants, that of being vulnerable humans, experiencing similar patterns of universal vulnerabilities, and seeking to bring more steady and meaningful contentment into our lives. The facilitating role of the MBP teacher is very much engaged in the group process by enabling the group to be as mutually inclusive, safe, empathic, and participative as possible.

This is very different to the more traditional 'top down' didactic approach that concentrates on the acquisition of knowledge and infers expertise on the part of the teacher. The learners in this system are 'receptacles to be filled by the teacher'[253]. Paulo Freire, the renowned radical Brazilian educationalist, in his famous classic 'The Pedagogy of the Oppressed', likens this to a 'banking' concept of education, in which the students are those that receive, file, and store the deposits (of knowledge), and therefore lack opportunity for creativity and transformation during the learning process.

> "Knowledge emerges only through invention and re-invention, through the restless, impatient, continuing, hopeful inquiry human beings pursue in the world, with the world, and with each other."[254]

253 Freire, 1970
254 Ibid.

A traditional top-down didactic education process will often have the teacher or lecturer at the front of the room and the students sitting in rows one behind the other. In an experiential learning process the chairs will usually be arranged in a circle with participants and the teacher/s sitting within the circle.

Two examples of MBP facilitating

Let us look at the examples of the nine dots puzzle[255] in MBSR (introduced in the first week as home practice), and 'Walking down the Street' in MBCT, which involves the whole group. Both are curriculum exercises that aim to highlight the role of perception, and these take place in session two[256].

Starting with the nine dots, the aim is explore the theme of perception by harnessing the group's engagement and involving as many people as possible in the discussion. Even though there is (hopefully!) someone in the group who is willing to share their solution to the puzzle, the learning comes out of the discussion within the group. The MBP teacher might pose questions to cultivate reflective curiosity. "What was it like to have this puzzle as part of your week's home practice?" They may use comments from the group such as, "I tried every which way to solve the puzzle and I just couldn't!", and turn them into questions that draw out the experience further, such as, "What did you try and what led you to give up? Did anyone else experience something similar?"

In doing this, the group is focusing on the experience of how and what they did as they approached the nine dots, rather than actually getting to achieve their goal of solving the puzzle (which is what most of them will want to get to). At some point the MBP teacher may well gather the discussion to a close with a summary of the teaching point, the headline 'take home' if you like – perhaps something like: "So in this mindfulness-based programme, we explore our experience rather differently than we might assume, and, learning to 'think outside the box', we become aware of the many assumptions we make as we approach something new". The exercise appears to run itself, with the nine dots up on the flipchart (or if online, using the whiteboard or PowerPoint), the questions that come out of the discussion, and lots of opportunities to include the whole group. It sounds very straightforward, which it can be, especially if there is some humour and fun in the mix. However, to get to this point with high levels of participation, some key facilitation skills are needed to hold and include as many group members as possible, through the use of questions, awareness of the whole group, bringing in group members by encouraging them to contribute, capturing everyone's contributions on the flipchart (as closely to what was said as we can so that everyone feels valued and heard), inviting reflection, summarising and recapping the learning.

255 https://amagicclassroom.com/uploads/3/2/3/0/3230875/9_dot_puzzle.pdf
256 Kabat-Zinn, 2013

Walking Down the Street is a curriculum exercise[257] drawn from Cognitive Behavioural Therapy and included in week two of MBCT. It explores the relationship between thoughts and feelings. The process involves a bit more structure than the nine dots puzzle, but in many ways it is similar in the learning that emerges from it. A flipchart with some columns drawn on the paper will be needed (or if working online, the whiteboard or a PowerPoint with text added). The task is then set up with a brief scenario: "You are walking down the street when, on the other side of the street you see somebody you know. You smile and wave, but the person just doesn't seem to notice and walks on round the corner, out of sight."

Then, as with the MBSR exercise, we facilitate the learning with a question, such as "What was your feeling when you failed to make contact with your friend?" The responses are gathered one at a time from different members of the group and written in the appropriate column on the flipchart (we probably have our own way of arranging this). Everyone who shares their feeling gets to see their 'feeling word' written up on the flipchart. This is important. It validates both their contribution and their experience. There may be times when somebody offers a word that doesn't quite fit the category that we are asking for. It may be necessary then to pause and gently suggest, "Maybe that's a thought, let's put that in the other column for now". Then, clarifying the task, we might add, "What would you feel when you fail to attract the attention of your friend?" In gathering information from the group in this way, we validate a range of experience from within the group, whilst at the same time making sense of any pattern that is emerging. Although we collect contributions from individual participants, we are holding the whole group in awareness, and including everyone in this process of gathering, acknowledging, and drawing out the patterns, so that eventually we can turn to the group and ask, "What do you make of that?"

It is as if by holding the group and facilitating the exercise, we are helping the learning to emerge from group members so that they draw their own meaning from the process and at the same time benefit from the meaning that other members of the group make. The group will have a range of responses. There is value in this shared exploring and hearing. I remember sharing a flipchart of this with someone who had been absent for the exercise. It made quite an impact on her, which she continued to refer to through the rest of the course. The fact that she could see all the group responses and learn from these in full view was crucial to her capacity to connect strongly with the learning.

At some point, we move briefly into more conventional 'teaching' by summarising the learning points. We are probably scanning the circle as we do, to see how this is landing in the group, letting the feedback we sense from the group tell us whether more is needed, or if that is enough. We are probably standing at the flip chart, feeling the feet on the solid of the floor

---

257 Segal *et al*, 2013, p160-164

beneath, holding the body, or if in front of a screen we are feeling our feet and their contact with the floor, so that as we gather responses from the group we are present and embodied. Kindly and clear holding is valuable in helping participants find the courage and confidence to share their ideas or ask questions.

The context of mindfulness-based programme facilitating

If we are to become more relevant to populations from communities that are currently seldom heard within mindfulness-based networks, we need to understand the contexts, norms and cultures of those we wish to reach. This might become central to the ways that we are able to connect with and hold the group. Using examples that authentically relate to the lives of the people we are teaching is important. This may be something we already do without giving it much thought. When I worked in South Africa, I learned to use examples that were relevant to life in the village I was staying in, such as carrying firewood, planting vegetables, collecting water, washing clothes at the river, caring for sick family members, and so on. These many daily physical activities offered opportunities for adapting everyday practices in their own way, that they could do together. Working with medical staff in health care settings is similar. We learn that doors are often opened by 'swiping' ID cards. In the busyness of the day, finding activities that happen regularly several times a day can help to interrupt things briefly, creating a gap that offers a choice of what to do next. Longer pauses or practices may simply not be possible, but using activities as cues to remember to briefly come back to anchoring practices can be invaluable if established as regular habits. These can then be reinforced within the group in and out of the MBP.

An MBP teaching colleague once worked with a team of highly paid lawyers in a big city. In looking for a practice that they could do together at work, they decided they could bow to each other as they passed in the corridor, and in doing so they would pause and come back to be present for a moment or two as they did. And this is what they came to love doing. Their bows were almost imperceptible, tiny movements of the head and the body, but known to the other as a kindly, mindful greeting, which to anyone not on the programme would be hard to notice. These tiny bows linked them to their practice and contributed to holding them as group members.

For MBPs to expand their relevance and reach further, we need sessions to be framed in the cultural settings, communities and activities that are relevant for the people we are teaching. It is how the MBP process will become accessible, empowering, and inclusive.

Supporting the holding of the mindfulness-based group (outside the sessions)

Up until now, in this overall holding section we have looked at:

- the different components involved in holding the group
- the intention of the teacher to hold the group
- understanding holding
- the practice of holding itself, as it is applied to inside out guiding, inquiry and facilitation.

We now briefly consider the ways that we can support ourselves as mindfulness-based teachers in this practice of holding the MBP group. We draw out three key approaches: reflection; supervision; and mindfulness practice 'on the cushion'.

Reflection

Whilst we are teaching a programme, we may find it helpful to spend some time reflecting on the group, perhaps on the way home in the car, on a walk the next day, or maybe at the breakfast table the following morning. We might devote a few minutes to this, perhaps capturing some thoughts in a journal, if you enjoy writing, or maybe with the use of a pro forma that lists the participants and has a space to include a sense of the group as a whole.

We can assume that the experience of each individual participant is in some way expressing something for the whole group. To gain insight into this, we might reflect on the roles people take in the group. Some of these may be well developed in some individuals, even a little overdeveloped at times. Examples might include:

- the person who steps forward and regularly wants to be inquired of first
- someone who tends to ask the tricky questions in the group
- the group member who is very caring to others, but rarely lets themselves feel feelings.

Then there are those with underdeveloped roles, perhaps contributing very little in the large group, or beginning to develop, such as starting to speak tentatively in the large group. Noting these different roles can guide us as to what the group is needing, leading us, as MBP teachers, to review these each week after each session, in the light of the group's and individual participants' holding needs.

Some questions to reflect on:

- How are the group roles changing since last week?
- Where are the movements in the developing roles?

■ How is the group becoming more confident?

As we review the changing roles, we can see them in the light of the group as a whole, not just acted out by one individual. We are gathering insights into what is needed to support these developing or emerging roles, sometimes being expressed on 'the edges' of the group. There may be a need to find ways of quietening the over-developed roles. This requires us as MBP teachers to listen out for the 'quieter voices' and maybe draw them out gently, so we tune in to respond to what the group as a whole, and the individual group members within it, need most.

There is another reflective tool we can use here.

> Imagine you are on the walk you take most days. You are passing the tree that you often look out for. As you walk past, you admire its bark, shape, spread and colour. You know it well; it changes as the seasons change, but its key features stay the same.

> What if you now walk now around the tree and look at it from the other side. How does it look? Is it recognizable as the same tree? What can you see? It is tempting to compare the two sides, judging which you like better, but if you look at this tree from this fresh perspective, with new eyes? What do you see?

By 'walking round the tree', we are seeking to bring a new perspective to the group and what it needs. We can also do this by imagining that we can see the group (and ourselves teaching) as if in a helicopter looking down from above. We are seeing how as MBP teachers we hold the group, and how group members are relating to the way we hold them, from this new vantage point. There's no judgement needed, just an interested and curious engagement.

Questions are invaluable, especially those that are quite simple and straightforward. What was happening when such and such said …? What was the feel of the group? How do I know? Rather than making statements such as 'it was like this', or 'it was like that', perhaps ask questions that offer the chance to get a sense of how it was. It can be helpful to start with one question and then move to another. The TLC[258] is an invaluable tool that can help to frame these reflections around groupwork skills and approaches.

We can have some challenging moments when teaching MBP groups, but if we can put things in place that support practice and reflection, they can sometimes prove to be rich sources of learning. They can change us as teachers from the inside out, and this invariably has a strong benefit for the group and the participants themselves.

---

258 Griffith *et al*, 2021: www.routledge.com/Essential-Resources-for-Mindfulness-Teachers/Crane-Karunavira-Griffith/p/book/9780367330798

Supervision

Issues affecting the MBP group are frequently brought to supervision sessions.

To explore this with our supervisor we can:

- Watch part of a recording of a session together.
- Explore some inner reactivity (sensations in the body).
- Generate some options for approaching the issue and the group differently.
- Inquire into regular practice and what it might be offering the teaching.
- Use the group animal exercise[259] to explore together what the group might need.

We bring our learning and growing edges in teaching MBP groups to supervision.

If groupwork is relatively new to us, it might be helpful to make a commitment with our supervisors to regularly look at the way we hold the group:

- at different stages of development
- in relation to overdeveloped/developing roles within the group
- in the context of challenging connections with individual participants
- at moments of trickiness and uncertainty.

Taking the group to the cushion

As MBP teachers, we may choose to take an individual group member who we currently teach 'onto the cushion' of our regular mindfulness practice. This intention might come to mind if there is some concern or lack of connection, or perhaps we feel we have been unskilful at some point. Equally, there may be times when we chose to bring the group as a whole to mind, maybe after a difficult session, or perhaps when there is a sense that the group needs something from us, as MBP teachers, that we have not quite connected with.

How might we do this? We explore some ideas around this in the next two chapters, but briefly here, we might simply bring the group or a group member to mind, remember the concern or issue we had and how that feels internally, and choose to breathe with any sensations that we find, bringing a kindly intention in on the breath for ourselves, the group and any individuals concerned. This may help to soften any tenderness around

---

259 See Chapter 9: Reading: body language

our teaching challenges, blending compassionate practice towards the individual, ourselves as MBP teachers, and the wider group as a whole.

Summary

"Inquiry is a skill that is an ongoing learning process."[260]

We find ways of cultivating our own style in the inquiry process that is flexible and responsive, staying in contact with what is happening on the inside (the MBP teacher's physical sensations), whilst holding the whole group in awareness on the outside. Horizontal and vertical inquiry are two styles of inquiry that can appear different, but which can also merge and flow into each other in a way that holds and facilitates the involvement of the whole group, yet explores the different layers of inquiry experience effectively, drawing out the learning for all.

In this last chapter within the holding section, we have been exploring ways of including, involving and holding the MBP group through different styles of inside out inquiry. Horizontal inquiry threads examples of the experience of practice around the group to facilitate inclusivity and normalise experiences amongst group members. Vertical inquiry focuses on one group member's practice experience in order to explore it more deeply to draw out the learning. Horizontal and vertical inquiry flow together, engaging the MBP group, sharing the sense of normalising, and cultivating inclusivity and shared learning within the group.

As MBP teachers, we learn to hold the group through awareness on the inside (body sensations, thoughts, etc) as we actively connect with, include, and are aware of the group on the outside. This chapter has included a section on facilitating the MBP group that explores the 'bottom up' inclusive process of drawing out experiential learning in order to maximise the participation of the group. As MBP teachers, we support this vital practice of holding the group through supervision, reflection, and personal practice.

---

260 Ibid. p59.

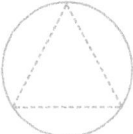

13. Online considerations

Gemma Griffith

In this chapter, we explore some of the practical skills needed to facilitate holding the group in an online environment. The other chapters in this book that focus on holding and launching the group are of course relevant to teaching online. There are, however, additional practical considerations for holding the group when teaching online, such as preparing participants, issues such as the participants having their cameras off or on, and the use of breakout rooms.

Some organisations have been running mindfulness-based programmes online for many years. In 2020 however, almost all MBP courses had to be quickly switched to be offered online due to the pandemic, and many MBP teachers (myself included) were surprised how rich the learning and connections in an MBP class could be. There are some evident differences between teaching online and teaching in person. This is especially the case when looking at the holding of the group, and how we create an online space which feels inclusive and supportive online, which, if done well, will facilitate participants' learning. It is important to clarify that the information in this chapter is specifically for teaching 'live' classes, with the whole group and teacher in the online space together, rather than courses that may be pre-recorded and offered online. In this chapter, we focus specifically on practical ways in which we can best hold the group online.

Preparing the group

When teaching online, it is important for MBP teachers to connect with individual participants, if possible, whether through an online orientation meeting or on the phone. This is to support the individual participants to take part as fully as they are able, and also to safeguard the container of the group, ensuring that, as far as is possible, people do feel part of a group that is learning together. Here we outline what participants need to know about equipment and safeguarding the space; this information can be offered in a written format as well as outlined in the orientation session.

Equipment

- We recommend that participants are reminded to join the teaching sessions using a laptop or desktop computer. Tablets and phones etc. are alternatives if a computer is not available, but their functionality is not as good, and therefore the individual may feel and be felt as not quite part of the group if they are unable to see everybody in the group on the screen at the same time, for example.

- It is good practice to check that participants test their internet connection, speakers, camera, and microphone before the session. This can be done as part of the individual orientation, during which potential issues can be addressed. For example if their face is difficult to see as they are sitting in front of a window, or are too close or too far away from the camera, suggestions could be given around moving position etc. so they are more visible to the group and can participate fully.

- At the start of each session we would encourage participants to check that the name on the screen matches their real name or the name they prefer to be called. This will help the group process.

The space

Participants may have quite different home contexts. This may range from those who live on their own or who can arrange to stay in a quiet place for the teaching sessions, to those with families, in shared accommodation, or with other caring responsibilities for whom this is much more difficult. Whilst acknowledging the challenges of finding a quiet space, it is helpful to suggest that participants find a dedicated space where possible (i.e. a room with a door), and to turn off any webpages that may distract them during the class, including work emails, etc.

For those that do not have a dedicated space, there are things they can do to help the holding of the container of the group. As MBP teachers, we might suggest that they try to arrange the following:

- Let people in their living space know that they are joining a teaching session, and ask, if possible, to keep any disruptions to a minimum.

- Wear headphones: this means that anyone sharing their living space cannot hear the teaching session. This is important for reasons of confidentiality; sometimes other group members may talk about their personal practice or similar, and it is important that this is not overheard by anyone else that they are living with.

- If possible, ask participants to make sure that anyone else in their space is not visible to the camera, or can be seen pottering around in the background. If there appears to be unknown people in the teaching space this can be challenging to others and may make the group boundaries unclear and break the safe 'container' of the group.

Teaching considerations

Practicalities

- Remind participants before each session what equipment or materials they need – such as sitting equipment/mats and pens and paper.
- Make sure participants have the log-on details handy so they can easily access them should they become disconnected.
- Share mobile phone details or email address so that participants can contact the MBP teacher should they be having internet connection problems or cannot log in.
- Ask participants to keep their microphone on mute unless specifically asked to do otherwise or unless they are in breakout groups. Remind participants that as MBP teacher, you may 'mute all' if there is a sound coming from somewhere. However, if they are 'muted' by their MBP teacher, they need to know that this is not personal, but has happened in order to ensure that the main focus of the session can be clearly heard by everyone.

Camera off or on?

This can be a controversial issue. Some MBP teachers insist on cameras being on at all times, and some are more flexible. In terms of the mindfulness-based group process, as MBP teachers, we might explain that it is preferable for participants to attend with their camera on all the time, if possible. Making this clear in the orientation and in any written documents that are sent out before the MBP starts is helpful, so that this is established as a norm in the group from the beginning. That said, there may be some circumstances that warrant exceptions either at the start or during the MBP course, such as a poor internet connection (turning a camera off can stabilise the connection so they can be heard more clearly), or participants who are not physically well enough to sit up to watch a screen, but who value listening and taking part. In these instances, it is important, with the participant's permission, to explain briefly to the group the reason why the camera is off. Also make a point of including those participants who are not visible or those with their cameras off to help them feel engaged and part of the group.

Camara off or on during formal practices?

It can help to be aware that some people may feel vulnerable lying down, sitting still, or moving with a camera on them, so for the formal practices it is possible to invite group members to keep the camera on, but give a choice as to whether they choose to sit in front of it. Depending on the group, it may be possible to offer a choice to even turn the camera off during formal practice, but taking care with how this is first introduced. In one of my classes in week one, I gave an open choice instruction (with trauma-sensitivity at the front of my mind) about how participants may choose to turn their camera off or on during formal practices, thinking that not many, if any, participants would actually do this. To my surprise, most participants then turned off their cameras for the first bodyscan practice which meant I had very little sense of how they were during the practice and the sense of the group practicing together was a little lost. This unfortunately then established a norm for the rest of the course, with most participants turning off their camera for the formal practices. I tried to encourage cameras on for practice numerous times for the rest of the course, but by then it was very difficult to get them out of this established habit and around half continued to turn their camera off during formal practices. So, what I now do is give a choice about angling the camera away from them if they so wish during a formal practice, rather than mention turning it off entirely.

Informal connections within the group

One of the downsides of online MBP groups is that there is little opportunity for participants to chat informally with other people in the group before and after the session unless the teacher makes arrangements to support this. In our experience participants find informal chat time helpful to make connections with other group members. Without making time for informal chats, the sessions can feel as if they start and end rather abruptly. It might be important therefore for the MBP teacher to find ways to help compensate for this. For example:

- Invite participants who would like to chat to arrive about 15 minutes before the class is due to begin, so they can be put into breakout rooms and have some time to connect together in small groups before the class begins. It is best to start this in week two: early enough on in the course to make this a regular option, but not before participants have had a chance to become acquainted. This can then be kept as an ongoing arrangement at the start of each session after that.

- At the start of every session, as a check in, group members might be asked to say something into the group. This could be quite brief – such as a word or phrase about how they are feeling that day. In this way, as MBP teachers, we can get a sense of what the group may need and be able to respond within the session accordingly. For example, if a number of participants report tiredness, extra movement practices can be included to help wake the body up – or the tiredness can be acknowledged as well as ways of working with this during formal meditation practice.

■ At the end of each session, group members might be encouraged to unmute their mic and say goodbye to the group, or to type any messages they may wish to make in the chat function. This is a way of everyone being invited to contribute to the ending of the session.

Breakout rooms

The use of small groups is vital to help build connections between participants, and breakout rooms allow us to do this when online. Many participants even say that some of the most meaningful interactions and learning on an online course took place when they were in smaller groups with fellow participants, and when no teacher was present. It may be that as many as 1-3 breakout groups are included in each session to help group members connect, and to keep participants actively engaged. Here are some things to consider when using breakout groups:

■ The use of breakout groups is particularly important in the first few sessions when the group is forming, so the group can begin to know other members of the group rather than rely on their connection with the teacher.

■ Do ensure that breakout groups are arranged with different people in them each time, so people have a chance to speak to everyone else on the course.

■ Give plenty of time for participants to speak together. It may take a couple of minutes for people to say hello and clarify the question, and we tend to go for around 10 minutes minimum for a breakout group (dependant on the task and how well the group know each other).

■ It is very helpful to give clear instructions about the questions to be discussed in the breakout rooms, putting any more complex instructions on a slide or in the chat box or in the broadcast function after they have joined the breakout room. This helps to give the MBP participants structure and clarity about what they are doing.

■ As MBP teachers, we cannot see what happens in a breakout room, so for safety reasons it may be best to have a small group size of at least three in the early weeks of the MBP. If people are placed in groups of two, there have been reports of participants feeling uncomfortable with just one other person, particularly if their partner is unwilling to engage that day. Towards the end of the course, when group members are known to us, and when participants know each other much better, breakout rooms of two may be suitable.

Adapting teaching exercises

Initially the absence of a flipchart may be very keenly felt, but as time passes and familiarity with the online platform increases, it may be possible to find many ways to adapt exercises so that they remain experiential and participative. For example:

- Using the whiteboard from the shared screen function allows the MBP teacher to annotate (add text or symbols) around a topic and include ideas from the group to be made visible to everyone.
- Holding paper up to the screen with one word or a picture on it is another way of sharing across the group – from group members to each other and to the MBP teacher
- Using PowerPoint slides, especially those that are colourful and relatively simple. The more complex and the more text on the slide, the less immediately accessible and participative it may be. These can also be annotated with text added as individual contributions from the group are offered.

Summary

Once we become more familiar with the online platform as MBP teachers, we may be pleasantly surprised with what is possible when teaching online. We may discover that many adaptations are possible, and whilst we may still miss the direct connecting that in-person MBP teaching offers, nevertheless MBP participants report rich experience of online shared learning, especially through the breakout rooms. As MBP teachers, particular care is needed when thinking about how best to hold and facilitate the online group process. This includes making time for informal connections between group members, ensuring everyone in the group can be seen and heard and so participate fully, and how to best use breakout groups.

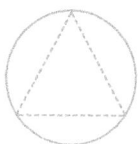

An interview with Pauline Gibbs

Pauline Gibbs is a Mindfulness Teacher and trainer in mental health, with over 25 years' experience of community projects in the voluntary and statutory sectors. She has been instrumental in introducing and developing various innovative and creative programmes in the UK within the NHS. Pauline recently set up MindfulBowl, London. Specialising in urban community settings and seldom heard voices, she is currently undertaking a project looking at the BPOC communities' access to Mindfulness in the UK.

Pauline is passionate about working with others in order to increase diversity among mindfulness teachers. She has been involved in this for quite a while. She started by speaking about her first introduction to mindfulness and how she came to realize that mindfulness complemented her contemplative Christian background very well.

Background: mindfulness

Pauline was first introduced to mindfulness around 2010 through an introduction to mindfulness course. She was interested to find that this course did not contradict her faith background. In fact, it helped her reconnect with her contemplative Christian faith.

> *"And I suddenly remembered who I was. I'm a contemplative Christian. I've done retreats. I've done silent practice for years. And I'd forgotten. I'd forgotten all of that side of me, and I suddenly remembered. And that's what the introduction to mindfulness reminded me of – me and who I was. It was so wonderful. Actually, I went and did the course again!"*

Following this, Pauline participated in an MBSR course and navigated the secular aspects of mindfulness practice with Buddhist ideas and her Christian faith, which helped her find her 'roots' alongside a community.

> *"And after a while, at the same time, I just really found I was becoming more and more rooted in who I am, and who I am as a Christian is at least half of who I am. I love my faith. I love what that means for me, and what I can then stand on with that. And I love coming together with others."*

Diversity within the mindfulness world

Pauline described her experiences within secular mindfulness and Buddhism as being mostly run by and with and for white people. She recounted a retreat she went to where the speaker talked about diversity but there was a distinct lack of it in the room. She shares how this felt to her.

> *"There's about 120 people there... And as he's talking about diversity, there were three non-white people there. Two of them were from Thailand, the other person was me. And I suddenly felt that this is just too much – even though this is an Eastern tradition being taught in the West. But there is no diversity here. At all."*

Inclusive teaching

A key question Pauline posed for white mindfulness teachers was to examine their social space and think about how their identity may offer them privilege. This recognition may then help them to 'open doors' to others.

> *"I'll ask you a question. What is it like to be white? What is it like to be English or French or American or whatever? What does that mean? It's these questions that we need to ask ourselves, because as a black person (and as black people) we're obsessed with these questions all the time – questions about our identity – and so we need to grapple with all of this... But most white people do not [think much about their identity]. So what is in your sphere of control? What are the seas that you're swimming in? My encouragement to you is to look at the seas that you're swimming in and ask yourselves, How can I make a difference in those seas? Can you make it possible for others to come and swim in here too? If you have access to the corridors that I (as a black woman) cannot get into? ... Where can you actually open doors? Where can you keep those doors open – and allow people to come through, whoever they might be?"*

Reaching diverse communities

Pauline thinks that secular mindfulness is difficult for some communities to access. She feels that active outreach programmes are needed to enable much better access. She thinks that listening closely to the people in these communities is our important first task.

"What [people involved in] mindfulness have done is that they've gone in with a colonial or a missionary attitude in how they deliver mindfulness. You need to go and listen first to what they tell you about their lives and what they need – and once you've understood that, you can be in a better position to offer mindfulness courses – but you need to go to them and not expect them to come to you."

Alongside listening and outreach, Pauline stressed how diverse representation among mindfulness teachers is key. Pauline knows of a few, but not many, other black mindfulness teachers. She spoke of how important it was to make training more accessible. She feels that lowering the expense of the training is one of the key elements to increasing diversity among mindfulness teachers.

"The thing that will be missing is that the people who deliver the teacher training look like you (white). So where are the black mindfulness teachers that are trained? Yeah, I am trained ... But black mindfulness trained teachers in this country? There are so few of us ... Let's look at what we can do to make it much more accessible so that people can see a viable training path. It is very expensive to train to become a mindfulness teacher."

As part of her work to increase accessibility and to support people from diverse backgrounds who want to train to be mindfulness teachers, at the time of the interview, Pauline was working with a charity (The Mindfulness Network) to deliver a level one mindfulness teacher training course that prioritised people from black, African, Asian, or Caribbean heritage.

"In 2022, we will be delivering a teacher training event to the BPOC community. And it will be our pilot. And the idea is to deliver this myself with support from the Mindfulness Network. So it's going to be accessible because that's my big thing! How do you make training accessible. The costs are being subsidised – this will help a lot. So that's exciting."

Pauline shared her long-term vision of how, as well as increasing the number of mindfulness teachers, it was important to have mindfulness teacher trainers from more diverse heritages.

"But we also need the trainers, so yes, first we teach them to teach ... but then we come to get to the next step to actually train them to

become trainers themselves. We need that so much if we are to succeed in having more BPOC teachers. So, my vision is pretty long term. It's going to take many years."

MBSR or MBCT do not explicitly cover social justice issues, and Pauline spoke of how it would be useful to include or adapt this so it is part of the curriculums, as well as having teacher-training organisations engaged in these issues.

"The other area that is so important to accessible/inclusive working is the element of social justice. For the future development of MBIs, this is essential and needs to be included as a part of their overall strategy (from governance, training to delivery). But in order to do this, we need to be listening to the communities we are engaging with as our first priority. What are they actually asking for? Do we understand the people and the lives of the communities we are engaging with? How do you work out what the needs and issues are?

My hope is that we will be working towards the day that we are able to develop MBIs that are holistic, and have social justice and systemic change at their core – and have MBIs that serve the community first, public systems second, and embody humility throughout."

Part Four:
Befriending the group

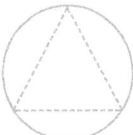

14. Befriending the mindfulness-based group

Trish Bartley

"Could a greater miracle take place than for us to look through each other's eyes for an instant?"[261]

Henry David Thoreau

In this chapter we explore the capacity of befriending as a practice to be cultivated and blended into every aspect of MBP teaching inside and out, that includes the personal practice of teachers themselves. In the chapter that follows this one, we move up close to what are called the Four Friends for Life[262], which bring a focus to the different qualities of befriending that we can cultivate.

Befriending is the final capacity within the inside out group model[263]. Befriending rests entirely on the intention to bring a friendly, appreciative, and caring attitude to the MBP group. It inclines us to engage the heart in our teaching. For this reason, it is best seen as a cultivation to be continuously developed, rather than a state to be achieved[264].

In the first capacity, Reading, we learn about the development of the group. There are theories that illuminate specific areas, and we can connect with existing MBP group research. Reading also moves us towards understanding some of the personal and social impacts that influence what group members bring with them into the mindfulness-based group. We look at the territory of body language and learn to read clues from participants about the group, and what it needs.

The second capacity, Holding, asks us to keep the group as a whole in our awareness as we teach. We learn to bring an embodied intention to hold all

---

261 Thoreau, 2016
262 van den Brink & Kostler, 2015
263 Griffith *et al*, 2019
264 Feldman, 2017

dimensions of the MBP, both inside and out. These involve the group, the individual participants, the programme and our own experience as teachers. Our purpose is to be ready to respond to whatever is needed, based on what we have sensed, read and understood. We are supporting the key enablers of safety and inclusivity within the group and their capacity to enable the learning of its members.

Befriending is the third and final capacity. We require each of these three capacities in every aspect of the teaching of MBP groups. However, in a very general way, we might say that Reading involves the mind, through understanding and applying some of the theories. Holding involves the body, in inside out embodying, awareness of the whole group, and a willingness to 'step forward' to support whatever the group needs. Befriending now includes the heart. In our original article, befriending was defined as "the practice of actively cultivating an attitude of compassion and friendliness to all experiences that arise while teaching (both inside and out)."[265] Underpinning all these three capacities is the mindful embodying of the MBP teacher.

As MBP teachers, we cultivate befriending towards all that arises on the inside within ourselves and the whole body-mind system, whilst at the same time cultivating befriending towards the mindfulness-based group members in the room or on the screen on the outside. Befriending accompanies holding with an attitude of friendly care and attention to all aspects of the MBP process, especially when our frailties and uncertainties, as MBP teachers, are making themselves felt. Indeed, the practice of befriending uncomfortable experiences is central to both personal and teaching practice. The first step is to notice the discomfort and that we do not want it, and then to become aware of the way we are pulled in different ways to try to avoid it. Finally, befriending enables us, as MBP teachers, to be able to stay with difficult experiences as they arise whilst teaching.

Befriending may come last of the three, but it has been there all along, threaded through all MBP teaching practice from the very beginning. It is included at the bottom section of the circle of the IOG model[266], representing how it underpins every aspect of teaching the mindfulness-based group. In this chapter we now explore befriending directly, by highlighting the need to bring intention to our work with MBP groups, in a way that is grounded and essentially caring and responsive. Authentic befriending brings an attitude of generosity, kindness, appreciation, and warm welcome. It starts as an intention and in time, with cultivation, becomes a congruent and integrated practice that flows into the group as an authentic way of being. In reality of course, these three 'capacities' are inseparable: reading, holding and befriending come together, with inside out embodying underpinning and supporting them all.

---

265 Griffith *et al*, 2019
266 Ibid.

Befriending overview

Befriending comes in many guises. As MBP teachers, we might first cultivate this through a warm welcome to people as they arrive at the start of the MBP. We set up clear ground rules with the intention of establishing boundaries that foster safety amongst participants. Later, as the group becomes more assured, qualities of friendly connection may move naturally into the MBP process and be as evident between group members as between teacher and participants. All these examples and many more are part of befriending. Befriending is not always soft and warm. At times, a stronger response may be needed when, for example, a group boundary is threatened. However, the intention behind this response is still aligned with establishing safety and inclusivity, and relating to experience inside the MBP teacher and out into the MBP group with care and kindness.

This cultivation of care and befriending is needed for all our teaching, in how we practice guiding and inquiry, and in the way we facilitate the involvement of the group in the curriculum exercises, small groups reflections, and whole group discussion. Sometimes, befriending might show itself in a glancing moment with a gentle look, or a tiny affirmation. At other times, a spacious, undemanding pause may be what is needed. Some of the kindest and most skilful inquiries can involve very few words. A moment can be held with the eyes, with a genuine acknowledgement of our shared humanity. "Yes, we all know this, don't we?" However, befriending is not something to plan or rehearse. As MBP teachers, we can only hold and renew our ongoing intention to teach in ways that embody kindness and care, knowing this is always what is most needed in the group.

Individual participants may well need specific befriending support at times. Some may struggle with the practice of mindfulness or perhaps connect with a troubling aspect of personal history. How we support them depends on the context of the group and what we agreed before the programme began. In some clinical programmes, external back up support may be available to individual participants. In courses open to the public, we might encourage group members to find a friend or family member to turn to. However, as MBP teachers, we are often best placed to offer friendly encouragement, as long as we are basing this on a mindfulness approach, and not straying into giving advice or providing a counselling role.

Befriending is inclusive

Earlier, we looked at the composition of MBP groups. We acknowledged that within the group space there may be people who appear confident and may readily contribute to group discussions. We might almost picture them in the 'centre' of the circle, inhabiting an assured 'mainstream' position.

There are also those whose presence may be quieter. They may feel isolated, as if there is no-one in the group quite like them, or they may naturally have an unobtrusive presence and enjoy listening more than speaking. As MBP teachers, one of our roles is to facilitate the participation of group members to bring about a healthy and equitable balance. There will always be folk who like to contribute more. Whilst this can be challenging when it becomes very pronounced, it can also be useful at times when there is a general hesitancy in speaking in the larger group. However, there are also times when it may be necessary to intervene, which in itself might be an illustration of caring for and befriending the whole group.

Whilst teaching on an intensive, online, mindfulness-based teacher training course of around 15 people, it was noticeable that the five men in the group were consistently contributing a lot more than the women. In most instances, when a discussion topic was aired in the large group, or when they were gathering themes from the breakout rooms, it was invariably one or more men who offered to feedback from the breakout group. About halfway through the sessions, during a reflective exercise, four of the men contributed one after the other and it was clear that the fifth man was getting ready to contribute next. The MBP teacher paused the process and gently asked the group if they had noticed any particular pattern to their discussion. After some contributions from the women that mainly related to the content of what had been said, the fifth man spoke up with, "All of us men have spoken one after the other and none of the women have had an opportunity to say anything yet". This gave the group a chance to reflect briefly on patterns of participation and whether gender had an influence in this group and in other groups in general. This took place without any blaming or shaming, and afterwards the balance of contributions was much more even, and the men seemed more aware of their part in the group as a whole.

As MBP teachers, we can seek to find ways of offering some gentle encouragement to those who seem to sit more on the edges of the group. This might come in the form of offering some friendly eye contact. We might acknowledge tiny gestures when they nod their agreement or smile at a comment made by someone else. We need to be appropriate with this, not singling anyone out for special treatment or exposing them in an obvious way, but finding subtle ways to look out for them, to hold them in awareness, offering a friendly helping hand when they look ready to say something. Reading the group is vital here, so that we are aware of patterns within the group, the stage of development it is at, and how individual group members seem to be finding the MBP.

As time passes and the group feels more comfortable, we often discover that those who tended to dominate the early sessions quieten down a little, and those who tended to be reticent at the beginning start to contribute a bit more. The MBP group as a whole is able to find its own balance in time. Individual differences can emerge and be included and respected once a safe group space has developed and group members feel included. Befriending has a big part to play in this.

Befriending may come last in the three capacities, but as we have said, it has been there all along. We learn to thread it into all of our teaching practice. Intention and integration are key to ensuring that befriending is authentic. In some contexts, and for some of us, this comes fairly easily. For others of us it may be more challenging. Much depends on our relational style, but even more on our practice. If we want to feel fluent in ways of befriending, the most effective way is to practice befriending ourselves and our own experience.

Befriending ourselves as teachers

We too need befriending as we teach MBPs, especially at times when we have been less than skilful or have said or done something that we really wish we had not. This can happen for us all, whether experienced or new to this work. A moment of thoughtless automaticity can quickly result in an unhelpful remark. The inner critic[267] then appears, ready to huff and puff and resume its ruminating. On these occasions, it helps to remember how normal this is, especially as a newish MBP teacher. We can notice and name the process: "Here you are again!" and do our best to substitute the inner critic for the learner, who is more discerning and supportive. We can reconnect with those core questions that remind us: "What is my intention in teaching this group? What it is that really matters to me in this work?" An adaptation of MBI-TAC known as the TLC[268] is a useful source of support for us as teachers. There is a section in the TLC where we can reflect on a challenging teaching moment in a non-judgemental way.

Supervision is another important support that hopefully offers a space to normalise painful moments and convert them into opportunities for rich learning and insight. Regular contact with our teaching peers and colleagues can help to build a supportive mutual space where there is potential to share safely and reflect together on the tender edges in our teaching roles.

"Being an MBP teacher asks a lot of us on a deeply personal level, and skilful engagement with reflective practice is key to our development."[269]

---

267 www.mindfulness-network.org/can-the-inner-critic-ever-be-a-help-a-mindfulness-teachers-perspective/

268 Griffith *et al*, 2021: www.routledge.com/Essential-Resources-for-Mindfulness-Teachers/Crane-Karunavira-Griffioth/p/book/9780367330798

269 Griffith *et al*, 2019.

Four Friends for Life

The following chapter offers some practices and teachings that help us to deepen our cultivation of the different aspects of befriending. Few of us as MBP teachers naturally and authentically embody befriending from the start of our MBP teaching practice (unless we had a pre-existing personal meditation practice that included kindness and care). However, there is value in reflecting on these befriending teachings and bringing them into formal and everyday practice, so that we can naturally and genuinely integrate them into our teaching of mindfulness-based groups.

Summary

Befriending is the last of the capacities in the IOG model[270], yet it has been there all along within mindful inside out embodying, reading, and holding. It brings qualities of the heart, of caring and kindness, into the MBP teaching practice, and is needed for all dimensions of the MBP including the individual group members, the mindfulness-based group as a whole, and the teachers themselves.

---

270 Ibid.

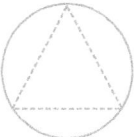

15. Befriending: four friends for life – kindness, appreciation, compassion and balance

Trish Bartley

"A valuable aspect of realising our common humanity is the cultivation of four emotional qualities that are boundless in their scope and exclude no one.... (We call them) .... the Four Friends for Life.'[271]

Erik van den Brink & Frits Kostler

This chapter moves up close to befriending, our last capacity in the IOG model[272]. Having looked at befriending in general terms in the previous chapter, we now explore some of the specific befriending qualities that as MBP teachers we seek to cultivate. We offer examples of ways that we can weave these into our teaching and into supporting us personally in our meditation practice outside the MBP. Eventually we might choose to foster an intention to embed these qualities fully into how we teach and how we live.

Roman Krznaric[273] defines empathy as "the art of stepping imaginatively into the shoes of another person, understanding their feelings and perspectives, and using that understanding to guide your actions".

Buddhist psychological teachings describe four modes of universal empathy that are called 'The Brahma Viharas', or Noble Abidings. We are indebted to Erik van den Brink and Frits Kostler for their secular translation of *The Four Friends for Life* that they have drawn from the Brahma Viharas[274]. We have made some slight adaptations to the ways that we articulate the different

---

271 van den Brink & Kostler, 2015
272 Griffith *et al*, 2019
273 Krznaric, 2015
274 Feldman, 2017

friends, which we call: Care and Kindness; Appreciation and Contentment; Compassion; and Grounded-ness and Balance. We see befriending as an overarching term that includes all four. We have included a number of recorded befriending practices - both a general overview and a recorded practice of each of the four friends for life. These can be downloaded at www.pavpub.com/teaching-mindfulness-based-groups-resources

It is important to emphasise that kindly befriending and mindful awareness are inseparable. It might be a great mistake for us to see the relational aspect of mindfulness practice as something extra to be added or in any way distinct or separate. Mindfulness is always kindly. Kindness, in the context of MBP teaching, needs present moment awareness to be wholesome and authentic. Without it, there is a risk of kindness becoming merely a technique or band-aid. To fully understand this, is to appreciate the centrality of the attitude that we bring to mindfulness teaching, for without the inclusion of kindly befriending, MBP teaching risks becoming dry, cerebral, disconnected and even cool.

Befriending speaks of our interrelatedness. We do nothing of value or worth on our own. This binds us to the narrative that joins the universal and the collective with the personal. The MBP is a place where this comes together in the group. Through developing a practice that involves the body, mind, and heart, we learn to care for our own experience, and through connection in the MBP group, we recognise and resonate with the experience of others, whether they are similar or different to our own. Relating, in this way, has been described as standing near, or coming alongside – which of course is the opposite of avoiding, ignoring, rejecting, or turning away.

A well-known anonymous saying (sometimes attributed to Albert Camus) speaks of what it is to be a friend:

'Don't walk behind me, I may not lead.

Don't walk in front of me, I may not follow.

Just walk beside me and be my friend'.

This illustrates the links we form in the MBP group space where we speak of 'we' and 'us' – rather than 'me' and 'you'. As MBP teachers, we may have more experience with the practice and understanding of the learning than our group members, but we are all vulnerable beings who struggle at times. There will never be a time when kindness is not relevant and necessary. However, as already mentioned, kindness is not a state to realize, but a cultivation to practice. We are told that whatever we cultivate will become the shape of our minds and the nature of our world. It may always be relevant to ask ourselves, "What am I cultivating in this moment?"

Perhaps we can approach the teaching of our next mindfulness-based group with an aspiration to relate to the group as if it were a microcosm of the entire world, which it is... and in doing so, intend for the MBP group to be the place where we develop kindly welcome, understanding, and empathy for ourselves and others.

The first friend for life: Care and Kindness

We start with the first friend for life which we call Care and Kindness. Care suggests a quality that involves protection and providing what is most needed. Care infers a gesture or an act that is free from harm. It asks for nothing back, so the offer of care is not motivated by any sense of reciprocity. Kindness is similar. The term suggests concern and consideration for the one we offer kindness to. Words like gentle, caring, and empathic might also come into our understanding of kindness. Some might want to include heartfulness when they refer to this friend for life.

We have been highlighting the value of including an intention to befriend the whole of the MBP – now we look at ways in which we can practice this. This relates to formal and informal practice – in the class space as we teach, outside in-between programme sessions, and in personal meditation practice.

Informal Brief Practices

During the MBP session – as teachers we might

■ internally wish the group well when we are holding the MBP process lightly, such as when the group is working in pairs or small groups.

This can help to soften our approach and reconnect with a sense of mindful, present moment awareness.

Outside the MBP sessions – we might

■ bring the group or a particular group member to mind and wish them well for a moment or two.

Formal Practice – we might

■ take the group to the meditation practice cushion throughout the eight-week programme, perhaps specifically bringing the group to mind at the beginning and at the end of the practice period[275] (sometimes known as 'bookending' a specific theme)

Words or phrases can serve as reminders, and we can choose our own words that support the context or special needs of the group we are teaching. If this approach appeals to you, you may decide to bring some words or phrases into your formal meditation practice – or equally you can use them silently in an informal way, for example on a walk or in a crowded area, or as you prepare for the session or during the session

---

275 This approach of bringing a particular focus to the beginning and the end of formal practice is sometimes known as 'bookending'.

itself. They help us to infuse different qualities into awareness and align us to the attitudes we wish to bring into our lives and into our teaching. It is important to understand that the purpose of these practices, however or wherever we do them, is to cultivate a connection with the quality we are focusing on. We are not seeking to feel anything in particular and if we find we feel very little, there is no need to have a sense of failure or inadequacy. We are simply aligning ourselves to qualities that connect us with befriending – and that in itself is enough.

There are different words or phrases that we might use to cultivate this first friend of Care and Kindness. Here are a few:

May the group be safe and well; May the group know peace; May the group rest in ease and kindness.

Or perhaps we can bring an internal well wishing to a specific group member inside or outside the teaching session.

Kim, may you be safe and well; Kim, may you be peaceful; Kim, may you rest in ease and kindness.

Whoever we cultivate this for, it is always important to include ourselves – perhaps the most challenging practice of all.

May I be safe and well; May I be peaceful; May I rest in ease and kindness.

If the phrases seem a bit cumbersome or unappealing, we can drop the phrases and use one a single word now and then, with a similar internal intention to wish well:

Safe; Well; Peaceful; Care; Rest; Ease; Kindness.

or any other word that speaks to you in this vein.

Remember that the words are just signposts – not to get us anywhere, but to help us anchor back into the intention to befriend.

Christina Feldman[276] encourages us to bring another phrase into this practice. This brings relatedness into these practices and links us to the context and present situation. We add the phrase '*In the midst of all this*' to any of those mentioned above, or to any of your own words or phrases.

In the midst of all this – care and kindness.

In the midst of all this – safe and well.

In the midst of all this – rest and peace.

There will be times when we do not feel as connected to a participant or the group as we would wish. Maybe there has been some storming or perhaps some trickiness. At these times, bringing this phrase into our befriending practice, whether formal or informal, in or out of the group, can deepen our

---

276 Feldman, 2017

intention to befriend (even if we do not feel anything as we are practicing this – maybe especially at those times).

In the midst of this – may we all be safe and well.

Many of us living within Western cultures are not used to cultivating kindness – especially towards ourselves. However, we can be reassured that the seeds of kindness already exist in us all. We have this potentiality waiting to mature and grow. The more that we cultivate this intention by bringing these qualities of friendliness and kindness into our teaching (and our lives in general), the more naturally they will be integrated. So, as best we can, we keep nurturing seeds of kindness, care, and warm relating – until they grow, woven into our very being. Remembering that our intentions to befriend need renewing, resetting, and adapting to changing contexts. It is all too easy, in the moment, to lose connection with care and kindness – much as it is to lapse into automatic pilot and forget to come back and be mindful.

As new MBP teachers, we are inevitably on the lookout for mistakes, and omissions. Much like our participants, attention lights up in the face of the difficult. It is so natural, when leading an inquiry and hearing about someone's pain or difficulty, to zero in and give the pain or thought a lot of detailed, and sometimes quite close attention. As we gain experience as teachers (and practitioners), we learn to shift this bias, into a more open, discerning and kindly awareness. Constancy of repetition is helpful – so that as we cultivate these intentions more often, for ourselves and the group, we are laying down new pathways. We are changing the shape of the habitual mind – moving from default reactivity into more skilful, kindly responding.

The phrases and words are reminders that we can also use internally as we are teaching, to connect with a sense of friendliness for yourself and the group, and be aware of the contact of the body with what it is resting on:

■ when we are up at the flipchart, waiting for someone to contribute
■ when guiding a practice during a natural pause between phrases
■ when the small discussion gatherings are happening

Remembering that cultivating kindly intentions are powerfully inclusive.

As we hold a group through the eight weeks of the MBP – we may choose to connect with an aspiration of relating to the current group as if it is linked to all other groups, also sitting in circles or joined on screens – exploring experience through the practice of mindful awareness. There has never been a better time for kindly awareness in the world.

In the midst of all this – may we all be safe and well.

The second friend for life: Appreciation and Contentment

We now move to the second friend for life – which offers us a focus on appreciation and contentment. In the Buddhist teachings of the *Brahma Viharas*, this is known as *Mudita*. Traditionally this comes third of the four – however we have chosen to take appreciation, sometimes referred to as appreciative joy, before compassion. We do this because appreciation and joy are especially resourcing[277] and will ready us for the third friend for life, which is compassion.

This second aspect of befriending speaks of happiness, of joy, and even of deep contentment. Appreciation lifts the heart and lets it sing, in moments when group learning is evident, connections are deepening, or when there is some shared laughter. Perhaps a sense of the befriending that we have been cultivating, joins with appreciation for the courage of the human spirit, and this can naturally morph into moments of inner joy. There is much to appreciate in the MBP group – every time someone explores their experience and discovers something new that will resource their lives – every time there is a ripple of shared understanding in what is being experienced. These are the moments when appreciation may be revealed. We spoke in the last section of friendliness, spilling out and being threaded through the group. In the same way, there are opportunities to sense the goodness and contentment in what is unfolding in the MBP – and see this ripple around the circle. We may find this happens naturally through the presence and humanity of the group.

As MBP teachers and practitioners, we know well that intentions to befriend do not necessarily come easily. It is part of human nature to fixate on the negative, and to let the door open to the inner critic, wishing things were better or different. It helps so much to look at the bigger picture. We know that all experience is in the process of changing. Nothing stays the same. We can have one MBP class where things seem to go beautifully. We leave the room at the end of the session and feel great joy that we are involved in doing this work and that the session has gone so well. Then the very next week, we meet again and somehow there is awkwardness and edginess in the group, and a lack of flow in us as teachers. Even so, can we appreciate that this is the way of things? Things change – and next week will be different again. Opening into the bigger picture that the group is still developing, that the practice and the learning is still happening, and that all the glitches that happen along the way are simply an inevitable and often useful part of the process.

So when an MBP session does not go as we would have wished, rather than switching off and choosing not to dwell on it, a useful exercise for MBP teachers could be to reflect on all who have helped us on this journey as

---

277 Much appreciation for my learning around this and many other teachings to Christina Feldman and Yuka Nakamura for their Brahma Viharas online retreat for the Bodhi College in 2021.

mindfulness teachers. Those who have taught us, those who have taught our teachers, the books, the retreats, the exchanges with colleagues, and all the participants that we have taught. They all contribute to the MBP teacher that we are now. The teachers who have taught us have been generous in sharing their skills and knowledge. This generosity illustrates the fact that we cannot do this work on our own. Throughout our lives, we are beholden to the incredible generosity of many beings.

> *"Before we leave home in the morning, we are already indebted to half the world."*[278]

> Martin Luther King

How many of us have lost a capacity for delight? Perhaps exhaustion and over busyness have contributed to a seemingly incessant feeling that we are not enough. We can find ourselves unfavourably comparing 'my' teaching with 'her' teaching, or this MBP group with the one before. What if we chose instead to cultivate appreciation by reflecting on the group soon after the end of each session? Perhaps we could deliberately remember some moment of ease, in us or the group – the moments of beauty, the times when there was connection and flow. By framing an intention to appreciate the lovely, we are befriending the MBP. And as with the cultivation of kindness, this will naturally flow into the group in time. It may even start in the group when someone speaks of their appreciation for being on the programme and belonging to the group.

Outside the MBP classroom, we can practice appreciating the ordinary – what is there under our noses – such as small moments of calm and steadiness. Spending time in nature can resource us and uplift the mood of mind, which can help us reconnect with an intention to teach for the benefit of others. In time, and with this ongoing cultivation, we will find joy and appreciation beginning to grow. And with this, we find integrity that does not focus on 'me' and 'mine' but includes a collective interrelatedness, of 'we' and 'us', where there is rich potential to appreciate and enjoy.

As we did before, it can help to have some phrases to remind us of our intention to cultivate appreciation and joy – to bring into personal practice, informally and internally whenever a suitable moment arises.

---

278 King, 1984

Practice of appreciation and contentment

In the midst of this, may I be joyful
May I be grateful for the opportunity to be doing this work – however it is going.
May I cultivate contentment

There are often spaces in the quiet moments of an MBP session – when we can appreciate the group. A gap in the teaching; or when the small groups are working – we can sit and gently appreciate the work that they are doing, the connections they are making. We can formulate a wish that this continues well for them.

May I appreciate what is here
May I feel joy in this work and in these people
In the midst of this, appreciating the good.

The third friend for life: Compassion

Compassion has become a mainstream term. An acquaintance of mine, who works for a large statutory health body, mentioned somewhat cynically that it greatly helps your chances when being interviewed for a job to use the word 'compassion' a number of times. At the other extreme, I remember hearing a talk many years ago that emphasised how rare true compassion actually is.

We learn from Buddhist teachings that compassion has two distinct aspects. One is *Anukampa*, which describes the poignant feelings we experience when we are touched by the suffering of others. This is often referred to as 'the trembling of the heart'. The second is called Karuna, when empathy moves into action, motivated by the wish to reduce suffering. These are the two sides of compassion, and we need both.

> *"At the heart of compassion is the invitation to turn toward suffering."*[279]

It is interesting to note that poignancy can arise when moved by the lovely and also when suffering or pain is present. We can feel touched by seeing or hearing something that is very beautiful, as well as by an experience that is very sad. The poignancy for the lovely relates to 'the second friend for life' – that of appreciation and joy. The poignancy that we feel when seeing or hearing about pain and suffering, connects us to compassion. These two are very interlinked. They seem to emanate from quite different encounters – yet easily overlap. A really lovely experience can quickly transform into one of sadness and a sense of loss that it may never happen again.

We are more likely to feel this empathic resonance when faced with the suffering of others. Our own suffering more easily moves us into reactivity, unless we cultivate compassion for ourselves. However, whether the

---

279 Feldman, 2017

suffering is our own or others, in order to act with compassion, we need to be well resourced – and this resourcing comes from renewing a sense of well-being and kindness, the first friend for life. When we feel exhausted or burnt out by the difficulties around us, within us, or within the group, we need to move back to the practice of kindness, offering ourselves reminders:

In the midst of all this, may I be safe and well,

In the midst of all this, may I rest in ease and kindness.

In the midst of all this … Safe. Well. Ease. Kindness.

As MBP teachers, it is not uncommon to feel burdened at times, with all that we hold in the group and in our lives. Failing to resource ourselves and pushing through in an attempt to force compassion, when all we feel is empty and numb is what is often termed as 'compassion fatigue'. Writing at this time, during the Covid-19 pandemic, it is clear that many front-line workers and carers are exhausted from many months of intensity. Their capacity for compassion is bound to be compromised. In a situation like this, when we move close to suffering, we can find ourselves quite closed down. We might also find this in a group member who describes themselves as feeling disconnected and separate from the rest of the world. It may be a time to gently acknowledge and widen out into the group and ask, '*does anyone else experience something like this?*' It is profoundly comforting to normalize experience – to connect with others and hear that they too can resonate with what has been described. In that moment, the isolation of blame and judgement is removed, and the possibility of interconnection is present.

Cultivating a sense of compassion, using similar contexts and times as we did with the previous two friends for life, we might use phrases such as:

May all beings find healing.
May all beings find peace.
May we all rest in care and compassion.

In the midst of all this, may I find healing.
In the midst of all this, may I know peace.
In the midst of all this, may I rest in care and compassion.

Once more, we are planting seeds of intention – this time to bring compassion to distress and difficulty. Compassion opens us to connect with 'others like me', 'others like us.' Using these reminders helps us stay connected with a wider sense of humanity and all that is happening in the world. We are practicing a willingness not to be indifferent. We are opening ourselves intentionally to be touched. We have no knowing how one person's suffering affects them, but compassion can be offered to the whole spectrum of suffering. It may be the person in the group that we feel most connected to. It may be the person we feel least connected to. Practicing in this way facilitates connection, especially with those we find hard to feel close to. We may not be able to feel truly caring for all our participants – but we can stand beside them and appreciate their struggles and feel compassion for their suffering. In time, as with the other qualities, the practice goes wider. We find that we can offer compassion to those we hear or see on the news, who are going through very difficult situations. We can reflect on what we can do to befriend our own struggles.

If we protect ourselves from the pain of others, we will not be able to befriend our teaching or the group when we encounter distress and pain in a group member. Compassion in action is more enduring than an emotion, which by its nature is bound to change. We may connect with a felt sense of compassion at times – and at others, feel very little connection at all. However, the feelings are not so important. What matters is a commitment to the intention to befriend whatever is arising in the moment in the MBP group. We practice turning towards and 'standing close' to respond to the difficult in a wise, kindly, compassionate and even fearless way, as best we can. It is a big ask – but one that we cultivate with each group that we teach, and each time we sit on the practice cushion.

When Jon Kabat Zinn gave a talk at an early CMRP conference at Bangor University many years ago, he spoke of his wish that people starting to teach MBSR might take a vow similar to the Bodhisattva vow, or perhaps something like the Hippocratic oath 'to do no harm', that medical doctors used to take. This inspired me at the time, and it touches me still – to vow to teach and practice in order to bring suffering to an end. It is an impossible aspiration, but it is an inspiring intention – and it is valuable to be reminded that this is not about 'me' and the calibre of 'my' teaching. This invites us to step into the role of MBP teacher as fellow practitioner, who is sharing a priceless resource that supports well-being. This also changes the focus that many teachers can experience, of not feeling 'enough' as teacher and practitioner, to doing what we can in this moment and the next.

We may notice that the heart seems to tremble most easily when we see images of suffering blameless people on the television or when we read something that has happened in the news. It can be much more challenging when faced with someone we have felt irritated by or frustrated with. It helps to remember that compassion rests on kindness and involves us in being willing to untie the internal knots and squabbles, the pulling away, and wanting things to be different. We may not manage to offer a compassionate response to everyone, but we can do our best to practice befriending inside and out – and not just with those we consider deserving. We can only start where we are – with a willingness to widen into awareness of a bigger picture and perhaps a new perspective.

A question we might ask ourselves in moments of challenge, uncertainty or difficulty, is what does this moment need?

Jim had been forced to retire early after getting cancer. He said that if anything could have gone wrong with his treatment it did. He described feeling flat most of the time. In the group, he often spoke in an angry resentful tone. It wasn't clear what he was getting from the programme – and as his MBP teacher, I felt unsure and anxious around him and was concerned about the effect he was having on the rest of the group.

I took my concerns to supervision. We agreed that what Jim needed most from me was compassion and kindness – so I spent time that week taking him onto my cushion in my personal practice, opening my heart to him and wishing him well. At some point, during the following session, Jim looked animated in a way I had not seen before. He wanted to tell us about his chickens. "I just stood there and watched them", he said. "I noticed my heart beating regularly, feeling quite good and strong – and my belly seemed warm and comfy. It felt almost good to be alive! I've not felt like that for a long while". I remember being quite amazed. I vowed to practice in that way more often!

The following week Jim looked awful. In due course, he shared with the group that a fox had got in and killed all his chickens. The group were clearly touched by his distress – and in different ways showed much care for him. He continued coming for the rest of the programme and became a leading light in the group – held in much affection by the others. He taught me a lot.

The fourth friend for life: Groundedness and Balance

In traditional Buddhist teaching, this quality is called equanimity. It includes and incorporates the other three qualities of kindness, appreciation, and compassion – and integrates them into the embodying of mindful awareness. As with the other friends for life, equanimity is a practice we need to cultivate for ourselves as teachers and practitioners. It is a little different from the other three – and needs them to warm it up, or there is a risk that it becomes distant, and cool. This is especially relevant as we support the group in launching and settling. Kindly equanimity is just what the group needs to feel safe enough to form connections – and over time, what MBP group members need as practitioners themselves.

The cultivation of equanimity appears right at the beginning of the eight-week course. For example: the body scan starts with an invitation to become aware of the contact points of the body with the floor. This cultivation of connecting with grounded-ness is core to equanimity. This is also evident in the brief grounding practice of feet on the floor, which we often introduce early in the first session to help participants settle. In fact, the cultivation of equanimity is at the root of all the practices that we share with our participants. In fostering the habit of 'coming back', whenever the mind wanders, we learn to establish an anchor – often in the breath, or some specific location in the body, such as the feet, the hands, or the seat. This proves foundational to the practice of mindful awareness within all formal and informal practice. In turn, this supports an abiding cultivation in the group that promotes steadiness, stability, and trust.

Within this, we are using qualities of grounded-ness and balance to describe this fourth aspect of befriending. Equanimity is not a word that is generally used in modern parlance, and equanimous even less – whereas grounding and inner balance suggest processes (rather than states) that we can easily understand and associate with, and they offer us gateways to understanding equanimity.

The Properties of a Mountain

The metaphor of the mountain is very helpful when exploring the quality of equanimity. Mountains have essential characteristics of being grounded and stable. They stand out on the horizon to display their shape, peak or peaks. They seem to have an enduring quality of remaining naturally constant, whatever changes are happening around them. However, when we look a little more carefully, it is their connection to the ground that enables them to be so stable and constant. In fact, as is often articulated in the 'mountain meditation practice' (first developed by Jon Kabat Zinn[280]), it is hard to separate the base of the mountain from the crust of the earth. They are so rooted into what they were once formed from, that it is impossible to tell what is the start of mountain and what is the ground that surrounds it.

This suggests that the quality of the mountain is not just calm – but also has a sense of abiding. Calm abiding. Grounded inner balance that is stable and enduring. This may be a helpful inspiration to hold in mind and body, amidst all the happenings in the MBP group and programme. As with the other friends for life, grounded-ness and balance is not a state to be achieved, but a cultivation to be practiced many times, over and over. The mountain has many challenges to 'manage' in order to maintain its calm abiding quality. The seasons rolling one after another bring different conditions of temperature, humidity, air pressure, rain or snow fall, wind and so on. Strong weather often converges around the mountain attracting thunder and lightning, storms, and wild winds. Sometimes thick mist descends and much of the mountain appears to disappear. However, all these different conditions do not affect the core stability of mountain. As the mountain meditation practice helpfully reminds us – "through it all, the mountain just sits". We can learn much from mountains.

This poem was composed by an MBP participant. It speaks of this quality which is referred to here as 'Mountain Man'.

---

280 Kabat-Zinn, 1994

Buffalo

Still they come, my thoughts
Trampling like a herd of buffalo
Through the green prairie of my mind
Leaving their black footprints in the smooth pasture

But I am Mountain Man
They do not scare me now
And I watch them moving by
With no more than passing interest

Geraint, 2009[281]

This poem infers that the mountain has a wide-open view and is able to see thoughts as buffalo, passing through the 'green prairie of the mind'. Relating this to the teaching of MBP, grounded-ness suggests strong support from the earth beneath. The connection with the ground offers a way of experiencing the energy of gravity that is drawing the weight of the body down. Balance suggests height, inner steadiness, and possibly even stillness at times – and a sense of open perspective and wide panoramic views. We can take in the bigger picture of the 'storms' when they arrive, the lovely moments of balmy weather, the different patterns of light and shadow playing across the faces of the group. From a centred, grounded place of inner balance, we can choose to see it all as the passing 'weather' of the group on the outside – and the passing 'weather' within each one of us as teachers, on the inside. Things come and go – and then something else appears. And through it all, our practice is to come back to embodied awareness, grounded and balanced as best we can – allowing things to be as they are.

There is a quality of constancy in equanimity. It suggests a trustworthy intention that whatever happens, we choose to come back home to be 'mountain man' which includes a warm heart of kindness. The term of equanimity also involves the notion of equalness – to be equally near all experience, whether pleasant or unpleasant – and equally near all people, whether we experience them as pleasant or not so pleasant. This is a huge undertaking! However, balance and perspective may help us here. Yesterday's lovely sunny moment is lost in today's rain shower. Both have their place in the wider scheme of 'weather'.

In the same way, it is not unusual for the pleasant participant who arrives with smiling enthusiasm at the start of the MBP to become the person in the group who gives us most challenge by the mid-point in the programme. We learn to notice our personal preferences and biases (for we all have them) – and as best we can, become aware and find ways to discover a middle ground between the extremes of wanting and not wanting things to be a certain way. We know that it is in our psychological DNA to give more

---

281 With many thanks to Geraint's widow Bridgette, who has kindly gifted TB this poem

attention to what is going wrong than what is going well. Remembering this as part of the human condition, we reconnect with our intention to befriend the moment with whichever 'friend' serves us best – and wisely we might start with a sense of grounded-ness and balance.

Equanimity is usually experienced as meditative and peaceful. It stabilises the other qualities of befriending – care and kindness, appreciation and contentment, and compassion – by grounding them in a way that is centred and 'earthed'. When things are going well, it is easier to be steady and find balance. However, when an MBP group is proving to be especially challenging, equanimity helps us avoid being sucked into the extremes of hopelessness and despair. It also protects us from becoming sentimental and overly pleased when things go well. Perhaps we can learn to be a little less involved – not in a way that is distant or cool – but by taking things less personally. It is not so much about *my* MBP group – although inevitably as teachers we have a significant role. It is much more about the group itself, the programme and all those who have contributed their learning and wisdom. This brings in the context of the MBP and all the implicit and explicit elements that impact on the success or otherwise of the outcomes for the group.

An MBP teacher who practices balance and poise may be better able to choose what is best in this moment – and find possibility in resting in not knowing. Many of our teachers and mentors commend 'not knowing' to us. Finding steadiness within not knowing allows for openness and gentle spontaneity. It can sometimes enable the most profound teaching practice of all.

We have phrases for the qualities of inner balance and grounded-ness for use in formal and informal practice. We might also use them as an intentional programme of practice over a period of time – or at particular times when teaching we can recite these phrases internally, perhaps at a pause place in the group.

May I cultivate inner balance and steadiness
May I accept things as they are
May I rest in not knowing

In the midst of all this, calm and ease
In the midst of all this, equalness with all things
In the midst of all this, grounded-ness and balance

May I rest with a peaceful heart in the midst of all this.

'*Out of the soil of friendliness grows the beautiful bloom of compassion, watered by the tears of joy, sheltered beneath the cool shade of the tree of equanimity*'.[282]

Longchenpa 1308-1363

282 John Peacock's translation in Feldman, 2017.

Summary

We have been exploring the cultivation of the Four Friends for Life:

- Care and Kindness
- Appreciation and Contentment
- Compassion
- Grounded-ness and Balance

As they relate to us as MBP teachers, both during the sessions themselves and to support our personal practice – formal and informal.

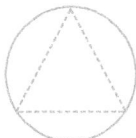

16. The ending of the mindfulness-based group

Trish Bartley

"In due course, after the poems have been read, we close the session. Taking our seats and coming to the breath, we link with everyone in the group for the last time... this moment marks the end of the course. We invite everyone to notice how this feels – and to connect with an appreciation of all the group has offered, wishing all group members well. Widening out, we offer our good wishes to loved ones who have made it possible to be here, and all those we know who are having tough times. Finally, we play with the possibility that this heart connection that we've gained through the group and our good wishes can reach down the corridors of the hospital and touch everyone who lies ill in bed. The sound of the bells closes our course and our final practice."[283]

In this last chapter, we consider the implications of the ending of the mindfulness-based group. It is interesting to notice how much emphasis we give to beginnings and, in comparison, how little we give to endings. In this chapter we look at how we might mark the last meeting of our mindfulness-based group and what needs to have led up to this last session to support an effective ending. We look at the use of ritual, and what specific processes might be helpful. As has been famously suggested by Jon Kabat-Zinn[284] and T.S. Eliot[285] no less, endings are also beginnings. We consider the potential for the interrelational skills and collaborative learning gained in the MBP group to move out into other contexts and networks – and how as MBP teachers, we might support that process.

---

283 Bartley, 2012
284 Kabat-Zinn, 2013
285 Referred to in Little Gidding (section V) in The Four Quartets. Eliot, 1963

Attitudes to endings

It may help to know that many people try to avoid endings, especially those that involve loss and uncertainty. If the mindfulness-based group has been successful, and if connections in the group that have been valued and offered rich learning, then a sense of loss at the ending of the group may be keenly felt by some people. This anticipated loss is bound to link with other losses, especially for those who have experienced recent or traumatic bereavements, relationship breakups, and any existing uncertainties, such as a change of job. Even if none of these are relevant, many group members may have found the sessions to be an anchor in their lives and the absence of this will be felt, especially at first.

For us, as MBP teachers, when a group member mentions at some point (even as early as at the halfway review in week five) that they will miss these Monday evenings or whenever they are being held, it is very tempting to reassure the group. We might find ourselves saying, "Not to worry, there will be chances to reconnect at follow up sessions". I am sure that many of us have made these sorts of remarks. I certainly have!

However, instead of offering reassurance, we might look at this as an opportunity not to discount the significance of the group and its ending, but to turn towards it and perhaps invite the group to reflect on what this ending might mean to each one of them – acknowledging the tendency to avoid goodbyes. We may find that by inviting the feelings in, whatever they are, that we are embodying a gentle turning towards what we tend to pull away from. In doing this, we can invite the group to acknowledge and feel their feelings in safety, held by the container of the group and by us, as MBP teacher. This allows group members to be able to express appreciation for each other, the group, the MBP process and teacher, and even for the practice of mindfulness itself. They can share what the experience has meant to them and fully own that, to take forward into whatever comes next.

Marking the ending: rituals and processes

In order to facilitate and appropriately mark the ending of the MBP group, many teachers employ rituals that we have developed and refined over time. I have heard of many examples:

- giving and sharing tiny jewel stones or pebbles (sometimes personally collected from the seashore with the group in mind)
- inviting group members to choose a little card that has a mindful saying on it
- giving out a small plant to each group member (which sounds lovely but unfortunately plants die, which may not be such a helpful memento!)
- sharing a simple thread bracelet with a bead on it.

The process of giving can be turned into a bit of a ritual if the group is meeting in person – for instance: as the bowl of objects gets passed around, each group member in turn might choose one of the objects for their neighbour and then pass the bowl on, for this to be repeated all the way round the circle. The MBP teacher might suggest that, as the object is chosen for each individual, it is coming as a gift or a blessing from the whole group, signifying good wishes from them all. All these little objects offer a way of capturing some aspect of the shared experience that can be taken away in material form: a stone in the pocket to touch and turn over in the hand; a saying to read and remember how it felt to sit in the group and practice together. Often it is not as specific as that – it may just capture a vague sense of remembering and reconnecting with something they valued.

Some MBP teachers invite their group members to write letters to themselves. This might include personal good wishes for the future (including their practice). This can capture some aspects of the MBP experience that they might want to remember, their intentions going forward for themselves personally, and their activities in the wider world. These letters then get posted back to each of them by their MBP teacher, some months down the line. This letter-writing tradition was first cultivated by early Mindfulness-Based Stress Reduction teachers in the US. Some teachers have adapted this into writing on postcards.

There are many other ways to mark the ending of a group. We used to have a mini party with MBCT for Cancer groups, to celebrate all that they had achieved in staying with the eight weeks of the course. Group members are invited to bring in small amounts of food or little nibbles (invariably finishing up as a veritable feast), and I would bring non-alcoholic fizzy drink for us all to toast the group with. Participants had been invited to write a poem about what mindfulness has meant to them as part of their home practice in week seven. They would protest that this was impossible to achieve and then many of them produced some stunning examples[286] that were read out during the 'party'. This was often an intimate process which needed courage and new creativity – yet most chose to do this. The process invariably feels meaningful.

In the service of what comes after the mindfulness-based programme

It is all too easy to forget that the whole point of the MBP, or even a brief taster session, is in service of what comes *after* the sessions have finished. As MBP teachers, we facilitate the learning of our group members in the hope that they will find ways to sustain their mindfulness practice in

---

286 Many are included in Bartley, 2012 and Bartley, 2017

everyday life – so that they make choices that resource them to manage difficulty and stress, and find ways to enjoy and appreciate what is wholesome and meaningful.

As we mentioned in the first chapter, the value of the MBP group might be realized long after the group has finished. There are two ways of looking at this. Firstly, the MBP group experience is often internalized, so that when individual group members practice mindfulness after the group has ended the group may come to mind. For example, when lying down on the floor engaging in a body scan practice, memories may naturally arrive of how it was to practice body scan with others in their group. If this is helpful, the former group member may well fold this into their practice on a regular basis. It can be tremendously supportive in continuing their individual practice to co-opt a sense of group support around them.

> "I was amazed at how much any awkwardness was diffused in the first session. The group was lovely; I felt invested in their future, not needing chapter and verse of their lives, but with a huge sense of wishing them well. Listening to the voice on the CDs always recalls the warmth and the positivity of the sessions."[287]

Of course, we cannot assume that all MBP groups are successful in supporting learning and connection – but the vast majority are, if as MBP teachers we have been able to care for the group in ways that support safety, inclusivity and kind, embodied presence. When we find ways of ending the MBP group congruently, learning has a chance of being integrated, and future intentions for sustaining practice can be shared in the group. It is then that the experience of connection can be acknowledged and honoured so that the group itself continues to support what follows in many ways, both direct and subtle – rippling out into aspects of group members' lives, possibly for a long time to come.

Summary

The ending of the mindfulness-based group needs some thought and care, perhaps with the use of personalised rituals or specific processes designed by the MBP teacher that serve to acknowledge what the group has offered during the learning, and to capture the sense of connection between group members. It can be helpful to acknowledge that endings are beginnings, and that the experience of having been in the MBP group may support ongoing personal mindfulness practice to benefit life beyond the group.

---

287 From Bridget's personal story – a participant in 2009 – and included in Bartley, 2012.

Conclusion

"Be patient towards all that is unsolved in your heart and try to love the questions themselves like locked rooms and like books that are written in a very foreign language. Do not now seek the answers, which cannot be given you because you would not be able to live them. And the point is, to live everything. Live the questions now. Perhaps you will then gradually, without noticing it, live along some distant day into the answers." [288]

Rainer Maria Rilke

We have covered a lot of ground in this book, and yet there is so much more to explore. This is the inspiration of groups – especially those rooted in mindfulness practice. This conclusion draws some threads together. We hope that what we have shared will support your teaching practice, generate your reflections, and turn up the volume of the group in MBPs. There is always further to go; deeper into the questions such as that Rilke invites of us above, and deeper into living the questions, which in time offer us meaning and connection.

We purposely designed the Inside Out Group (IOG)[289] model to be straightforward to remember. We want MBP teachers to hold a sense of the model as they teach, with the capacities of inside out mindful embodying, reading, holding, and befriending. Each of the capacities relies on and relates to the others. They are interdependent. We have attempted to flesh out the model and explore the practice and process issues in a bit more depth than was possible in the IOG paper[290]. Gemma Griffith in her chapters[291] shared some valuable knowledge about what we know thus far about mindfulness-based groups, how the pedagogy of MBP groups has developed, and what others have shared that is relevant around the theory of groups and the way they develop over time. We hope that this book makes a worthwhile contribution to the MBP group body of literature – and that the theory that we have included informs the teaching practice, just as the teaching practice we have written about is informed by embodied and grounded qualities of the heart.

We offer two questions to kindle reflections as we conclude this book.

1. **What are you taking away?**

    As you have been reading, what has landed with you that you want to remember and choose to take away with you? Reflecting back on your

---

288 Rilke & Norton, 1934.

289 Griffith *et al*, 2019 : https://link.springer.com/article/10.1007/s12671-019-1093-6

290 Ibid.

291 Gemma's chapters referred to here are Chapter three - The evolution of pedagogical theory, Chapter four – The research, and Chapter seven – Reading the mindfulness-based group (theory).

motivation for reading this book, have your learning aspirations been met, and how might you capture them now in order to inform what you want to take forward into your teaching?

2. **What are your next steps in relation to teaching mindfulness-based groups?**

    It may be that what you take from this book is not new at all but confirms the significance of what you already know. This can be very rewarding learning. However, for newer MBP teachers, it might be worth going through the different parts of the IOG model to see what you might want to investigate further. Have you found any new emphases that you wish to capture and bring into your teaching? Is there one capacity that needs a little more developing that you might explore as a theme in supervision?

    Whatever you draw out of this book, we encourage you to blend your new learning into existing skills, resources, and experience with groups and with MBPs. And from that mix, do what makes sense, has coherence, and fits with a rationale for the context and the people that you are teaching. Our intention for this book is that it will serve to nurture your reflections, questions, and ideas, rather than be a textbook that suggests how things ought to be done.

New priorities

We have sought to open doors to important developments that relate to social and environmental agendas. If these matter to you, it may be worth reflecting on how you can harness the potential of your mindfulness-based groups to engage with these issues. There seems to be a number of approaches (and there will be more we have not thought of):

■ We can learn to integrate contextual issues into the curriculum exercises, routine activities, and everyday mindfulness examples (such as choices around food, exercise and active transport; recycling, caring for and enjoying nature; reaching out to people from different communities etc.). The mindfulness-based group will naturally generate ideas that are relevant to these and offer support to help put new behaviours in place.

■ We can include material from social agendas and incorporate these explicitly into the MBP itself – perhaps by offering programmes (for example in a climate change context along the lines of Bruce Barrett's team Mindful Climate Action programme[292]). The group will again be an important source of inspiration, learning and mutual support.

■ We can also facilitate reflective discussions in either of the formats above, around what the group itself has offered the process of learning

292 Barrett *et al*, 2016

mindfulness together. This would bring explicit awareness of the various group skills to light (by the group itself) – and how they may serve them in their families, networks, communities, and social action groups (if they are involved in them).

And finally...

We hope that this book has offered some answers. We also hope that it has generated some reflections and asked some questions. Most of all we hope that it has kindled an interest in the vast potential of the mindfulness-based group, so that the ripples from your groups can spread out far into individual participants' lives and out into the world, benefitting connections wherever they are made.

> *"We are made for goodness. We are made for love. We are made for friendliness. We are made for togetherness. We are made for all the beautiful things that you and I know. We are made to tell the world that there are no outsiders. All are welcome..."*

Desmond Tutu 1931 – 2021

We wish you well with your teaching of mindfulness-based groups. May they be a source of rich inspiration and learning for you, and all your group members.

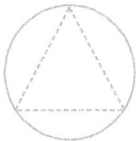

17. A personal postscript

Trish Bartley

"As long as there is poverty in the world, I can never be rich. As long as diseases are rampant, I can never be totally healthy. I can never be what I ought to be until you are what you ought to be. This is the way our world is made. We are interdependent."[293]

In this last chapter, I want to share a little of my personal experience of teaching mindfulness-based groups, offer a particular inspiration that links to this, and see if there are any meaningful threads that give further hope around the personal and collective development of well-being, and what is most needed in the world.

Whilst writing this book, I have often found it hard to capture the fullness of what can be present in the experience of the group. I have long held something of a passion for group work and have often wondered what it is in groups and groupwork that is so significant to me. In my experience, groups are never straightforward or predictable. They can be frustrating, illusory and even disappointing, yet there can also be some special moments in the mindfulness-based group, when a sense of 'me' with all the anxieties, uncertainties, inadequacies, and wanting recedes, and a larger sense of connectedness emerges.

When this happens, there seems to be a natural flow that connects up the members of the group, the leader/teacher, the learning, and the process of the group. The various challenges move into the background. The experience in the room or on the screen seems to slow down and smooth out. As the mindfulness-based group moves into what we might call 'optimal functioning', it seems to shift into another level of development, where there is a possibility of open, warm, interrelatedness. Individual group members lose none of their freedoms – and importantly there are no particular products or group outcomes to be sought or realized – yet at times a felt sense of being part of a greater whole emerges. Things seem to move beyond

---

293 King, 1984

the individual self and the individualism of the self and connect into a wider and fuller presence, where goodness and love can be found.

> *"Love is that condition in the human spirit so profound that it empowers us to develop courage; to trust that courage and build bridges with it; to trust those bridges and cross over them so we can attempt to reach each other."*

Maya Angelou

The narrative of flow

There are stages in the lifespan of everything, including the group. I find that the early times of a mindfulness-based group are a little like setting up a mindful sitting practice – when we strongly invest in the foundations of the body in contact with the ground, being held by the earth itself. Launching the group needs similar foundations of arriving, grounding, settling, welcoming, connecting, and embodied holding. It may be tempting to cut back on this – but in giving each group the best start, conscientious and careful beginnings are needed.

Later, after the group has got going, I often experience doubt (frequently around the halfway point). Confidence ebbs and I question why I ever thought I enjoyed working with groups! Connection seems decidedly glitchy. It is easy to forget that this is a familiar phase and I tend to work too hard to try to bring connections through. If I have been wise, especially when working solo, I have set up support and with the reassurance of kind connection, like arms that hold us when we falter, I pause the drama, remember the pattern, and carry on with embodied intention and trust.

> *"Those with the wisdom to do so will heed their hearts and draw strength from relatedness."* [294]

In a short time (often overnight in intensive trainings, or from one session to another in MBPs), calmer waters prevail. This reminds me of the process of little streams or tributaries flowing separately until they come to the place where they converge. At those points of joining, the water gets agitated. Eddies and undercurrents jostle for position until there is enough space for the water to flow more evenly, safely contained by the twin banks of the river. Looking back, it becomes obvious that the conscientious and careful beginning is just what was needed for the individual tributaries to find their way to where they connect up. For without that, and the inevitable currents that disturb the waters, the river would never find a way to become a river, or do what it needs to do to make its way down to the sea.

---

294 Lewis *et al*, 2000

Making fine music

Classical music is a particular interest of mine. One of my personal (if rather unusual) mindfulness-based group mentors is an Italian conductor called Claudio Abbado, who died in 2014, aged 80. Listening to his music and watching recordings of his conducting, I marvel at the way he enabled the orchestral musicians to listen deeply to each other. A classical orchestra is often over 100 strong and yet he gave his players apparent freedom to express themselves through the music, whilst holding the ensemble together by clearly being exquisitely present, embodied, and aware. He apparently prepared for concerts with incredible care, conducting long works from memory, which enabled him to maintain a visual and intuitive rapport with the players in his orchestras.[295]

I find this combination of expression, awareness, and connecting of the individual with the whole, very inspiring. It is rare, and yet maybe there are some small faint echoes in a mindfulness-based group that flows and 'sings as no-one ever has'.[296]

Making meaning from the mindfulness-based group

In these reflections, I have been looking a bit more at what the experience of belonging to an 'optimally functioning' mindfulness-based group might offer. We considered the value of the group in the first chapter, drawing out the pro-social and ethical orientation of mindfulness practice and the current interest in mindfulness from social scientists, in the fields of climate change research and social justice.

Dipping into various development theories, it is noticeable that most focus wholly on the self, whilst some theories include a relational paradigm, usually some way towards the 'top' of the system:

- Maslow's Hierarchy of Needs[297] originally had five levels, from the basic physical need for shelter to self-actualisation. It was only later that he included a level that linked with service to others, and values that go beyond the self.

- Robert Kegan's Constructive Development Theory[298] has six stages of consciousness that are concerned with the way people organise their

---

295 This is a link to Abbado conducting a short clip of Beethoven's Symphony No 6, 'The Pastorale'. https://youtu.be/m6iKHI5vVZE and here is another short clip of The Firebird Suite by Stravinsky. https://youtu.be/fCwDudQeGRU

296 Rilke, 1996

297 Maslow, 1943

298 Kegan, 1982

thinking, feeling and social relating[299]. His final stage, Interindividual Balance, orients towards 'co-constructing experience together'[300] and tolerating 'not knowing' as an opportunity to grow and connect.

■ Ken Wilbur, in Integral Meditation[301], draws out three tiers and nine stages of 'growing up, waking up, and showing up'. He believes that when 10% of the population gets to their highest tier (Integral), "we can expect the most profound tipping point in the history of humanity… [that results in] a truly inclusive, non-marginalising society."[302]

There are also some radical new theories in very different academic development spheres, which seem to have resonance and potential here.

■ Thomas Malone, Anita Williams Woolley and their colleagues are looking at Collective Intelligence[303] and asking questions such as 'Why do some groups perform better than others?' They suggest that the groups that have higher levels of collective intelligence are more socially and emotionally perceptive, cognitively diverse, and communicate and participate more equally.

■ In his recent book *The Constitution of Knowledge: A Defense of Truth*[304], Jonathan Rauch looks at the sphere of global politics and the threat to modern democracy. His philosophical grounding of 'reality-based community' suggests that it is crucial for the moral development of society to progress towards "less social violence, more social participation and a wider circle of dignity and toleration."

■ Finally, in her latest book *Seven and a Half Lessons About the Brain*[305], Lisa Feldman Barret writes a chapter that explains how our brains "secretly work with other brains." She suggests that we co-regulate each other in a number of ways. "This hidden co-operation keeps us healthy, so it matters how we treat one another in a very real, brain-wiring way."

These themes share a good deal with those that we have been writing about in this book. Perhaps it is possible in the future to see many more broad-based groups, gatherings, and networks finding a role for mindfulness to support how they work together. This could offer personal and relational benefits for the individuals involved. Groupwork practice that includes the role of mindfulness, and the mindfully embodied presence by the group leader could be developed. And on a meta level,

---

299 Erikson, 2006

300 Kegan, 1982

301 Wilbur, 2016

302 Ibid.

303 Woolley *et al*, 2015

304 Rauch, 2021

305 Feldman Barret, 2020

we might learn more about how mindfulness practice in groups supports relational skills, pro-social values, and ethical behaviours in and beyond the group[306].

Until we know more, for now, let us rest with confidence in knowing that the experience of the mindfulness-based group is of value to the world, and see where it goes.

> *"Irrepressible hope is rising in my heart… a growing sense of collectivity … we are taking stock of what is truly important and concluding that so much of it is what we share rather than what we can own individually. A quiet rebellion is growing… Humanity is so much more complex than what we are led to believe… May there continue to be a decline of the cult of the individual – and his or her wealth and fame. Let us be confident to be happy to live modest lives that are guided by our values – with balance and humility."*

Guy Singh-Watson[307] (December, 2020)

---

306 Making progress in this meta layer will benefit the personal and the groupwork practice layer

307 Guy Singh-Watson is founder of Riverford organic farmers, a B. Corp. cooperative that has won many awards.

References and bibliography

Adichie, C.N. (2014). *We should all be feminists*. Fourth Estate.

Analayo. (2003). *Satipatthana: The direct path to realization*. Windhorse Publications.

Asante, M.K. (1988). *Afrocentricity*. Africa World Press.

Baer, R., (2015). Ethics, Values, Virtues, and Character Strengths in Mindfulness-Based Interventions: A Psychological Science Perspective. *Mindfulness*, **6**(4),956-969. https://doi.org/10.1007/s12671-015-0419-2

Bateson, G. (2000). *Steps to an ecology of mind*. The University of Chicago Press.

Battle, M. (1996). The Ubuntu theology of Desmond Tutu. In L. Hulley., L. Kreetzschmar., & L. Lungile Pato. (Eds.), *Archbishop Tutu: Prophetic witness in South Africa*. Human & Rousseau.

Barrett, B., Grabow, M., Middlecamp, C., Mooney, M., Checovich, M.M., Converse, A.K., Gillespie, B., & Yates, J. (2016). Mindful Climate Action: Health and Environmental Co-Benefits from Mindfulness-Based Behavioural Training. *Sustainability*, **8**,1040. https://doi.org/10.3390/su8101040

Bartley, T. (2003). *Holding up the sky: Love, power and learning in the development of a community*. Community Links.

Bartley, T. (2012). *Mindfulness-based cognitive therapy for cancer: Gently turning towards*. Wiley-Blackwell.

Bartley, T. (2017). *Mindfulness: A kindly approach to being with cancer*. Wiley-Blackwell.

Bauman, Z., & Donskis, L. (2013). *Moral blindness: The loss of sensitivity in liquid modernity*. Polity Press.

Berne, E. (1963). *The structure and dynamics of organizations and groups*. Lippincott.

Bion, W.R. (1961). *Experiences in groups and other papers*. Routledge.

Bion, W.R. (1967). *Second thoughts*. Karnac.

Bisseling, E. M., Schellekens, M. P. J., Spinhoven, P., Compen, F. R., Speckens, A. E. M., & van der Lee, M. L. (2019). Therapeutic alliance-not therapist competence or group cohesion-contributes to reduction of psychological distress in group-based mindfulness-based cognitive therapy for cancer patients. *Clinical Psychology & Psychotherapy*, **26**(3), 309–318. https://doi.org/10.1002/cpp.2352

Bonebright, D. A. (2010). 40 years of storming: a historical review of Tuckman's model of small group development. *Human Resource Development International*, **13**(1), 111–120. https://doi.org/10.1080/13678861003589099

Bowden, A., Norton, K., & Griffith, G. M. (2020). Do Trainee Mindfulness Teachers Practice What They Teach? Motivation, Challenges, and Learning Gaps. *Mindfulness*, **12**, 970-982. https://doi.org/10.1007/s12671-020-01565-6

Bowlby, J. (1988). *A secure base*. Routledge.

Brandsma, R. (2017). *The mindfulness teaching guide*. New Harbinger Publications.

Bregman, R. (2020). *Humankind: A hopeful history*. Bloomsbury Publishing.

Bretherton, I. (1992). The origins of attachment theory: John Bowlby and Mary Ainsworth. *Developmental Psychology*, **28**(5), 759–775. https://doi.org/10.1037/0012-1649.28.5.759

Bristow, J., Bell, R., Nixon, D. (2020). Mindfulness: developing agency in urgent times. The Mindfulness Initiative. https:www.themindfulnessinitiative.org/agency-in-urgent-times/

Broks, P. (2003). *Into the silent land*. Atlantic Books.

Bruner, J. (1960). *The process of education*. Harvard University Press.

Buber, M. (2010). *I and Thou*. (R.G. Smith trans). Martino Publishing.

Burlingame, G. M., Seebeck, J. D., Janis, R. A., Whitcomb, K. E., Barkowski, S., Rosendahl, J., & Strauss, B. (2016). Outcome differences between individual and group formats when identical and nonidentical treatments, patients, and doses are compared: A 25-year meta-analytic perspective. *Psychotherapy*, **53**(4), 446–461. https://doi.org/10.1037/pst0000090

Cairns, V., & Murray, C. (2015). How do the features of mindfulness-based cognitive therapy contribute to positive therapeutic change? A meta-synthesis of qualitative studies. *Behavioural and Cognitive Psychotherapy*, 43(03), 342-359. doi:10.1017/S1352465813000945

Canby, N. K., Eichel, K., Lindahl, J., Chau, S., Cordova, J., & Britton, W. B. (2020). The Contribution of Common and Specific Therapeutic Factors to Mindfulness-Based Intervention Outcomes. *Frontiers in Psychology*. https://doi.org/10.3389/fpsyg.2020.603394

Cassidy, J., & Shaver, P. R. (2002). *Handbook of attachment: Theory, research, and clinical applications.* Rough Guides.

Chambers, R. (1983). *Rural development: Putting the last first.* Longman Scientific & Technical.

Choudhury, S. (2015). *Deep diversity: Overcoming us vs. them.* Between The Lines.

Covey, S. (1989). *The 7 habits of highly effective people: Powerful lessons in personal change.* Simon & Schuster.

Craig, P., Dieppe, P., Macintyre, S., Michie, S., Nazareth, I., Petticrew, M., & Medical Research Council Guidance. (2008). Developing and evaluating complex interventions: the new Medical Research Council guidance. *BMJ*, **337**, a1655. https://doi.org/10.1136/bmj.a1655

Crane, R. (2009). *Mindfulness-based cognitive therapy.* Routledge.

Crane, R.S., Eames, C., Kuyken, W., Hastings, R. P.1, Williams, J.M.G., Bartley, T., Evans, A., Silverton, S., Soulsby, J.G., Surawy, C. (2013). Development and validation of the Mindfulness-Based Interventions: Teaching Assessment Criteria (MBI:TAC), *Assessment*, **20**(6), 681-688. https://doi.org/10.1177/1073191113490790

Crane, R.S., (2016). Implementing mindfulness in the mainstream: Making the path by walking It, *Mindfulness*, **8**(3), 585-594. https://doi.org/:10.1007/s12671–016–0632–7

Crane, R. (2017). *Mindfulness-based cognitive therapy* (2nd ed.). Routledge.

Crane, R.S., Brewer, J., Feldman, C., Kabat-Zinn, J., Santorelli, S., Williams, J.M.G. & Kuyken, W. (2017). What defines mindfulness-based programs? The warp and the weft. *Psychological Medicine*, **6**, 990-999. https://pubmed.ncbi.nlm.nih.gov/28031068/10.

Crane, R. S., Soulsby, J. G., Kuyken, W., Williams, J. M. G., & Eames, C. (2021). The universities of Bangor, Exeter & Oxford manual of the mindfulness-based interventions teaching assessment criteria (MBI-TAC) (version 2018). Mindfulness Teaching Skills. https://mbitac.bangor.ac.uk/documents/MBITACFullPAGESFINAL6.7.21.pdf

Crane, R.S., Karunavira., & Griffith, G.M. (2021). *Essential resources for mindfulness teachers.* Routledge.

Cormack, D., Jones, F.W., & Maltby, M. (2017). A "Collective effort to make yourself feel better": The group process in mindfulness-based interventions. *Qualitative Health Research*, **28**, 1–13. doi:10.1177/1049732317733448

Dana, D. (2018). *The polyvagal theory in therapy: Engaging the rhythm of regulation.* W.W. Norton & Company.

Erikson, E.H. (1997). *The life cycle completed.* W.W.Norton.

Erikson, K. (2006). The constructive developmental theory of Robert Kegan. *The Family Journal: Counselling and Therapy for Couples and Families*, **14**(3), 290-298. https://doi.org/10.1177/1066480706287799

Fehmi, L., & Robbins, J. (2007). *The open-focus brain: Harnessing the power of attention to heal mind and body.* Trumpeter.

Feldman Barret, L. (2020). *Seven and a half lessons about the brain.* Picador.

Feldman, C., & Kuyken, W. (2019). M*indfulness: Ancient wisdom meets modern psychology.* The Guilford Press.

Feldman, C. (2017). *Boundless heart: The Buddha's path of kindness, compassion, joy and equanimity.* Shambhala.

Frank, P., Fischer, D., & Wamsler, C. (2019). Mindfulness, education and the sustainable development goals. In W. Leal Filho., A. Azul., L. Brandy., P. Ozuyar., & T. Wall (Eds.), *Quality Education, Encyclopaedia of the UN Sustainable Development goals*. Springer.

Frankl, V.E. (1984). *Man's search for meaning: An introduction to logotherapy.* Simon & Schuster.

Freire, P. (1998). *Pedagogy of freedom: Ethics, democracy and civic courage.* Rowman & Littlefield.

Freire, P. (1970). *The pedagogy of the oppressed.* (trans. Ramos, M. B.). Penguin Books.

Fromm, E. (1962). *The art of loving.* Unwin Paperbacks.

Galante, J., Friedrich, C., Dawson, A. F., Modrego-Alarcón, M., Gebbing, P., Delgado-Suárez, I., Gupta, R., Dean, L., Dalgleish, T., White, I. R., & Jones, P. B. (2021). Mindfulness-based programmes for mental health promotion in adults in nonclinical settings: A systematic review and meta-analysis of randomised controlled trials. *PLoS Medicine,* **18**(1), e1003481. https://doi.org/10.1371/journal.pmed.1003481

Gilbert, P., & Chodon. (2013). *Mindful compassion: Using the power of mindfulness and compassion to transform our lives.* Robinson.

Gilbert, P. (2010). *Compassion focussed therapy.* Routledge.

Gilbert, P. (2010). *The compassionate mind: How to use compassion to develop happiness, self-acceptance and well-being.* Constable.

Goodall, C. (2020). *What we need to do now: For a zero carbon future.* Profile Books.

Green, L. (2012). Transformative learning: A passage through the liminal zone. In A. Bainbridge & L. West (Eds.), *Minding a gap: Psychoanalysis and education* (pp. 199-216). Karnac.

Griffith, G.M., Crane, R.S., Karunavira, & Koerbel, L. (2021). Reflective practice framework: The mindfulness-based intervention: Teaching and learning companion (MBI:TLC). In R.S. Crane., Karunavira, & G.M. Griffith (Eds.), *Essential Resources for Mindfulness Teachers* (pp. 125-148). Routledge.

Griffith, G.M. & Karunavira. (2021). Science and Theory. In R. S. Crane. Karunavira, & G. M Griffith (Eds.), *Essential Resources for Mindfulness Teachers* (pp. 200-213). Routledge

Griffith, G. M., Bartley, T., & Crane, R. S. (2019). The Inside Out Group Model: Teaching Groups in Mindfulness-Based Programs. *Mindfulness,* **10**, 1315-1327. https://link.springer.com/article/10.1007/s12671-019-1093-6

Grossman, P. (2015). Mindfulness: Awareness informed by an embodied ethic. *Mindfulness,* **6**, 17-22.

Harari, Y.N. (2018). *21 Lessons for the 21st century.* Penguin Books.

Hawken, P. (2008). *Blessed unrest: How the largest social movement in history is restoring grace, justice and beauty to the world.* Penguin Books.

Hawken, P. (2021). *Regeneration: Ending the climate crisis in one generation.* Penguin Books.

Hay, J. (2015). *Group processes* (module workbook). Hertford: Psychological Intelligence.

Heron, J. (1989). *The facilitator's handbook.* Kogan Page.

Hutchinson, J. K., Jones, F., & Griffith, G. M. (2021). Group and common factors in mindfulness-based programmes: A selective review and implications for teachers. *Mindfulness,* **12**, 1582-1596. https://doi.org/10.1007/s12671-021-01596-7

Hunt, C., & West, L. (2006). Learning in a border country: Using psychodynamic ideas in teaching and research. *Studies in the Education of Adults,* **38**(2), 160-177.

Hunter, D., & Rewa, J. (2020). *Leading groups online: A down and dirty guide to leading online courses, meetings, training, and events during the coronavirus pandemic.* Daniel Hunter.

Imel, Z., Baldwin, S., Bonus, K., & Maccoon, D. (2008). Beyond the individual: group effects in mindfulness-based stress reduction. *Psychotherapy Research: Journal of the Society for Psychotherapy Research,* **18**(6), 735–742. https://doi.org/10.1080/10503300802326038

Jarvis, P. (2009). *Learning to be a person in society.* Routledge.

Jung, C.G., & Jolande, J. (1953). *Psychological reflections: an anthology of the writings of C.G. Jung, selected and edited by Jolande Jacobi.* Pantheon Books.

Kabat-Zinn, J. (1994). *Wherever you go, there you are.* Hyperion.

Kabat-Zinn, J. (2000). Indra's net at work: The mainstreaming of Dharma in society. In G. Watson,. S. Batchelor., & G. Claxon (Eds.), *The psychology of awakening.* Samuel Weiser.

Kabat-Zinn, J. (2013). *Full catastrophe living: How to cope with stress, pain and illness using mindfulness meditation.* (Revised ed.). Piatkus.

Kabat-Zinn, J. (2019). *Mindfulness for all: The wisdom to transform the world.* Piatkus.

Kegan, R. (1982). *The evolving self.* Harvard University Press.

King, M.L. (1984). *The words of Martin Luther King: Selected by Coretta Scott King*. Fount Paperbacks.

Knowles, M. S. (1980). *The modern practice of adult education. From pedagogy to andragogy*. Englewood Cliffs: Prentice Hall.

Kocovski, N. L., Fleming, J. E., Hawley, L. L., Huta, V., & Antony, M. M. (2013). Mindfulness and acceptance-based group therapy versus traditional cognitive behavioral group therapy for social anxiety disorder: A randomized controlled trial. *Behaviour research and therapy*, **51**(12), 889-898.

Krznaric, R. (2014). *Empathy: Why it matters, and how to get it*. Rider Books.

Krznaric, R. (2020). *The good ancestor: How to think long term in a short-term world*. WH Allen.

Lakey, G. (2010). *Facilitating group learning: Strategies for success with diverse adult learners*. Jossey-Bass.

Laska, K. M., Gurman, A. S., & Wampold, B. E. (2014). Expanding the lens of evidence-based practice in psychotherapy: a common factors perspective. *Psychotherapy*, **51**(4), 467–481. https://doi.org/10.1037/a0034332

Lean In & McKinsey. (2020). *Women in the workplace report*. McKinsey & Co.

Leopold, A. (2021). *Think like a mountain*. Penguin Books.

Lewin, K., Lippitt, R., & White, R.K. (1938). Patterns of aggressive behavior in experimentally created social climates. *Journal of Social Psychology*. **10** (2): 271–301. doi:10.1080/00224545.1939.9713366.

Lewis, T., Manini, F., & Lannon, R. (2000). *A general theory of love*. Vintage Books.

Lindeman, E. (1926). *The meaning of adult education*. New Republic.

Lovelock, J. (2021). *We belong to Gaia*. Penguin Books.

Luborsky, L., Rosenthal, R., Diguer, L., Andrusyna, T. P., Berman, J. S., Levitt, J. T., Seligman, D. A., & Krause, E. D. (2002). The dodo bird verdict is alive and well—mostly. *Clinical Psychology: Science and Practice*, **9**(1), 2-12.

Maathai, W. (2020). *The world we once lived in*. Penguin Books.

Macy, J. (1991). *World as lover, world as self*. Parallax Press.

Macy, J., & Johnstone, C. (2012). *Active hope. How to face the mess we're in without going crazy*. New World Library.

Malpass, A., Carel, H., Ridd, M., Shaw, A., Kessler, D., Sharp, D., Bowden, M., & Wallond, J. (2012). Transforming the perceptual situation: a meta-ethnography of qualitative work reporting patients' experiences of mindfulness-based approaches. *Mindfulness*, **3**(1), 60-75. doi:10.1007/12671-011-0081-2

Mantzios, M., & Giannou, K. (2014). Group vs. single mindfulness meditation: Exploring avoidance, impulsivity, and weight management in two separate mindfulness meditation settings. *Applied Psychology: Health and Wellbeing*, **6** (2), 173–191. doi:10.1111/aphw.12023

Maslow, A. H. (1943). A theory of human motivation. *Psychological Review*, 50, 370-396.

Matoba, K. (2021). Global Social Witnessing: An educational tool for Awareness-based systems chance in the era of global humanitarian and planetary crisis. *Journal of Awareness-Based System Change*, **1**, 59-74. https:// doi.org/10.47061/jabsc.v1i1.548

Matiz, A., Fabbro, F., & Crescentini, C. (2018). Single vs. group mindfulness meditation: effects on personality, religiousness/spirituality, and mindfulness skills. *Mindfulness*, **9**(4), 1236–1244.

McCown, D., Reibel, D., & Micozzi, M. S. (2010). *Teaching mindfulness: A practical guide for clinicians and educators*. Springer.

McCown, D. (2013). *The ethical space of mindfulness in clinical practice: An exploratory essay*. Jessica Kingsley Publishers.

McCown, D., Reibel, D., & Micozzi, M.S. (2016). *Resources for teaching mindfulness: An international handbook*. Springer.

McCown, D. (2016). Stewardship: Deeper structures of the co-created group. In D. McCown, D. Reibel, & M.S. Micozzi (Eds.), *Resources for teaching mindfulness: An international handbook* (pp. 3–24). Springer.

McGilchrist, I. (2009). *The master and his emissary*. Yale University Press.

McLeod, S.A. (2018). *Maslow's hierarchy of needs*. Retrieved on 4/12/21 from https://www.simplypsychology.org/maslow.html

Mehrabian, A. (2007). *Nonverbal communication*. Aldine Transaction.

Mezirow, J. (1990). *Fostering critical reflection in adulthood: A guide to transformative and emancipatory learning*. Jossey-Bass.

Mezirow, J. & Associates. (2000). *Learning as transformation: Critical perspectives on a theory in progress*. Jossey-Bass.

Mezirow, J., & Taylor, E.W., and associates. (2009). *Transformative learning in practice: Insights from community, workplace, and higher education*. Jossey-Bass.

Mezirow, J. (2012). Learning to think like an adult: core concepts of transformation theory. In E. D. Taylor, P. Cranton & Associates (Eds.), *The handbook of transformative learning: Theory, research, and practice* (pp. 73-95). Jossey-Bass.

Morgan, P., Simpson, J., & Smith, A. (2015). Health care workers' experiences of mindfulness training: a qualitative review. *Mindfulness*, **6**(4), 744–758.

Ogden, P. (2015). *Sensorimotor psychotherapy: Interventions for trauma and attachment*. Norton.

Rauch, J. (2021). *The constitution of knowledge: A defence of truth*. Brookings Institute Press.

Ricard, M. (2013). *Altruism: The power of compassion to change yourself and the world*. (C. Mandell & S Gordon Trans.). Atlantic Books.

Rilke, R.M. & Norton, M.D. (1934). *Letters to a young poet*. Norton.

Rilke, R.M. (1996). *Rilke's book of hours: Love poems to God*. (trans. by Barrows, A. & Macy, J.) Riverhead.

Roos, C., Stein, E., Bowen, S., & Witkiewitz, K. (2019). Individual gender and group gender composition as predictors of differential benefit from mindfulness-based relapse prevention for substance use disorders. *Mindfulness*, **10**(8), 1560–1567. https://doi.org/10.1007/s12671-019-01112-y

Rotenberg, V.S., & Arhavsky, V.V. (1987). The two hemispheres and the problem with psychotherapy. *Dynamic Psychiatry*, **20**, 369-377.

Saad, L.F. (2020). *Me and white supremacy: How to recognise your privilege, combat racism, and change the world*. Quercus.

Salzberger-Wittenberg, I. (2013). *Experiencing beginnings and endings*. Karnac.

Salzberger-Wittenberg, I., Williams, G., & Osborne, E. (1993). *The experience of teaching and learning*. Karnac.

Santorelli, S. (2010). *Heal thy self: Lessons on mindfulness in medicine*. Harmony.

Sears, R. W. (2015). *Building competence in mindfulness-based cognitive therapy*. Routledge.

Segal, Z. V., Anderson, A. K., Gulamani, T., Dinh Williams, L., Desormeau, P., Ferguson, A., Walsh, K., & Farb, N. A. S. (2019). Practice of therapy acquired regulatory skills and depressive relapse/recurrence prophylaxis following cognitive therapy or mindfulness based cognitive therapy. *Journal of Consulting and Clinical Psychology*, **87**(2), 161–170. https://doi.org/10.1037/ccp0000351

Segal, Z.V., Williams, J.M.G., & Teasdale, J. (2013). *Mindfulness-based cognitive therapy for depression* (2nd ed.). The Guilford Press.

Schein, E.H. (2013). *Humble inquiry: The gentle art of asking instead of telling*. Berrett-Koehler Publishers.

Schlapobersky, J.R. (2016). *From the Couch to the Circle: Group-Analytic Psychotherapy in Practice*. Routledge.

Schroevers, M.J., Tovote, K.A., Snippe, E., & Fleer, J. (2016). Group and individual Mindfulness-Based Cognitive Therapy (MBCT) are both effective: A pilot randomized controlled trial in depressed people with a somatic disease. *Mindfulness*, **7**, 1339–1346. https://doi.org/10.1007/s12671-016-0575-z

Sol, J., & Wals, A.E.J. (2015). Strengthening ecological mindfulness through hybrid learning in vital conditions. *Cultural Studies of Scientific Education*, **10**, 203-214. doi:10.1007/s11422-014-9586-z

Shapiro, S. L., Carlson, L. E., Astin, J. A., & Freedman, B. (2006). Mechanisms of mindfulness. *Journal of Clinical Psychology*, **62**(3), 373–386. https://doi.org/10.1002/jclp.20237

Shafak, E. (2020). *How to stay sane in an age of division*. Profile Books (in association with the Welcome Collection).

Tarrant, J. (1998). *The light inside the dark: Zen, soul and the spiritual life*. Harper.

Tarrant, J. (2008). *Bring me the rhinoceros: And other zen koans that will save your life*. Shambhala.

Tate, K. J., Newbury-Birch, D., & McGeechan, G. J. (2018). A systematic review of qualitative evidence of cancer patients' attitudes to mindfulness. *European Journal of Cancer Care*, **27**(2), e12783.

Teasdale, J., & Chaskalson, M. (2011). How does mindfulness transform suffering? The nature and origins of dukkha transformation of dukkha. *Contemporary Buddhism*, **12**, (1), 89-102.

Teasdale, J., & Chaskalson, M. (2011). How does mindfulness transform suffering? The transformation of suffering. *Contemporary Buddhism*, **12**, (1), 103-124.

The Work that Reconnects. (2021): An exploration of de-escalating patterns of harm in white dominant spaces [Webinar]. https://workthatreconnects.org/.

Thoreau, H.D. (2016). *Walden or life in the woods*. Penguin Classics.

Thornton, C. (2016). *Group and team coaching: The secret life of groups*. (2nd ed.) Routledge.

Thunberg, G. (2021). *No one is too small to make a difference*. Penguin Books.

Tillich, P. (2000). *The courage to be* (2nd ed.). Yale University Press.

Treleaven, D.A. (2018). *Trauma sensitive mindfulness: Practices for safe and transformative healing*. W.W.Norton.

Tuckman, B. W. (1965). Developmental sequence in small groups. *Psychological Bulletin*, **63**(6), 384-399. https://doi.org/10.1037/h0022100

Tuckman, B.W. & Jensen, M.A.C. (1977). Stages of small-group developmental revisited. *Group & Organization Studies*, **2**(4), 419-427. https://doi.org/10.1177/105960117700200404

Tutu, D. (1972). 'Viability' in *Relevant theology for Africa*: Report on a consultation of the Missiological Institute at Lutheran Theological College, Mapumulo, Natal. 12-21

van Aalderen, J. R., Donders, A. R. T., Giommi, F., Spinhoven, P., Barendregt, H. P., & Speckens, A. E. M. (2012). The efficacy of mindfulness-based cognitive therapy in recurrent depressed patients with and without a current depressive episode: a randomized controlled trial. *Psychological Medicine*, **42**, 989-1001.

van Agteren, J., Iasiello, M., Lo, L., Bartholomaeus, J., Kopsaftis, Z., Carey, M., & Kyrios, M. (2021). A systematic review and meta-analysis of psychological interventions to improve mental wellbeing. *Nature Human Behaviour*, **5**, 631-652. https://doi.org/10.1038/s41562-021-01093-w

van den Brink, E. & Kostler, F. (2015). *Mindfulness-based compassionate living*. Routledge.

van den Brink, E., Kostler, F., & Norton, V. (2018). *A practical guide to mindfulness-based compassionate living: Living with heart*. Routledge.

Van der Kolk, B. A. (2009). Developmental trauma disorder: towards a rational diagnosis for chronically traumatized children. *Praxis Der Kinderpsychologie Und Kinderpsychiatrie*, **58**(8), 572-586.

Wall Kimmerer, R. (2021). *The democracy of species*. Penguin Books.

Wamsler, C., Osberg, G., Osika, W., Hendersson, H., Mundaca, L. (2021) Linking internal and external transformation for sustainability and climate action: Towards a new research and policy agenda. *Global Environmental Change* 71:102373. Online.

Walsh, Z., Böhme, J., & Wamsler, C. (2020). Towards a relational paradigm in sustainability research, practice, and education. *Ambio*, 1-11.

Wamsler, C., Schapke, N., Fraude, C., Stasiak, D., Bruhn, T., Lawrence, M., Schroeder, H., & Mundaca, L. (2020a). Enabling new mindsets and transformative skills for negotiating and activating climate action: Lessons from UNFCC conferences of the parties. *Environmental Science and Policy*, **112**, 227-235. https://doi.org/10.1016/j.envsci.2020.06.005

Wamsler, C., Wickenberg, B., Hanson,H., Alkan Olsson, J., Stalhammar, S., Bjorn, B., Falck, H., Gerall, D., Oskarsson, T., Simonsson, E., Torffvit, F., & Zelmerlow, F.(2020b). Environmental and climate policy integration: Targeted strategies for overcoming barriers to nature-based solutions and climate change adaptation. *Journal of Cleaner Production*, **247**, 119-154. https://doi.org/10.1016/j.jclepro.2019.119154

Wamsler, C., (2018). Mind the gap: The role of mindfulness in adapting to increasing risk and climate change. *Sustainability Science*, **13**, 1121-1135. https://doi.org/10.1007/s11625-017-0524-3

Wampold, B. E., & Imel, Z. E. (2015). *The great psychotherapy debate: The evidence for what makes psychotherapy work*. Routledge.

Wilber, K. (2016). *Integral meditation: Mindfulness as a path to grow up, wake up, and show up in your life*. Shambhala.

Williams, J. M.G., & Kabat-Zinn, J. (2013). *Mindfulness: Diverse perspectives on its meaning, origins and applications*. Routledge.

Williams, J. M.G., & Penman, D. (2011). *Mindfulness: A practical guide to finding peace in a frantic world*. Piatkus.

Williams Woolley, A., Aggarwal, I. & Malone, T.W. (2015). Collective intelligence and group performance. *Current Directions in Psychological Science*. Vol **24**(6) 420-424. https://doi.org/10.1177/0963721415599543

Wilson, K.G. & Dufrene, T. (2010). *Things might go terribly, horribly wrong: A guide to life liberated from anxiety*. New Harbinger.

Winnicott, D.W. (1971). *Playing and reality*. Penguin Books.

Woods, S. L., Rockman, P., & Collins, E. (2019). *Mindfulness-based cognitive therapy: Embodied presence and inquiry in practice*. New Harbinger Publications.

Wreford, L., & Haddock, P. (2019) *Mindfulness and social change*. https://www.opendemocracy.net/en/transformation/mindfulness-and-social-change/

Wright, D.S. (2009). *The six perfections: Buddhism and the cultivation of character*. Oxford University Press.

Wyatt, C., Harper, B., & Weatherhead, S. (2014). The experience of group mindfulness-based interventions for individuals with mental health difficulties: A meta-synthesis. *Psychotherapy Research*, **24**(2), 214-228. https://doi.org/10.1080.10503307.2103.864788

Yalom, I.D., & Leszcz, M. (2005) *The theory and practice of group psychotherapy* (5th ed.). Basic Books.

Young, E. S., Simpson, J. A., Griskevicius, V., Huelsnitz, C. O., & Fleck, C. (2019). Childhood attachment and adult personality: A life history perspective. *Self and Identity: The Journal of the International Society for Self and Identity*, **18**(1), 22–38.

Practice recordings

We have recorded a few practices to accompany this book. They link to specific chapters or sections and are designed as support to MBP teachers within teaching sessions or on the practice 'cushion' between teaching sessions. These can be downloaded at www.pavpub.com/teaching-mindfulness-based-groups-resources

Chapter 1 - The value of the mindfulness-based group

Intentions Practice

Part One - Inside out embodying

Feet on the Floor

The Pause

The Pause and Feet on the Floor combined

Part Two - Reading the group

Bringing the Group to Mind

Part Three - Holding the group

Inside Out Guiding

Part Four - Befriending the group

General guidance to befriending practices

First friend for life

Second friend for life

Third friend for life

Fourth friend for life